1

9/8

PO 20871

THE
CANTING
CREW

A volume in the
CRIME, LAW, AND DEVIANCE
Series

THE CANTING CREW

LONDON'S CRIMINAL UNDERWORLD 1550–1700

JOHN L. McMULLAN

RUTGERS UNIVERSITY PRESS
NEW BRUNSWICK, NEW JERSEY

Library of Congress Cataloging in Publication Data
McMullan, John L., 1948–
  The canting crew.

  (Crime, law, and deviance)
  Bibliography: p.
  Includes index.
  1. Crime and criminals—England—London—History.
  2. London (England)—Economic conditions. I. Title.
  II. Series.
  HV6950.L7M35 1984   364.3'09421'2   83–11191
  ISBN 0-8135-1022-8

For Nanette Juliano
without whose encouragement, support, and
understanding this book would never have been written

CONTENTS

PREFACE

Writing a book like this is more often than not a cooperative effort. I should like to single out those to whom I am most conscious of indebtedness: Paul Rock, who first suggested that I might consider looking into this topic and who provided advice and criticism of great value; Professors Hubert Guindon, Kurt Jonassohn, and Robert Ratner, who read earlier versions and aided in the clarification and development of my ideas; Roberta Hamilton, who took a particular interest in this study, painstakingly criticizing all versions of my manuscript and providing excellent editorial advice; Jo-Anne Fiske, whose suggestions on how best not to write English saved me from errors; and Nanette Juliano, who helped me with bibliographical matters and carefully and precisely prepared the typescript.

I made some good friends while doing the research for this book, Bob Davis, Nigel Williams, Pete Murry, and Michael Nicholson, each in his own way, made me feel welcome and provided emotional and practical support. Most of all, Nanette Juliano shared the good and the low times of this project. Her confidence and encouragement prevented me from failure and isolation; it is to her that I owe my greatest debt.

THE
CANTING
CREW

A volume in the
CRIME, LAW, AND DEVIANCE
Series

1

INTRODUCTION

This is a study of crime in sixteenth- and seventeenth-century London. Although the description and analysis of criminal process and organization from 1550 to 1700 (with particular emphasis on the Elizabethan and Stuart years) are central to the study, its basic aim goes beyond this: to further our understanding of how persistent crime developed and maintained itself in an economic, legal, and political context. The criminal classes of the period have received the attention of serious historians, who have tended either to exaggerate the strength of persistent criminal organizations or deny that they existed. On the one hand, an uncritical assessment of the criminal classes has characterized them as numerically vast, organizationally cohesive, and socially dangerous. Elaborate hierarchies of roles, rules, and power relationships allegedly coordinated much criminal behavior. Criminal groups were said to have been horizontally linked in city- and nationwide arrangements. The metaphor of the "fraternity" encouraged historians to think in terms of a criminal conspiracy.[1] On the other hand, more recent historical research has challenged the idea that a criminal underworld existed. The febrile imaginations of contemporaries and the gullibility of historians apparently contributed to erroneous reconstructions. Professional roguery and its attendant organizational configuration, we are now advised, were unlikely in the extreme.[2] This book is intended as a contribution to the debate; it argues against both these positions and contends that professional organized crime did exist, but in a local contained form, at least in London. By examining theft practices and the world of prostitution, I hope to lay bare the nature of criminal group formation, the features of a wider criminal infrastructure, and the operations of criminal markets. Moreover I analyze criminal organization from a wider sociohistorical perspective, focusing on: (1) how the interplay between the economy, the legal order, and the labor market affected criminal opportunities, relationships, and networks; (2) how geopolitical organization structured criminal groups and institutions; (3) how decentralized state social control shaped the underworld; (4) the fragmented and negotiated character of crime and crime control; and (5) mediations between public and private spheres and the consequences for power and markets in organized crime.

My focus is almost entirely on London. All accounts seem to agree that it was a social and geographical monster, vastly larger than other English towns. It was the center of trade, commerce, law, and politics. It had the largest casual labor market and was the undisputed center of conspicuous consumption and the satellite entertainment industries. It is doubtful if a criminal underworld flourished elsewhere, at least to the same degree. For London provided a unique environment for crime: a large amount of accessible money and other valuables; a sizable and transient population; and an anonymous and relatively protected social setting.

Such research is not without its pitfalls. The major difficulty is that evidence about the topic is slender, especially for London. Although some legal and city records for some of the period have survived, we really have no criminal statistics. Moreover, there is little systematic knowledge about the organization of London courts or about the law-enforcement process. A history of pardoning and policing is lacking. We are left in the main with contemporary descriptions and assessments of crime and criminals, many of which are incomplete and difficult to evaluate. Some are clearly dubious. We face here an acute version of two general problems of historical research: validity and reliability. We cannot be sure that what contemporaries claimed to have reported was in fact so, and one must thus take care to avoid being directly hoodwinked. Certainly some accounts were exaggerations and partial plagiarisms.[3] Other documents may fall into a similar category without this being obvious. Sources may be decoys, jokes, or disguises. We must wonder about the adequacy of descriptions, the motives of authors, and our own interpretations. We are dealing, then, with elusive and unmeasurable evidence that is difficult to situate and understand. Because of the skeletal nature of the evidence, I have, where possible, tried to corroborate it by seeking out different types of evidence. Certainly much of value has emerged from the sifting of materials, and the assembling of vocabulary, impressions, and accounts does enlarge one's knowledge of crime.

The terms of reference pose a further difficulty. The meaning of the words crime, criminal, and criminal organization in this period is problematic. Certainly they lacked precise legal definition. Jurists spoke more regularly of felonies, trespasses, and sins.[4] Yet the words crime and criminals had current usage, referring primarily to thieves and vagabonds whom the authorities disposed of with haste. Contemporary pamphleteers, dramatists, and legal officials alike spoke of criminals as outside community standards, a separate social group whose members were identifiable by discrete language, dress, residence, and social habits—and by their dishonest means of livelihood. Other illegal acts, such as assault, rumormongering, drunken misbehavior, and creating a nuisance, were not usually included in what was understood as crime. They were more readily tolerated and were managed by different courts and subject to different juridical procedures and punishments.[5] Similarly, "white-collar" offenses (fraud, extortion, or embezzlement), carried on as sidelines by reputable craftsmen, professionals, and law enforcement agents, while prevalent, seldom entered into the commonsense notion of crime. These intriguing forms of crime remain outside the scope of this book. The criminals we are dealing with here are pickpockets, cutpurses, thieves, confidence-cheats, fences, panderers, and prostitutes who have controversially been termed the Elizabethan underworld.

A further issue of definition arises in connection with contemporaries' references to specific areas and institutions. It is not always clear whether a reference to London meant the entire metropolis or the City of London proper. More confusing, however, were references to particular streets, districts, and institutions. It was not possible to produce detailed maps of the crime areas. The evolution of criminal districts corresponds uneasily with surviving maps; I was able to plot main thoroughfares, but little else. However, no real difficulty is presented by this shortcoming in that the descriptions are sufficiently full to illuminate a social ecological understanding of crime.

An objection might also be raised with regard to the notion of policing. The term is probably an anachronism for this period. Certainly there were no counterparts to present-day types and methods of police work. The policing that did exist was rudimentary: amateur, volunteer, and reluctant, and the idea of policing must be used with care.

A word of clarification is also needed about my use of related legal documents. Historians in particular may feel that my reluctance to draw upon quarter sessions, petty sessions, ecclesiastical courts, mayors courts, and county records is misplaced, since such documents are increasingly being used as indicators of crime and lawlessness. Yet archival information for the early modern period (particularly the indictment files), is sparse and in need of decoding, and presents a most bewildering pattern. Many indictable cases, never went to the requisite courts, but were dealt with in other civil or religious contexts, or were resolved by extrajudicial means. Moreover, the costs of prosecution, the reluctance of ward and parish constables to present offenses, the inducements to kin, friends, and even court personnel to settle disputes informally, and the discretionary social discipline available to employers, landowners, and clergy, meant that court action was a sanction of last resort and is, I think, a dubious measurement of "real" crime. Furthermore, while these flawed records could be used in combination with other social data, I have strong doubts about their utility for reconstructing the organizational properties of crime.[6] They informed me about individual criminals and rates of crime, but seldom did they reveal much about criminal skills, technology, tutelage, or institutions. Thus the legal records were not particularly helpful to the major subject of this book: the wider internal and external features of criminal organization.

My research is also intended as a contribution to historical criminology. Interdisciplinary in its construction, it explores what sociologists and criminologists have been reluctant to study: criminal phenomena over time. Thus, my work addresses itself to this lacuna in the field of deviance and crime and claims a fit with the existing studies on eighteenth- and nineteenth-century crime. But the book does have another purpose and that is to open up a broader sociological perspective on the historical reconstruction of criminal underworlds. Much of what is now being called the social history of crime is impressive in its detail and scope, but seems to lack analytical imagination. In part this is because historians are astonishingly reluctant to familiarize themselves with the theoretical or topical discourses developed by criminologists and sociologists. By reexamining old assumptions and questioning existing formulations, I hope to push back disciplinary frontiers, and challenge the alleged novelty of modern aspects of crime by offering a new interpretation of the London underworld.

The study begins with an attempt to place crime and criminal organization within an overall perspective of economic development in London. The opening chapter examines the London environment, paying particular attention to the ways in which commercial capitalist development created a unique structure of criminal opportunities. This is followed by an analysis of the London labor market and how it helped produce a criminal population. I also dwell here upon the regulation and legal censure of an outcast population, unraveling some of the ironies of the mediation of law for social control. The next chapter describes and analyzes the importance of territoriality for crime. I map out the ecological zones of London crime and stress some of the implications: protection, shelter, neutralization of the law, and the growth of intermediaries. Chapter Five examines the coercive apparatus of the state: watch and ward, privy council, city marshalcy, and militia forms of domestic policing, drawing out the effects of decentralized crime control upon the organization of crime. The next two chapters are concerned with what I have called the "canting crews" themselves. This phrase is borrowed from the criminal cant of the period and refers to the coordination and teamwork implicit in crime. These chapters use broadsides, criminals' confessions and short biographies, dramatists' descriptions of gambling, confidence cheating, and other crime, and canting dictionaries (dictionaries of criminal argot) to develop a coherent interpretation of criminal process and organization. Calling the book *The Canting Crew* highlights the *organized* features of crime and underscores the importance I have placed in my historical reconstruction on the language of crime as an expressive lexicon. By focusing on criminal cant I try to piece together the technology and division of labor of crime, relations between formal criminal organization and the larger underworld, criminal institutions, and the structure of power and markets in the underworld. Finally, the last chapter focuses on the mediation of criminal organization. I analyze, as far as my sources permit, the informal systems of state pardons, rewards, and patronage in order to establish connections between criminal structures and processes of social control. Particular attention is paid to the growth of middlemen entrepreneurs in crime: fences, thief-takers, and informers, and to their roles in translating law into social action and transforming criminal practices into coherent organizational forms.

2

THE MAKING OF
AN UNDERWORLD

Introduction

This chapter has two main tasks. One is to outline a perspective on the development of London in the context of the commercial revolution of the sixteenth and seventeenth centuries, a perspective that can serve as a background for the rest of the study and especially for understanding economic, demographic, and social contexts. The other is to relate the importance of urban growth to the opportunity structure of crime. This will help identify the nature of a surplus criminal population (a topic to be taken up in the following chapter), and pave the way for an understanding of its territorial and organizational character.

Population Growth and Economic Change

The period between 1550 and 1650 was a time of immense and probably unprecedented economic and social upheaval in England.[1] But patterns of change were unsystematic and uneven. London, in particular, underwent intensive upheavals. Simply stated, it became the economic center of the country.[2]

In tackling this development, it is useful to examine the contours of the essentially parochial English economy. Communities were small and production was for local markets. Consumption was limited to a narrow range of goods and services and tied to regional output.[3] Production per head was low, the division of labor and techniques of production were simple, and capital investment was minimal. National and personal incomes were minuscule, savings were virtually nonexistent, the economy was almost entirely at the mercy of natural forces, and labor power was the most important element of production.[4]

Two major factors unleashed the process that transformed London into the center of economic activity. First, a population explosion increased the demand for basic goods, enlarged the consumer goods market, stimulated new investment, and spurned innovations in the technology and organization of labor.[5] Firm statistics do not exist, but between 1500 and 1620 the population of England and Wales nearly doubled from 2.5–3 million to 5 million. This increased the labor force and enlarged the towns and cities, especially London. Population growth was fairly steady in rural areas until 1620, but in the early seventeenth century, population growth in the provinces began to fall off.[6] Plague, emigration, harvest failures, and commercial crises combined to hold down population increases. A new pattern took shape, in which the North, the West Midlands, and London became centers of population growth.[7] Differential fertility, but more likely the preference accorded London by wayfarers and migrants, stimulated new mobility patterns. From 1500 to 1650 the population of London increased eightfold.[8] It grew from 60,000 in 1550 to between 320,000 and 340,000 in 1634, and to 350,000 by 1650.[9] By the late Stuart period London was absorbing 8,000 or so new migrants every year.[10] At the beginning of the sixteenth century it was five times the size of the largest provincial town, but by the mid-seventeenth century it was between ten and fifteen times as large.[11]

The second factor unleashing this process of social change was the expansion in nonlocal trade. Foreign trade in general expanded, particularly from 1508 to 1551 and from 1603 to 1620, stimulating local production.[12] Increasingly, England imported commodities. A vigorous market in linens, silks, and assorted foods and beverages was spawned. The expansion of trade did not depend primarily on the efficiency of exporting industries and competitive marketing. Rather, import-led trade patterns favored commercial enterprises that traveled abroad to discover and import foreign commodities. Such a shift from competitive manufacture to trading cartels severly dislocated the economy, spelling the decline of provincially based economies, unable to compete with London. Indeed London became the relay station for long-distance trade and for a lively reexport business. The metropolis waxed fat at the expense of regional capitals.[13] With this growth of trade and commerce, the Thames environs enjoyed a heyday of prosperity. London-based shipyards and dock-related small industries expanded sharply. As a result of geographical and commercial shifts, industrial reorganization occurred. The centrality of London to long-distance trade routes encouraged a multiplication of small consumer goods industries, in particular, the silk and sugar establishments which demanded a large seasonal labor force.[14] By the mid to late sixteenth century London had emerged as the focus for new overseas trading markets.

London and the Capitalist Marketplace

The character, importance, and consequences of economic and demographic changes for London need to be elaborated with emphasis on three major processes. First, London was transformed into the largest labor exchange in the country. An essential feature of pre-capitalist social formations had been the balance between land and population. Peasant farming in the fourteenth and fifteenth centuries was the economic mainstay of a prosperous aristocracy, town life, and some intercontinental trade. Agricultural production was local, technology primitive, and yields low. Technical and social relations fettered the growth of more elaborate agriculture production. We have already seen that a peculiar pattern of population growth created pressure on the land, bringing about a transformation in the available labor supply. Although the sources of this growth are not well understood, the emergence of a rural surplus was of primary significance.[15] Driven from the land, partly because of the reluctance of the English landowners to subdivide their holdings, a landless agrarian class emerged, part of which was transformed into

9

town and city populations.[16] These new populations in turn stimulated the agricultural sector, increasing the demand for agricultural
surplus. The demands of food markets, particularly London's, trig-
gered further capital penetration of the countryside and encouraged
further land enclosures.[17] The masterless populations, out of work
and out of shelter, were a permanent fixture. As Slack has observed,
"London was the magnet whose growth imposed its influence on
the patterns of mobility elsewhere."[18]

London was preferred for several reasons. The outparishes and
suburbs of the city provided havens for expanding domestic and exporting industries. Existing apprenticeship rules, negligible taxes,
and immunity from city regulations encouraged industry, particularly leather making, sugar refining, glass making, dyeing, brewing,
and shipbuilding.[19] More seasonal employment was available in
London than elsewhere. The size of London as a home market and
its access to foreign markets also favored it as a center of commerce
and industry. Town dwellers drifted to the city as the cloth export
trade became dominated by the London merchants. Urban laborers
moved with the marketplace. Combined with the rural surplus they
placed increasing pressure on the metropolis. The plentiful market
days and fairs of the capital were further boons for masterless populations, offering opportunities for work, including trading, debt col-
lecting, and thievery.[20] More social support facilities were available
in London than in other urban areas. Inns and alehouses were plentiful, and lodgings and food could be easily procured. The city, by
its size and anonymity, provided a location in which those pushed
out of one place could start afresh. In the winter vagrants could hole
up in the suburbs' unregulated barns and alehouses and engage in
subsistence activities, some illegal.[21] Moreover, the multiplicity of
better organized charity foundations attracted and held the unemployed and the destitute in the capital.[22] One unintended consequence of the advanced experimentation in social services was "that
relief . . . attracted hordes of beggars to the city instead
of reducing their numbers."[23] London became the magnet for the
ejected migrants of smaller towns. The enforcement of Tudor poor
laws sent strangers to the capital. This reserve army of the unemployed was a volatile group and ranged from 20 percent of the
city population in stable times to over 50 percent in times of seasonal depression.[24]

Second, London evolved into the largest single consumer goods market in England, probably in Europe. As the largest center of population in the country it had a substantial home market. Citizens were increasingly becoming users and earners of cash, thereby stimulating the demand for food and raw material imports. A large and steady demand for goods and services was created. The range of goods and services available was extended, and as the increased sales of goods and services added to more purchasing power, the standard of living rose.[25]

What differentiated London from other European capitals were the variety and volume of its consumer goods market. A widened demand for household goods, textiles, building materials, pottery, and hardware resulted. Craft production and the building trades enjoyed irregular cycles of boom and bust. Such a market was not to be contained; rural dwellers became to some extent cash customers, for goods produced and supplied outside their area, particularly from London. Even goods produced outside London in regional centers were funneled through the metropolis for "finishing touches" and redistribution.[26] London, in the apt words of E. J. Hobsbawm, was the pivot of a national market "for 'middling' goods, unlike the city in continental states."[27]

A more significant feature of the London market was that goods were cheap. As a result, "they penetrated a considerable way down the social scale."[28] Tobacco, textiles, and sugar, for example, were consumed by the middle and lower ranks of the city population. Although a specialized trade in articles of grace and luxury continued, the growing economic importance of the city depended upon its inexpensive consumer goods market.[29] A variety of portable commodities became more available, particularly linens, silks, and cotton-based articles. The "snapper-up of unconsidered trifles" as Shakespeare put it, could make a steady living from such minor commodities.[30]

Moreover, the consumer goods market both promoted and was stimulated by the elaboration of a system of communication that tied London to all parts of the provinces: systems of roads, carrier paths and cart trails, and waterways and canals were developed to handle the increased flow of raw materials and finished products.[31] Imports, exports, labor, raw materials, and manufactured goods were distributed through the capital. Social networks based on the buoyant trade spawned by the London market emerged. Inns, taverns, and shops evolved in a distribution system that was tied to the metropolis. News and people moved more easily. The Stuart inn came into prominence as a social institution, functioning as a hotel, warehouse, bank, auction room, place of exchange, scrivener's office, coach and wagon station, and information depot.[32] In particular, the expansion of the consumer goods market enlarged a traveling class of traders, badgers, cartmen, and merchants. Population change, commercial expansion, and communication fed one upon the other. The importance of London to the rest of the country was intensified; the capital became the finishing center par excellence.

Third, as the burgeoning center of finance, trade, government, and law, London emerged as the focal point of conspicuous consumption. Three factors made it so. First, it was the political headquarters of the country. Government and crown were increasingly established in Westminister. Second, the seats of law were located in the London environs and the age of the late Tudors and early Stuarts was a litigious one. Third, the elevators of social mobility were concentrated in London: high government, the law, trade, finance, the professions, and prestigious marital circles.[33]

London's development as the center of politics, law, and social mobility encouraged economic activities drawing the noblemen, the gentry, and the skilled professions to the city. Centralized schemes of credit, finance, and government made entrepreneurship and capital accumulation less risky. Capital flowed into the city from both the declining provincial centers and the newly acquired trading markets.[34] The nobility and the rising gentry were particularly ostentatious about the use of their newly acquired wealth. Although some of their capital was invested in productive enterprises, much was spent on pleasure and luxury. By the late sixteenth century London's emergence as the center of conspicuous expenditures had altered its social character.[35]

Three major effects can be discerned. First, the increased urban activities of the gentry and nobility fostered the rapid expansion of the lay professions. As the center of law, finance, and politics, London and adjacent Westminster were meccas for career-minded lawyers, doctors, clerks, and writers. Law suits were common and increasingly located in prerogative courts in London. The seasonal and more permanent residence of the wealthy created enlarged demands for medical, legal, commercial, and leisure institutions.[36] A spectacular rise in the numbers of lawyers occurred as property and land claims increased. Between 1534 and 1650 the crown seized most of the revenues of the church and immediately placed church lands and property on the private market. Some 25 to 30 percent of the land of the entire country was released from previous legal restrictions. The result of the free land market was a "massive transfer of land by purchase and sale."[37] In addition, bans on the use of private violence to settle disputes favored the growth of political and legal action. Between 1590 and the 1630s the number of lawyers called to the bar at the Inns of Court increased by over 40 percent. Similarly, solicitors and attorneys expanded by over 400 percent from 342 in 1578 to 1,383 by 1633.[38]

Changes in the occupational structure were considerable. As noted, the upper classes gained as a result of their commercial prosperity. Increases in the number of landowners, high fertility rates, and casual practices toward the sale of office and honors trebled the numbers of the ruling elites.[39] The number of peers rose from 60 to 160, of baronets and knights from 500 to 1,400, of squires from perhaps 800 to 3,000, of armigerous gentry from perhaps 5,000 to around 15,000.[40] In part this class grew at the expense of the clergy, and it also contributed to the upsurge of the secular professions. A new middle class, clerical and administrative, oriented and tied to the state, became an important avenue of social mobility. It is estimated that by 1640, court and royal bureaucracies employed some 600 civil servants.[41] The revolutionary decades undoubtedly increased the state bureaucracy. In particular, social control agencies were expanded. Tax collectors, excisemen, customs officers, and assorted military officers were members of burgeoning administrative professions. Stone estimates that by 1690 there were 6,000–8,000 local and central officeholders with incomes over £50.[42] The medical profession also showed sustained and dramatic growth in London. One estimate places the average number of doctors, surgeons, and apothecaries practicing medicine between 1603 and 1643 at 1,000.[43] The nobility also spent considerable sums on education.[44] In London, educational centers were constructed or enlarged to handle the influx of the children of the gentry.[45] As Fisher has noted, "Admissions to Gray's Inn . . . which had amounted to only two hundred in the third decade of the sixteenth century had risen to seven hundred and ninety-nine in the last and to twelve hundred and sixty-five in the ten years between 1611 and 1620."[46] By the reign of Charles I, London had displaced Oxford and Cambridge as the educational center for the offspring of the country gentry. So pronounced was the expansion that it produced an educated gentry and aristocracy in excess of the capacity of church and state to absorb them. Many remained, with their wealth, in the city attempting to curry political favor and find political employment.[47]

Associated with the rise of secular professions was the expansion of an economy of ostentatious display. Revenues were increasingly spent upon luxuries. London's social circles set the tone for ruling elites throughout the country. Capital was directed into grandiose edifices, gardens, and parks suited for the leisure activities of the wealthy.[48] Entire residential areas were built up to house the substantial immigration of rural gentry. To a large extent the demands for accommodation were met by the hotel and catering trades who waxed fat on the wealth of the gentry. Great inns and stately taverns, as well as humble cookshops and victuallers, expanded and rejuvenated their businesses. But private building flourished also, and segregated gentry communities contained five- or six-story mansions, elegantly decorated and lavishly furnished with expensive items. Many were "double, triple, even quadrupled-fronted structures . . . enriched with elaborately carved balconies and bay windows."[49]

Perhaps the most important effect of the new wealth was the expansion of the entertainment industries. Enterprises supplying luxury goods, pretentious apparel, and foreign foodstuffs were stimulated. Specialized markets expanded to accommodate higher-class sectors of the population. At the same time London's mass consumer market was also growing. Although selectivity was preserved, tastes nevertheless percolated downward. The supply of entertainment and leisure activities underwent commercialization. Vast networks of gaming ordinaries, bowling alleys, alehouses, lodging houses, and pleasure gardens emerged to cater to the gentry and professional classes. Such institutions were known for the opportunities they provided for high spending, gambling, and illicit sexual activities. Above all, commercial theater became a private business supported in some measure by the surplus wealth flowing into the city.[50] The new commercial leisure activities supported employment in service, retail, provisionary, and catering trades. While members of the urbanized and semiurbanized gentry of Elizabethan and Stuart times were the major consumers, conspicuous consumption, like consumer goods, penetrated the social order. The "middling sorts" and the "meaner orders" made persistent use of the common taverns, alehouses, cheap ordinaries, and victualing shops that increasingly spotted the London landscape. Commercial theater was also stratified according to income and class.[51]

London Upside Down: Opportunities for Crime

English society between 1500 and 1700, in the words of Lawrence Stone, "experienced a seismic upheaval of unprecedented magnitude." Widening opportunities and rapid social change were persistent features of the times, particularly during the "century of mobility 1540–1640."[52] I have outlined the major implications for London. Yet there existed a related but distinct underside to London's importance and development. The city in Christopher Hill's apt phrase also afforded "better prospects for earning a dishonest living. In the late sixteenth and early seventeenth centuries men suddenly became aware of the existence of a criminal underworld."[53] London emerged as the urban equivalent of the greenwood forest—an anonymous refuge providing routine avenues for persistent crime. The masses of consumer goods displayed in open stalls and shops made petty theft easy. The concentration of a large population living near or below the poverty line, little influenced by religious or moral ideology, provided criminal work groups with ready-made material. The institutions of leisure and entertainment were the haunts of pickpockets, confidence cheats, and prostitutes. The patrons of such pleasure resorts—the gentry and the rising professionals—were the abundant and lucrative targets of the thief and the cony-catcher (confidence trickster, gamester, and dice cheat).[54]

Five major factors enhanced the opportunities for crime. London afforded: (1) wider structural opportunities for theft, (2) a secrecy of operations, (3) established criminal habitats, (4) networks of criminal association, and (5) an elaborate black market for disposing of stolen goods.

The Expansion of Criminal Opportunities

London between 1550 and 1650 held large concentrations of wealthy residents. Increasingly, the city became the locus of the business activities of the gentry, the nobility, and the emerging professions of lawyers, doctors, and administrators. Their lives followed fixed routines, and they frequently carried valuables and money on their persons and exchanged them in open public places. Such persons and transactions were accessible targets and attracted confidence cheats, pickpockets, cutpurses, and swindlers. Because legal practices and commerce were carried out at regular times and at set locales the thief could plan his crimes.[55] Not only were targets accessible, they were confined to set quarters and walks of the city. The fact that locations tended to be fixed and the density of social interaction provided camouflage for the expert thief and cony-catcher. The craft of pickpocketing acquired a regularity and stability that mirrored the places, seasons, and daily habits of the wealthier classes. As Robert Greene explained in "A Notable Discovery of Cozenage":

> The cony-catchers, apparelled like honest civil gentlemen or good fellows, with a smooth face, as if butter would not melt in their mouths, after dinner when the clients are come from Westminster Hall and are at leisure to walk up and down Paul's Fleet Street, Holborn, the Strand and such common-haunted places, where these cozening companies attend only to spy out a prey who, as soon as they see a plain country fellow, well and cleanly apparelled, either in a coat of homespun russet or of frieze, as the time requires and a side-pouch at his side—"There is a cony" saith one.[56]

Moreover, dress codes made it easier to take advantage of wealthy clients. Elizabethan society was acutely conscious of dress as an earmark of social position. This made the respectable and the wealthy visible, but it also provided a cover for the criminal. Playing the part of respectable citizens—mastering their manners, life style, and conversation—was the working tool of "gentlemen thieves" and confidence tricksters. Thus, the swindler recruiting clients for dice games sought out his victims according to dress and gained his victim's attention by the embellishment of his own personal apparel. "Haply as I roamed me in the church of Paul's now twenty days ago . . . there walked up and down by me in the body of the Church a gentleman, fair dressed in silk, gold and jewels, with three or four servants in gay liveries all broidered with sundry colours, attending upon him. I advised him well, as one that pleased me much for his proper personage, and more for the wearing of his gear." The well-dressed gentleman and his entourage, the narrator victim informs us, were but a team of skilled dice cheats.[57]

Shoplifters were attracted to the mercers', goldsmiths', and haber-dashers' stalls and shops. The penetration of cheap luxury items to the middle and lower levels of the social structure meant that many people carried portable objects that could be profitably pilfered. A steady dishonest wage could be earned from the petty opportunistic theft of scarves, cheap jewelry, silks, linens, and metal artifacts. Gentlemen's quarters, decorated with conspicuous artifacts were favored targets. But equally important, Elizabethan and Stuart London offered a growing mass of clients and artifacts from which a thief could take small but regular amounts sufficient to confirm him in a steady practice. The intermeshing of trade and communication through London ports and waterways bolstered criminal opportunities. As the quantity of trade increased, river piracy and dock-related crimes became common. While much of this may have been employee theft—the work of amateurs—some was undoubtedly that of experts. Certainly the highways and numerous inns around London were lucrative markets for highway robbers. According to Cockburn, the adjoining county of Hertfordshire "attracted large numbers of highwaymen lured by the rich pickings on the main roads out of London . . . some robberies yielded unusually high sums of money or quantities of silver plate, a fact which may indicate the planned assault of a particular traveller."[58] And Harrison says that few robberies were committed without the assistance of innkeepers and chamberlains, who found out which men were worth robbing and what direction they were traveling in; some even infiltrated the party, guiding the journeyers into the robber's hand.[59]

Little protection could be provided against petty forms of theft and deceit. Coercive institutions, as I discuss later, were not equal to the task of ferreting out and interning the urban criminal. The criminal had a wide and varied market to exploit—one that could support him on a full-time basis.

Anonymity of Operations

Like other major European centers, London contained a myriad of diverse social universes. Socially, it was set off from other towns and from the scattered rural communities. London was highly stratified, and the contrast between rich and poor was particularly evident. Gregory King calculated in 1688 that the landowners and professional classes, though only 5 percent of the population, enjoyed a larger portion of the national income than did all the lower classes (which he estimated at over 50 percent of the population) put together.[60] Geographically, London was divided into contrasting social worlds. Ancient boundaries marked off various living spaces. Mazes of parish, craft, royal, and municipal privileges overlay administrative ward definitions. An eccentric geometry segregated wealthy and poor, professions and lesser trades, workshops and living quarters. Competing jurisdictions and rights rendered London a loosely ordered collection of microcosms. Donald Lupton described it succinctly: "She's [London] certainly a great world, there are so many little worlds in her: She is the great beehive . . . I am sure of England; She swarms foure times in a yeare, with people of all ages, Natures, Sexes, Callings . . . She seems to be a Glutton, for she desires always to be Full"[61]

The urban landscape and its importance to crime are analyzed later. For the present, it is necessary to introduce London as a city of dense and shifting population conglomerates. The adventurers, the ambitious, the discontented, the restless, the distraught, lived in and passed through the metropolis. Material gain was a primary motive as was the pursuit of leisure and entertainment. It is estimated that perhaps one-sixth of the total population spent at least part of its lives in the metropolis, many returning to their countryside parishes with newly acquired urban values.[62] "True Londoners," born and bred within the city, were apparently a small portion of city numbers. The growth of the metropolis was founded, then, upon the immigration of large and varied groups; peasants, craftsmen, yeomen, foreigners, soldiers, gentry, vagrant migrants, and rogues. These influxes stretched traditional living quarters and upset the old patterns. Indeed London pulsated with energy because it was an alternative to the constrictions of traditional agrarian society. "London is one of the freest places for their going abroad, without any questioning them what they are, for if they pay for their lodging or other charges they need not remove."[63] It represented, then, a place in which a degree of independence and liberty not found in rural social relations was available, a place in which a new start could be made. An urban citizen, for example, was less likely to be someone's servant. This should not be idealized. Parishional and corporate guild bodies certainly provided some order to urban London but urban life was freer and more diverse than rural life. Towns and cities possessed their own privileges and freedoms. Walls, separate magistracies and law, autonomous financed powers, and territorial liberties were some of London's prominent features. Because of its size, density, and heterogeneity London often served as a means of social escape. The expanding suburbs, in particular were a refuge for the discreditable.[64] Within the fabric of the social order of the city was threaded a large number of morally contrasting areas. Metropolitan London was a series of free zones in which "moderate libertie and lawful place of safties" could be found.[65] With loose bonds of social order and sporadically monitored, the metropolis offered anonymity. A thief, pickpocket, or confidence cheat easily acquired protection. Detection and social exclusion were unlikely. Safety, while relative, was enhanced by the diversity of urban life. The growing impersonality of relationships made identification and apprehension difficult. As Samaha has noted, "living near to London made it easy for criminals to slip across the border into the city and get lost among its teaming nameless faces. This was especially true as the period [1558–1603] progressed and the population expanded."[66] The risk of being caught was thus minimized, and criminal practices could acquire a stable routine. Opportunities for safe and persistent forms of crime were strengthened by the social protection the city afforded.

London, then, not only provided a marketplace for widened criminal enterprises, it was an environment with huge variation in habits of living. The dynamic and pluralistic character of the city fostered greater access to illegitimate means. In particular, it harbored entrenched criminal districts and associations.

Criminal Habitats

Behind the triple safeguard of moats, embankments, and ramparts, London revealed a peculiar ecology. A combination of customary privilege, weak communal policing, decentralized administration, and outright defiance, led to a complex city geography. Like Paris, London evolved as an agglomeration of monitored and unsupervised enclaves. The city center and main squares were usually a wealthy and tightly knit pattern of wards and parishes.[67] Elsewhere looser relationships prevailed. Of particular importance were the ecclesiastical domains within the city borders and the liberties and outparishes in the suburbs. Frequently they were urban palatines,

19

providing temporary and permanent refuge for lawbreakers, debtors, and felons. Such territories, in churchyards, asylums, bedlams, and other welfare principalities, were thriving deviant centers by the fifteenth century. Within them congregated people engaged in an array of discreditable criminal crafts, and exhibiting considerable entrepreneurship in violence. They thus constituted distinct neighborhoods outside the patterns of traditional authority.[68] During Elizabethan and Stuart times, the criminal palatines expanded, absorbing migrant populations, and in conjunction with the growing suburbs, they became the residential quarters of thieves, prostitutes, beggars, and casual laborers.

The significance and internal features of these criminal territories are analyzed in Chapter Four. It is sufficient to note here that a tradition of criminality was to be found within these precincts that offered organization, leadership, new oaths, laws, specific argot, and supportive facilities to criminal trades.[69] Such territories provided a group basis to marginal, oppositional, and criminal activities. Moreover, the criminal sanctuaries were effective bases of operation from which crimes could be planned and criminal skills routinized and passed on to succeeding generations. Like other city corporate bodies the cutpurses, thieves, prostitutes, and cony-catchers possessed their own versions of seigneuries collectives which lent a shape and stable structure to urban crime.[70] Criminal areas were mirror reflections of trade and guild quarters, and, as we shall see, they borrowed from the legitimate trades some of their characteristics: division of labor, collective styles, particular codes of behavior, and work discipline.

Criminal Associations and Networks

The increasing size and density of London's population in the late sixteenth and early seventeenth century made it easier for criminals to become concentrated enough to form discrete social networks of their own through which the skills and techniques of crime could be refined and generationally transmitted. We have seen that the London marketplace attracted a considerable casual labor pool. Seasonal variations in employment, periodic economic crises, and general insufficiencies in the job market meant that London harbored a rootless migratory population. Approximately 90 percent of the inhabitants of London were "artisans and urban poor"; of those about 13 percent were young men and women who hired out as domestic servants. A further 8 to 10 percent were regular transients—drivers, pack horsemen, petty chapmen, traders, and provincial merchants—who floated in and out of the city.[71] Students and disbanded soldiers and mariners by the thousands composed a large part of London's mobile population. In addition, hosts of wage earners and part-time workers drawn from the rural poor assisted artisans and craftsmen, particularly in the building trades and on the docks. Some 40,000 persons[72] were employed on the Thames and in the port of London. Common laborers, unskilled in trades, also represented a large marginal employed section of the labor force. It was particularly difficult for women, who were banned from guilds and crafts, to find permanent employment. Even the skilled workers—artisans, handicraftsmen, and mechanics—were linked with the poor. The traditional organization of crafts and guilds was on the wane. Competition from unregulated corporations destabilized and disrupted existing production practices. A devaluation of old skills and a drift into insecurity and poverty for the skilled worker were pervasive.[73] Estimates of urban pauperism in England and Western Europe place about one-quarter to one-half of the city inhabitants below subsistence levels.[74] As Pound has observed, "in virtually every English town of any size, the wage earners made up some 40% of the taxpayers. Combined with the really destitute, they totalled at least half and in extreme cases up to three-quarters of the population, and were a potentially dangerous element in society."[75]

Surviving censuses for Sheffield and Norwich reveal that the begging poor composed almost one-third of the town population. Moreover, the begging jobs they were supposed to be following were often fronts for discreditable activities.[76] London exhibited the same pattern. According to one estimate in 1602, there were some 30,000 "idle persons and masterless men" in the city. Perhaps one out of seven inhabitants was unemployed or unemployable.[77] Countless others remained in poverty despite casual or even full-time labor. Grinding poverty was acute and it contained the seeds of criminality. "There were broadly speaking two categories of poor: those prepared to work if given the opportunity, and those determined to avoid it at all costs. The latter group contained a whole host of individuals, ranging from the professional beggar on the one hand to the thief and murderer on the other."[78]

London was particularly well suited to an underworld of crime. It was the major milieu within which membership and organization could expand. It concentrated those with legitimate skills that could be transformed into criminal techniques. The expanding inchoate networks of hotel, catering, and transport workers were strategically located to tip off targets, and collude with thieves and prostitutes in providing information, assistance, shelter, and merchandising arrangements.[79] Tools such as gilks, ginnys, and cuttle-bungs could be readily acquired from dispossessed and sympathetic craftsmen in need of financial assistance.[80] The expanding entertainment industry facilitated a trade in illicit commercial sex.[81] Ordinaries, ale-houses, taverns, and playhouses were the haunts of thieves, tricksters, fences, and prostitutes. Middleton provided description of one such criminal haunt.

> There [a rogues' ordinary] was your gallant extraordinary thief that keeps his college of good fellows, and will not fear to rob a lord in his coach for all his trancher-bearers on horseback; your deep-conceited cutpurse, who by the dexterity of his knife will draw out the money, and make a flame-coloured purse show like the bottomless pit, but with never a soul in't; your cheating bowler, that will bank false of purpose, and lose a game of twelve-pence to purchase his partner twelve shillings in bets, and so share it after the play, your cheveril-gutted catchpoll, who like a horse-leech sucks gentlemen: and in all your twelve tribes of villany.[82]

London was also the mecca for wayfarers and for disbanded soldiers and mariners. Both these groups had for centuries possessed refined subcultures in which ruse and stealth were important elements. These itinerant occupational groups possessed unique languages, songs, rituals, and beliefs. The groups were partly autonomous, distinct but not completely severed from the meaning system of the culture at large. In particular, soldiers and sailors were versed in the ways of gambling, cheating, and theft. Such subcultures were important backcloths against which embryonic criminal institutions and relationships could take shape.[83] By the seventeenth century military styles of address were used among thieves. References to captains of thieves and to headquarters, divisions, ranks, badges, and soldiers were not uncommon.[84] The large bodies of ballad singers and sellers, centralized in London, were skilled in persuasive salesmanship that easily shaded into fraud. Their street wisdom was useful to thieves, informers, and blackmailers, but more directly, their capacity to draw and distract large street crowds made them convenient allies for pickpockets and robbers. London's domestic servants, growing in number as the gentry increased its residence in the city, were another group likely to assist in crime.[85] As insiders in wealthy residences they were accomplices of thieving teams. Many were seasonally employed women who drifted into a casual or enduring life of prostitution.

The magnetic nature of London made it a breeding ground for the dispossessed. The fragmented social order and the diversity of urban worlds in the context of widening criminal opportunities set the conditions for a criminal occupational community. Mobility loosened social mores and bonds. Countervailing traditions of deviance and crime took root in an economy of urban expansion.

A Criminal Marketplace

In addition to anonymity, opportunities, low risk, favored sanctuaries, and criminal allies and support, the expanding metropolis also provided a lucrative market for the disposal and distribution of stolen property. This function was crucial and is examined in greater depth in Chapter Six. For the moment it is important to note that the commercial growth of London was mirrored by the expansion of a criminal marketplace. It is unlikely that other English towns, lacking London's size and heterogeneity, could support such an institutional arrangement. The expanding metropolis was particularly well suited to the reselling of stolen goods. Because it was the crossroads of the country, travelers were continually passing through, and thieves or their receiver-patrons could easily dispose of their takings to such populations. More usual outlets were peddlers and the shops being set up in increasing numbers in the streets and at fairs, in which thieves self-fenced their goods. Similarly, the expanding leisure trades, the hotel industry, and the catering trades were convenient stalling-kens where stolen articles were stored and later distributed. The centrality of London and its importance as a port also contributed to the rapid circulation of goods. Articles could be dropped off quickly and disposed of quickly. Distribution reached into the hinterland, and the tracing of stolen goods was difficult.

Equally important for the thrust of criminal activities was London's loose network of fencing partners who helped thieves dispose of their goods. Often they functioned as patrons of crime, directing the organization of thieving.[86] Such brokers ran houses at which information, contacts, alibis, and shelter were provided. The risks of self-fencing were eliminated by this use of intermediaries. Many brokers of stolen property were themselves strategically placed to funnel the "takes" into wider legitimate markets. The attendant at the alehouse and tavern, the bawd of brothels, the cartmen of the markets, and the small shopkeepers had a ready clientele, which enabled them to mix regular business with routine illegal distribution. Thus separate fencing businesses lent a shape to crime; they provided a working method, a locus of exchange between disreputable activities and the legitimate world. The fencing business in London widened the avenues for the flow of stolen goods. In the context of weak policing institutions, fences sometimes came to play public roles. They developed new and simple markets, the most obvious and important one being to return stolen property to its rightful owners. The system of returning stolen property for a commission allowed some fences to open permanent offices and warehouses for the recovery of stolen property, which thief and victim were encouraged to patronize. The institutionalization of such regular intermediaries, by guaranteeing that outlets would be available, encouraged thieves to steal regularly.

London, then, was unique in providing what Cloward and Ohlin refer to as a structure of illegitimate opportunities.[87] That is, the metropolis provided by means of differential association its own specific type of opportunities and life styles distinct from legitimate ones. In particular, it afforded widespread access to illegitimate means. Countries that are now undergoing similar transitions to urbanization seem to develop similar patterns of criminal opportunities which are ecologically based and organized. As Clinard and Abbot concluded in their comparative survey of crime, "access to illegitimate means . . . the heterogeneity, complexity, asymmetry, anonymity, impersonality, and individuality of urban life create situations not only for young migrants but for those in positions of economic and political power in regard to motivations, opportunities, rationalizations, and the lack of effective legal controls to support the breaking of formal laws."[88] London offered exactly such a supportive ground for criminal opportunities in the form of available wealth and commodities, colleagueship, techniques of operation,

24

protection and immunity, and market rationality. In addition, as I discuss later, crime was encouraged by features of the legal and political order itself. Gaps and irregularities in the enforcement of social control led to official negligence and corruption which undergirded criminal ventures.

3

THE LABOR
MARKET, THE LAW,
AND CRIME

Introduction

To a considerable degree, London's growth as a consumer market was parasitical, feeding off the radical redistribution of wealth occurring in the provincial economy. This provides a major clue to an understanding of the London labor market. "London's commercial success in the sixteenth century relied heavily on cannibalizing the trade of provincial ports, while much of its growing population was underemployed and could only be supported by an unhealthy expansion of marginal service activities."[1] Not only did London attract a disproportionate share of disfranchised and unemployed men, women, and children, it seldom could employ or support these populations. Thus, the underemployment characteristic of the economy of the period was magnified in the metropolis. In industry this condition arose from the "absence of fixed capital equipment capable of operating independently of the immediate interference of nature."[2] The irregular demand underlying much of London's economy generated reliance on a casual unstable labor base. Labor turnover was high and subject to considerable seasonal variation. Climatic conditions, transportation difficulties, delays in the delivery of supplies and raw materials, and irregular and inconstant demands for products further exacerbated the underdeveloped nature of the economy. This had serious implications for the social structure of London and for the formation of a criminal population. This chapter begins by looking briefly at the nature of the casual labor market in London, then examines the process of legal censure, and finally, describes the effect the law had on the creation of a criminal underclass.

The Casual Labor Market and the Social Structure of London

Within London a peculiar structure of casual labor emerged. Although the English economy as a whole was plagued by a long-term tendency toward underemployment, London was also profoundly affected by sudden short-term economic transitions: the eviction of the rural surplus population, the return of disbanded soldiers, mariners, and private retainers, immigration from the Continent, periodic trade slumps, and price-wage imbalances. These factors, combined with the seasonal nature of production and consumption central to a service economy of leisure, produced an inescapable casual labor problem. Here I explore the nature of production as it relates to the London poor and the creation of specifically criminal associations and transactions.

An analysis of the major industries of London—consumer goods, the port industries, and the construction trades—reveals the irregularity of the labor process resulting from the inconstant production demand and difficulties related to the supply of capital, the availability of materials, and the technology of travel and communication.[3] The hotel, catering, and leisure trades were particularly tied to seasonal fluctuations in demand. The gentry's London season ran from October to June and directly affected the employment of servants, hostelers, barmen, cooks, tailors and dressmakers, and the entertainment industry.[4] Cloth workers were also prone to seasonal unemployment with their peak production rates around the high consumption periods of Christmas and Easter.[5] The fuel workers and those carmen connected with the transportation end of the coal trade suffered from a slack period in summer. The importance of London as a finishing center for consumer wares implied a small-scale industrial base dependent on receiving already worked-on goods and raw materials from the provinces.[6] Supplies had to come long distances and were subject to seasonal interruptions. The shipping of grain and timber ebbed and flowed irregularly, and the arrival on the docks of imported goods fluctuated according to seasonal sales. London was important as a food market, and trades tied to the transportation, processing, and distribution of foodstuffs were subject to the vagaries of nature. Bad harvests meant little work and possible starvation. The seasonal interruption of the supply of partly finished products and raw resources was further affected by climatic conditions and by the poor transportation technology.[7]

Seasonality also affected labor by interrupting the production process itself. Irrespective of demand and the supply of raw materials the building trades were regulated by climatic factors. Cold, rain, and snow shortened working hours and reduced output.[8] The new domestic industries of the city suburbs outside the regulations of the livery companies were particularly affected by seasonal employment. Attracted by the tax benefits of escaping city jurisdiction, their industries—sugar refining, glassmaking, alum and dye works, copper and brass mills, clock making, weaving, printing, and the silk trade—made use of cheap labor without providing the benefits of apprenticeship.[9]

This underlying seasonality of production was amplified by social custom. The right to leisure was deeply embedded in community claims that overrode an interest in income maximization. The patterning of daily work developed out of a tradition of laxness. Holidays and religious and communal ceremonies were frequent, long, and irregular, disrupting the regularity, consistency, and intensity of labor practices. A rhythm of time and work discipline so necessary to steady production had not yet developed.[10]

The seasonality of production did not always imply a seasonality of employment. Some trades were capable of maintaining a nucleus of regular workers, hiring casual workers only at peak periods. Others diversified their products, but most hired labor periodically for short durations. Some dovetailing of one seasonal occupation with another did occur. Day laborers regularly relied on agricultural work as well as domestic handicrafts.[11] But markets were unstable and severe cumulative effects of seasonality persisted, producing irregular employment for the London laboring class. Indeed, the sheer availability of mobile labor meant a continual glut of the labor market. So plentiful were the unskilled in London, that the House of Lords in 1621 drafted an act to restrain any further migration into the city.[12] But skilled apprentices, artisans, traders, and journeymen were also linked to the casual labor market. Their skills could easily go out of demand, and they often slipped into poverty.[13] Their wages could fall as much as twelve months in arrears.[14]

Estimates for the size of the problem vary, but the sudden and volatile nature of the variation is clear. Trade depressions, natural climatic events, harvest disasters, and plague often plunged the city into severe crises. At any one time a substantial sector of London's population was out of work. Conservative figures place the stable surplus labor force at 20 percent, but this shot upward at times of seasonal depression to as high as 50 percent.[15] When this large surplus labor pool was combined with trade slumps and natural catastrophes, a solid basis for organized mobs was prepared.[16] Historical research on later periods indicates that such structural underemployment remained a pervasive feature of the Hanoverian and Victorian London economy.[17]

Through a crude catalogue of the composition of London's population, it is possible to prize out the strata that fed the pool of the demoralized London poor. A central feature was the continual population of migrants pushing in and out of the city. By the early seventeenth century most Londoners were first-generation immigrants to the city.[18] Authorities referred to the majority of the city's population as the base multitudes, the meaner sort, or the lower orders. Such collective labels often encompassed 80 to 90 percent of the population and included a jumble of artisans, semiskilled laborers, apprentices, and paupers. Skilled and unskilled workers were seldom differentiated.[19] There is warrant, however, for drawing a broad distinction between as many as five social strata within the lower orders of the city:

1. The master craftsmen, artisans, and small shopkeepers of the city and the petty tradesmen with stalls in markets.
2. The skilled journeymen and apprentices. The dividing line between these groups and the strata above and below was very fluid. Some were upwardly mobile, achieving the status of master through skill or marriage. Many remained journeymen and spent their lives at the edge of poverty.

3. The mass of common workers—semiskilled or unskilled—who knew only the rudiments of a trade: the day laborers, cooks, bakers, victuallers, servants, tanners, clock and river workers, founderers, bricklayers, coachmen, chimneysweeps, and cartmen.
4. The host of irregular transients and small traders who constantly moved through the city on a larger orbit of activity—the postriders and carriers with wagons, hundreds of other transportation workers, drovers, pack horsemen, petty chapmen, and mariners by the thousands, watermen, bargemen, sailors—who may have amounted to 8 percent of the city's population.
5. Finally, the submerged and roaming populations of beggars and vagrants, the miserable unemployed and unemployable, the old and masterless, part-time servants said to compose 13 percent of London's urban poor, the poorest of the immigrants, the criminal rogues, and those who tended to be called "idle persons and masterless men," of whom there were reckoned to be some 30,000 in 1602.[20]

Life for the mass of London's inhabitants was difficult, brutal, and violent, and a constant struggle against disease, poverty, and death. Conflicts within and between social groups were intense. The bonds of status, obligation, and employment that once guaranteed position in the chain of things were dissolving. Social mobility in both directions was a heightened fact of life within the London metropolis. There was some leveling of prestige distinctions between court, gentry, greater merchants, and secular professions. Yet the overwhelming trend was one of downward social mobility.[21] The gaps between rich and poor widened, as did the differences within social groupings. Thomas Nashe proclaimed that "in London, the rich disdayne the poor. The Courtier the Citizen. The Citizen the Countryman. One occupation disdayneth another. The Merchant the Retayler. The Retayler the Craftsman. The better sort of Craftsman the baser. The Shoemaker the Cobler, the Cobler the Carman."[22]

This social mobility did more than fracture established arrangements of rank and status. The content of work was altered. The transition to a commercial capitalist economy transformed masterlaborer relations which affected not only the expanding service and leisure occupations but also traditional craft production. The institution of apprenticeship in particular was altered. Sons of gentlemen no longer able to live on land rent and other capital surpluses sought out trades and, with what wealth they had, set up as middle merchants and tradesmen. Thus, poorer apprentices were blocked from promotion and became part of an ever-growing transitory class of journeymen. Their channels of mobility blocked from above, they spent their lives as part of a wage-earning, declassed poor.[23] The destabilization of labor was not peculiar to the tertiary sector, it was also rooted in the emerging capitalization of social relations within manufacturing and retailing industries. As Hill has noted, the putting-out system of production in London was built around a "standing pool of unemployed labour."[24] Thus, the predominantly domestic household system of production operated more and more on assumptions calculated to meet a seasonally structured market. Employers routinely had more workers on the books than normally required to enable them to meet seasonal fluctuations in demand. Moreover, workers were often paid in kind that was valued at inflated prices. They were encouraged to obtain raw materials on credit. Indebtedness was cultivated to create dependency. Bargaining power was nonexistent. Hours were long and work and wages irregular. In slump times surplus workers were thrown onto parish relief.[25] Wage labor and poor relief legislation arose in unison and complemented one another. Poor laws encouraged the payment of low wages which had to be supplemented by relief from parish coffers if the families of laborers were to survive.[26]

The importance of the London casual labor market was bolstered by two other major economic factors: monetary inflation and declining real wages. Although these factors acted as a stimulus to the export clothing trade, whose prices lagged behind those of continental competitors, they savagely depressed the living standards of the lower half of the population.[27] The general price level rose five times between 1530 and 1640, with food and fuel prices rising more dramatically than those of other commodities. Real wages declined in some trades by over half.[28] These problems, combined with the pressure to forsake land and holdings and the availability of rural-based labor, which further served to keep wages down, meant that London was burdened with an increasing number of desperate demoralized poor who were tied into a widening orbit of economic instability. Pamphleteers and preachers talked of men, women, and children dying of starvation on the streets of London. Those making up the 'begging poor' were not merely "wandering tribes," they were also stable urban paupers.[29] The casual labor market embraced wide sectors of the economy. Few skilled artisans, master craftsmen, or petty tradesmen were likely to become unemployed. Some small men of property, and to a greater degree their wealthier counterparts—the peers, gentry, and larger merchants, and the professional and managerial elite of lawyers and clerics—probably benefited from the price spirals of the sixteenth and seventeenth centuries.[30] However, the common laborers, the small traders and carriers, and the domestic servants, more likely than not became and remained pauperized.[31] Cyclical fluctuations did at times relieve economic pressures. Some trades found temporary solutions. Other crafts barely survived. But, for many Londoners, seasonal unemployment with its dependence on the arbitrary whims of supply and demand was a way of life.[32]

Four factors combined to keep the supply of labor chronically in excess of demand. First, there was a continual flow of excess labor from rural areas and foreign countries. Second, there was a ready supply of surplus workers because of general transformations in the transition economy and the seasonality of employment in various crafts and work. Third, the penetration of outside labor into the London market as a result of short-term crisis and fluctuations was continual. Finally, there was a high degree of circulation of part-time laborers around jobs within the London casual labor market. These factors often intermeshed, and temporary pulls to the city were frequently a prelude to perpetual imprisonment within the London casual labor market.[33]

Two further peculiarities of the structure of the London labor market need to be mentioned. First, the age composition of the unskilled population was particularly low. The effects of the dislocation of commerce and industry upon the mass of the population drove more and more children into the labor market. The data on vagrants indicate that many were children and adolescents. Approximately one-quarter of all migrants were between the ages of eleven and twenty.[34] And in the case of Salisbury, two-thirds of those set on work schemes were under fifteen.[35] As Hill has noted, "child labour existed long before the factories in the form of home industries."[36] Certainly contemporaries were alarmed about keeping the young at labor. Justice Lombarde observed in 1582 that "many young persons not altogether evil at first" were abandoning their trades and becoming migrants.[37] The sudden disruption of cottage-based industries deposited increasing numbers of children on the London wage market. Unskilled and unlikely to be apprenticed, they were forced into the dead-end occupations associated with routine intermediary tasks such as messengers, porters, carmen, and errand boys. Some substitution of juvenile for adult labor probably occurred. The young were regularly singled out for specific monitoring in the vagrancy acts of 1536, 1547, 1549, 1572, and 1597.[38] They were usually given corporal punishment or apprenticed to work.[39] The City of London experimented with work schemes, hospitals, and transportation as means of managing the surplus child population.[40] Between 1618 and 1622 close to 300 vagrant children were deported from London to Virginia as a cheap labor force.[41] This did not alleviate the problem of semicriminal children. In 1632, the Corporation reported that 773 poor children were at Christ's Hospital, and approximately 50 vagrants were bound over as apprentices to work in Barbados and Virginia.[42]

A second striking feature of the London labor market was its sex composition, women being well represented. Data on migratory populations suggest a drift of women into the casual wage-earning sector of the economy.[43] London was an economic magnet for single women seeking work, and females outnumbered males thirteen to ten.[44] The refusal of guilds and of the city crafts to apprentice women narrowed occupational opportunities and confined many to "housewife trades"—brewers, bakers, and cooks—for which they were poorly paid. Women were particularly prominent in the victualing and vending trades; by far the greatest number worked as domestic servants for the wealthy, or at private inns.[45] Many women drifted in and out of prostitution and thieving. Henry Peacham warned the young, "You young men, avoid all whores; and you young women, avoid becoming such."[46]

Fueled by the decline of provincial ports, the outflow from the countryside, the breaking up of large estates, and the disbanding of continental armies, London's casual labor supply outstripped demand. Trade and commercial enterprises, although expanding, could not accommodate the available pool, and underemployment was chronic. Seasonality of production and employment ensured a reserve population of cheap labor. Irregular production, fluctuating prices, and declining real wages opened up a wide divide within the city. The London poor, in Engels's apt term, were a demoralized poor. A section of them drifted into deviant and criminal trades. Moreover, it is important to notice that they were defined as an occupational group, and in numerous tracts, statutes, and acts, their activities, language, and life style were described as discrete social phenomena rather than as lower-class deviations.[47]

Regulating the Outcast: Law and Order

The casual labor market in London created considerable problems of social control, and its management was a major preoccupation of municipal, state, and parish authorities. Often surveillance, regulation, and sanctions involved cruel coercion. A primitive legal code evolved that substituted harshness for philanthropy. Social reforms combined unevenly with legal censure. On the one hand, the poor laws demanded strict discipline and severe punishment. On the other, they recognized the necessity of a comprehensive social policy. The workhouse stood in the shadow of the torturer. The myriad of work schemes, ad hoc parish relief, and punishments points up the gravity of the problem, and the desperate quality of the solutions reveals the tenuous character of state control during the Elizabethan and Stuart periods. Social problems were managed by a peculiar artifice of law and censure—one that was difficult to translate into action and that had consequences for crime. What follows is an examination of poor law legislation, an assessment of enforcement, and an evaluation of the role of the law in the establishment of a criminal underclass.

But first a note on order and power is necessary. Internally, English society was structured hierarchically. The least powerful, the casual poor and masterless, were the objects of an elaborate scheme of surveillance and repression, which monitored their movement, labor, and social behavior. The powerful, on the other hand, were seldom accountable for their actions; they could violate the law with impunity.[48] The significance of this distinction was bolstered by the prevailing vision of social order, a vision infused with "the corporeal analogy of society."[49] This metaphorical imagery defined Elizabethan society as a commonwealth with distinct contours and an inner structure of dissimilar yet related parts. As W. R. D. Jones has noted, "socio-economic ideas and projects . . . were embedded within an organic ideal of society which still upheld differentiation of status and of function, equity of distribution as well as efficiency of production, delegation of power and of property in trust."[50] The social order was largely constituted by groups who had local loyalties and who performed fixed roles. "No land and no man without a land" was the leitmotif.[51] Groups wedded to masters and stable communities with stable obligations were the accredited segments in the body politic. The morally reputable had a defined place in the long accepted chain of patron-client subordination. Those without masters, on the other hand—rogues, vagrants, beggars, cottagers, squatters, itinerant traders and laborers, women seeking work, and disbanded soldiers and mariners—formed a disreputable underworld. Often they were defined as inferiors, mean, and on occasion social menaces. Indeed, in a corporealist vocabulary, the dispossessed were endowed with a pathological status, as akin to parasites and plagues. Crowley compared them "to corrupted humours in a body" and went on to say that forceful purgation was an essential remedy.[52] Cheke referred to vagrants and the "loitering poor" as but "a boil in a body, nay like a sink in a town," the implication being that poverty and disenfranchisement were the causes of disorder.[53]

Neglect and corruption on the part of the higher orders, though criticized by religious thinkers, were not considered of much social consequence, but the outcasts were thought to be less than fully human, deserving qualitatively different and unique treatment.[54] A fear of civil disobedience or even social resistance was widespread. The seasonal poor, the unattached, and the itinerant were without a manifest connection to the political order. Because they were base, they merited less legal respect than those who were gentlemen or of the middling sort. Becon described the prevailing notion of social justice: "The inferior members to envey the principal part of the body . . . The servant to rule the master, the inferior to rue against his sovereign, the subject to disobey his governor . . . The brainsick, yea rather the brainless head to attempt redress of matters in a commonweal, unsent, uncalled O preposterous order."[55] It was generally assumed that large segments of the poor and masterless would be punished as a matter of course, perhaps even hanged, that the wandering, the rootless, the gypsy, the beggar were preordained for whippings, the stockades, and the rope. It was the status of the offender, not the offense, that defined the meaning of illegality and crime.[56] In control of the justice system the powerful easily acquired immunity from the effects of their own laws. As Samaha has noted, the privileged often committed great crimes but seldom were they caught or punished. "The law could not even reach the upper classes' lowest ranks, if they wished to cast it aside. In general, it seems they [gentry] came to court when they wanted to do so and not otherwise."[57] For lesser offenses, the poor were maimed and executed. As Dekker complained, "many lost their lives for scarce as much coins as will hide their palm, which is most cruel."[58]

The growth of the casual poor became an integral part of the problem of law and order. The sixteenth century did not discover poverty but found it taking new shapes, appearing on a larger scale and in a more concentrated form. Particularly noticeable during the latter half of the sixteenth century were the urban poverty associated especially with London and the large textile towns, and the rural poverty linked to the instability of the agricultural hinterland.[59] It is the former that is of chief interest here. The persistent yet fluctuating and growing casual labor market represented the major social and political problem for the London authorities. The management of the London poor was determined by a policy toward law and order that had as its central tenet the suppression of vagrancy, mendicancy, and crime. The incredible mass of legislation produced between 1550 and 1700 has been examined elsewhere,[60] but I would like to indicate the main landmarks of the legislative history, evaluate their importance, and draw out the implications for the criminal underclass.

Legislation against the Poor

Before 1530 there were few laws governing vagrancy, although several municipalities had for half a century been dealing with the problems caused by "poverty . . . and his cousin necessity."[61] The existing laws were simple and reflected the medieval attitude that "poverty was at once a blessing, a challenge and a chastisement."[62] Poor relief was in the hands of ecclesiastical authorities, or was a matter of private charity. By giving alms the wealthy received a meritorious status. They acquired grace by fulfilling their Christian duty. Monasteries, not the courts, were the major institutions assisting the dispossessed.[63]

A distinction was often made between genuine and feigned or wilful poverty. The origins of a legal typology of the poor can be traced at least as far back as the Ordinances of Labourers of 1349, where they existed within an essentially repressive framework.[64] In the sixteenth century, however, under the influence of humanist social thought, a more elaborate classification and treatment emerged. Recognition of the need for more involved control of the poor was combined with an understanding of the economic and social causes of poverty. In practical terms, this resulted in laws that mixed social reform and work discipline.[65] Preoccupied with the problems of the dispossessed, particularly with their social control, the authorities evolved a doctrine of corporate responsibility that minimized private charity and maximized self-improvement and communal duty.[66] The sixteenth-century laws against vagrancy reflected this thrust for discipline, social betterment, and corporate responsibility. Early legislation directed that all suspicious dispossessed should be detained until sureties could be found. Vagrants were divided into two categories, sturdy and impotent. The latter were to be recognized as legitimate poor. They were licensed and permitted to beg for assistance. The former were forbidden to wander. They were made to work, put in the stocks, whipped, maimed, and even executed.[67] This rudimentary legal framework was built upon in the course of the sixteenth century. The dramatic transformations in economic and social life led to a growing appreciation of the continual need for careful and vigorous differentiation of the causes of poverty, which resulted in more elaborate poor laws, classifications, and modes of treatment, and to the realization that systematic organized poor relief was an essential state priority. This new view came about primarily because "on the one hand, accelerating changes in the economic organization of society led to an increase in poverty which was either rootless or not attributable to natural catastrophe—both characteristics which were potentially dangerous to peace and order. On the other hand, men saw those institutions which—with all their defects—had traditionally been responsible for the relief of destitution in the past now crumble between the pincers of decay from within and attack from without."[68] But more was involved. Behind visible fear and decay, intangible processes were at work fostering direct legal initiatives: (1) the gradual movement of responsibility from religious to secular authority, (2) the decline of ecclesiastical institutions and the emergence of civil contexts, (3) the shift from voluntary gifts to compulsory poor rate assessments, and (4) the growth of a central political authority.[69] The central issue for this discussion is that the problems of social stability were increasingly a matter for civil institutions, in particular the Elizabethan state. As Jones has argued, "the significance of the State as guarantor of law and order . . . increase [d] as reverence for a divinely sanctioned rigid social hierarchy diminished."[70] The regulation of the poor, once a responsibility of church and guild-sponsored programs, now became enshrined in an increasingly imperialistic legal code. In turn, law as an institution acquired increasing symbolic and instrumental importance. Its practices were akin to a civic drama in that they ritualistically shored up the social order.[71]

To understand the character of the legislative explosion against the poor, it is necessary to consider the statutes of 1530–1531. The poor without papers and outside their districts, and all persons able to work who were caught begging, were stigmatized as undeserving. They were to be punished, then sent back to their place of residence and either put on relief or set to work. Specific low-life occupations were similarly cast outside the margins of propriety. Proctors (collectors for charities, usually authorized, but often in an ambiguous position), shipmen, fencers, minstrels, pardoners, players, and the like were to be whipped two days in succession. For a second offense the undeserving poor and those practicing disreputable crafts were to receive further similar punishment and, in addition, were to be put in the pillory and have an ear removed. For a further offense they were to undergo more whippings and have the second ear removed. An amendment to this statute in 1536–1537 made it a felony punishable by death to be guilty of vagrancy a third time, and this remained in force until 1547.[72] In this year, the two earlier statutes of the 1530s were repealed and replaced by much harsher legislation.[73] All ablebodied persons without work were adjudged de facto vagabonds. Their former masters might legally transform them into personal chattel for two years. As such, they were branded, chained, whipped, and forced to work. The masterless poor were to be made collective chattels of the local community, also for a two-year period. If they escaped, they were branded with an S and made slaves for life. A second escape resulted in death as a felon. This body of legislation, although severe, was difficult to enforce and was repealed two years later.[74] The statutes of 1530–1531 were then revived and remained in effect until 1572.

The statute of 1572, the product of six years' debate and organization, was an elaborate legal artifice. In response to increasing vagrancy and social disorders, it provided an even stricter punitive system for sturdy beggars and inaugurated a compulsory poor rate to assist the respectable poor. This law contained the well-known differentiation between the poor by physical affliction, the poor by economic circumstances, and the poor by their own idleness.[75] Moreover, it vividly described the ranks of sturdy rogues and vagrants. The list of disreputable poor included proctors without licensed authority, idle persons indulging in crafty and unlawful games (pickpockets, dice cheats, etc.), all unaccounted for ablebodied persons who were not working, common laborers who refused to work, counterfeiters of passports and licenses and users of the same, unlicensed shipmen, discharged prisoners, soldiers and sailors, all fencers, bearwards (bear trainers), players, minstrels not affiliated to reputable persons, and finally, all itinerant peddlers, chapmen, and jugglers unless licensed by two justices of the peace, one of whom had to be from the shire in which they resided. The penalties were severe and applied to those over fourteen years old. For a first vagrancy violation, offenders were to be whipped and burned through the right ear or recruited as indentured labor for one year. For wandering, loitering, idling, or begging a second time, the punishment was death as a felon unless they could be apprenticed to a master as indentured labor for two years. For a third offense, the penalty was death without right of labor or benefit of clergy. Further legislation, enacted three year later, provided for some parish assistance in setting sturdy rogues to work. It urged the provision of work materials (stocks of wood, iron, hemp, etc.) and the construction of parish workhouses. The famous poor laws of 1597 and 1601 were simply modifications of these statutes of 1572 and 1575.[76] They moderated the punishments and made more explicit the methods for financing poor relief and for establishing the ablebodied at work. These poor laws remained virtually unaltered throughout the seventeenth century. The changes that were made, particularly at the time of the later settlement acts, strengthened the formal procedures for moving and certifying migrants,[77] but did not alter the legal typology of the poor.

It is difficult to assess the significance of this welter of poor law legislation. At one level, government, law, and policing agencies attempted to fashion a concise moral world whose horizons and character were clear. Poverty in general was made equivalent to a lack of grace.[78] A large number of offenders, offenses, dubious occupations, and practices were recatalogued and thrust to the periphery of the social order. Many lesser offenses were made capital. The concept of "vagrant rogue" was used indiscriminately to describe several categories of poor: the work shy, migrant workers who followed their jobs from place to place, beggars who solicited on the streets or from door to door, and habitual criminals who mingled with these wanderers and encouraged and schooled novices among them. The poor laws actively promoted the idea that vagrants were petty criminals who led other wayfarers into illegal activities and incited them to riot.[79]

The poor law statutes expanded the use of criminalization as a control mechanism in three ways. First, the coverage of the law was extended. The problem of poverty became inextricably mixed with that of unemployment. Instead of using the old division of the poor into the impotent and the willfully idle the law now embraced those who were marginally employed or in search of work. Second, the new statutes codified harsher penalties for traveling unemployed populations. Although these provisions were aimed at the professional rogues and focused on common theft, the effect was to make all wandering tradesmen and traveling workers a suspect class with little legal protection. Such statutes could be used to coerce a wide range of wayfarers.[80] Stigmatized by the law as dangerous and criminal, the poor were increasingly demoralized. Finally, Elizabethan and Stuart poor laws, unlike previous vagrancy regulations, centralized policy at the state level, by insisting that the central government assume a coordinating function in administering enforcement.[81] While the actual practice of such a coordinating role was checkered, it did represent a form of state intervention in local parish and borough affairs. Such a policy provided an early example of enlarged nationwide crime control, mirroring the increased involvement of the state in guild and church organization.[82]

The coercive and segregative tone of the poor laws was bolstered by new perceptions about poverty. The view that the poor deserved kind treatment from society because the social order had not treated them well was replaced by a harsher, more disciplinarian attitude. Almsgiving was decried and replaced by work schemes. Labor was enforced and monitored. Children were trained to work. Hard work was rewarded. Those who remained poor were a cursed generation "bent to all mischief."[83] "He makes a beggar first that first relieves him" became an increasingly popular refrain. "As for the legacies to the poor . . . as for beggars by trade and election, I give them nothing; as for impotents by the hand of God, the public ought to maintain them; as for those who have been bred to no calling nor estate, they should be put upon their kindred.[84] The "wicked poor," in the words of one pamphleteer, should not only be condemned and excluded but "must be purged away by the hand of the magistrate."[85] Socially outcast, "the honourable will abhor them, the worshipped will reject them, the yeomen will sharply taunt them, the husbandmen utterly defy them, the labouring men bluntly chide them, the women with a loud exclamation wonder at them, and all children with clapping hands cry out at them."[86]

Punishments became more severe and ceremonial. Sermons, mobile gallows, dying speeches and confessions, whipping campaigns, proclamations, and search and arrest tactics ritualistically emphasized the magnitude of the separation between the reputable and the disreputable. The poor laws were a form of social censure that received legitimacy from the policies arrived at by the government and the employing class.[87] As Hill and Stone have noted, the poor faced the thrust of regulation which the rich avoided.[88] But the outcast was not entirely cut off from the world of legitimacy. The multiplicity of statutes, the frequency with which laws were enacted, and the accumulation of criminal definitions and punishments were a constant and at times majestic affirmation of the social order. Yet, at another level, everyday enforcement practices were inadequate to the tasks. The margins between good and evil did become blurred, and the law itself was open to considerable bargaining. Before expanding this argument, I would like to discuss a second body of law directed specifically against the "criminous classes."

Legislation against the Criminal Classes

In addition to the legislation against vagabondage, there was a series of laws directed at thieves and cony-catchers. These laws recognized that picking pockets and illegal gaming had become discrete criminal crafts, the practitioners of which were linked together for support. Picking pockets was described in statutes as akin to a craft mystery with routinized skills, roles, and working places. One law is worth quoting at length.

> Where a certain kind of evil disposed persons commonly called Cutpurses or Pickpurses, but in deed by the laws of this land very Felons and Thieves, do confer together making among themselves as it were a Broth-

erhood or Fraternity of an Art or Mysterie, to live idle by the secret Spoil of the good and true Subjects of this Realm and as well at Sermons and Preachings of the Word of God, and in places and time of doing service and common Prayer in Churches, Chapels, Closettes and Oratories, and not only there but also in the Princes Palace House, yea and presence, and at the Places and Courtes of Justice, and at the times of Ministration of the Laws in the same, and in Fair, Markets and other Assemblies of People, yea and at the time of doing of Execution of such as been attained of any Murder, Felony or other criminal cause ordained chiefly for Terror and Example of evil doers, do without respect or regard of any time, place or person, or any fear or dread of God, or any law or punishment, under the cloak of honesty, by their outward apparel, countenance and behaviour subtley, privily, craftily and felonously take the goods of diverse good and honest Subjects from their persons by cutting and picking their purses and other felonous slights and devices, to the utter undoing and impoverishment of many.[89]

The penalty for such crimes was death as a felon without right of labor or benefit of clergy.

Although this was the most severe and direct of all the statutes against theft, the state made repeated efforts to restrain the operation of thieves. Legislation was directed particularly at controlling the spread of taverns and alehouses. Lists of tavern keepers were drawn up. Instructions were circulated forbidding unlawful activities and proclaiming strict working hours. There were edicts against playhouses, the stews, sporting events, and the crowds and traffic in specific city locales, all of which warned of criminal activities: theft, cony-catching, and prostitution.[90] City areas were identified in the legislation as criminal dominions, and justices of the peace were enjoined to survey and regulate them directly.[91] More systematic as a legislative code were the laws against gaming. By the mid-sixteenth century there were numerous statutes and proclamations against dicing, bowling, card games, half-bowl, tennis, and tables.[92] Yet, despite the statute books, "gambling diverted the attention of the labouring poor . . . Men gambled on cards, dice, horses, foot races, bear baiting, cock fighting and a host of similar pastimes."[93] Moreover, a system of patents afforded protection to gaming facilities and permitted what the laws otherwise forbade. Hence, the government licensed what it could not restrain. The patent of 1576, permitting exclusive royal control over gambling houses in London puts the problem succinctly: "seeing the inclination of men to be given and bent to the aforesaid pastimes and play, and that secretly or openly they do commonly play, and that no penalty of the laws or statutes aforesaid have therefore restrained them."[94] Such patents were akin to monopolies and had the effect of undermining the legal statutes. They were purchased and farmed for profits by court favorites, and were the source of continual conflicts between municipal and state governments. The economic benefits all went to crown-sponsored patrons, while the costs of the crime and disorder associated with gaming houses fell on the municipal authorities. Gambling institutions also became the principal fields of operation of card and dice sharpers and cozeners.[95]

The granting of monopolies over licensing was ostensibly a social-control measure. For keepers of the play and groom-porters the ability to issue licenses, control the manufacture and distribution of dice, tables, and cards, and prevent various forms of fraud was one of the perquisites of office.[96] For example, royal patents awarded to Thomas Cornwallis required that he award his licenses with caution and ensure that authorized agents did not suffer frauds or allow suspected persons to frequent gaming premises. The patent empowered him with a right of sanction. He set fines and penalties on those who gamed unlawfully.[97] A second patent awarded to him twenty years later increased his powers in regard to preventing deceit and cozenage. It maintained his monopoly privileges and allowed for the surveillance of gambling institutions to discover abrogations of legal statutes and of the patent. In addition, dice makers allegedly responsible for much cozenage were placed under direct supervision. Craftsmanship and retailing were to be strictly monitored under the patent. Fines for making or vending false dice were set at 3s.4d.[98]

There is some reason to suppose that the awarding of patents to control licenses was not entirely effective. According to City of London records, licensed gaming houses and bowling alleys remained plentiful and disorderly. They produced health problems and were the regular haunts of pickpockets, thieves, cozeners, and prostitutes.[99] Privy Council and the London Court of Aldermen reported that despite statutes and patents, the manufacture of false dice continued unabated. Committees were formed to investigate haberdashery shops, patrol licensing procedures, and survey gaming establishments.[100] Enforcement was inconstant, proclamations and orders were continually renewed, and the implication is that dice fraud and confidence cheating went on regularly, if clandestinely.

Playing cards, like dice, were regulated by monopolies issued under patent, and control was a matter of private patronage. Licensed restraint rather than outright coercion was the mode of operation. Monopolies were sold to court favorites and then speculated on for profit. Thus Ralph Bowes and Thomas Bedinfield paid 100 marks a year to obtain official control over the importation and manufacture of playing cards in England.[101] The privilege empowered them and their successors to search, license, and impose sanctions. A lucrative business could be formed from fines. Indeed, since patents were awarded for limited durations there were strong incentives to sell licenses, collect fines, and generally maximize short-term personal gain. The licensing system provided ample opportunities for corruption and fraud, as criminals could easily impersonate patent officials and extort fines illegally. Cony-catching was shielded by royal protection. The ambiguities and loopholes in the law provided "excellent chances for booty . . . with rogues blackmailing other rogues in the card business, and compounding for fines and penalties."[102] The legal machinery was malleable, and revenues to the crown were balanced against due process. The law, particularly as it applied to theft and cony-catching, was equivocal and complex and exploited by the knowing: "The most important reason for the cony-catchers' immunity from legal interference was what we should call . . . 'graft.' They had influence in high places."[103] Thus, officials at all levels who administered the criminal law invented and indulged in practices that sometimes nullified legal intent. The widespread use of prerogatives and patents made the law susceptible to bargaining and collusion.[104]

Enforcement, Supervision, and Translation

To return to the enforcement of the law, one mode of regulation flowing from the welter of legal initiatives was the construction of concise moral boundaries. Specific populations were ritualistically excluded from the moral order, and their habits were legally proscribed. The poor laws were thus symbolic, maintaining and affirming the relationships of power and privilege. Yet as the discussion of legislation against thieving and cony-catching has implied, the consequences of the law were less than its intentions. This does not mean that the poor laws were without coercive effect. Their avowed design was to hold the "base multitudes" of casual labor in place, to build around them statutes that barred their movement.[105] Many of those statutes brought awful results. Some were written in blood. The cartmen and the hangmen did a steady business.

But the effects of this legislative venture were not clear-cut. Everyday enforcement and supervision practices suggest that legal censure was negotiable. The state's power to criminalize should not be exaggerated, and the regulation of the outcast was seldom straightforward or uncomplicated. Territorial anomalies, for example, affected rural and urban enforcement. Central direction was weak, and certain corners of the land were unsystematically supervised. Coastal areas, the rugged north country, commons, fens, and forest lands were relatively free from the influence of the courts. Frequently they were unpatrolled and had recourse to their own legal designs.[106] The very mobility of the casual labor pool made overall state authority difficult to assert. The "mean people" of the woods and commons detached themselves from established legal practices. Cottage communities on wastes and commons near forests were "nurseries and receptacles of thieves, rogues and beggars." Such territories, unruly and lawless, were the breeding grounds of crime—"the very spawn of rogues."[107] Inside London, criminal habitats supported considerable resistance to legal domination. They thrived in the interstices of weak and ambiguous social control processes. It was difficult for the law to penetrate such criminal districts. As both Leonard and James have observed, the regionalization of poor law administration encouraged partisan loyalties and contributed to an enforcement system lacking in coherent design and bureaucratic efficiency.[108] The lack of a central, efficient communication system within the judiciary further weakened legal enforcement.[109]

The efficacy and morality of the justice system itself also rendered the law open to particularistic translations. As Samaha has noted, "the comments of upper class Elizabethans . . . and the draconian felony laws are misleading, because neither reflects what actually happened to individuals who committed crimes. An enormous attrition in the number of suspected felons brought to public notice took place from the time an offense was committed and a convict was hanged, a fact that drastically diminishes the impact of the brutal felony laws in the sixteenth century."[110] In general, legal penalties, technicalities, and inducements combined to create an elaborate system of legal bartering. In the first place, not all crimes were reported. Communal attitudes and pressures, the intricacies of composing indictments, mistrust of policing officials, the high costs of presentments, and the loss of time associated with criminal prosecution worked against use of the legal system to redress injuries.[111] Furthermore, losses were seldom restored, and the criminal justice system based on public retribution did not encourage pursuit of wrongdoers. One Somerset justice of the peace estimated that 80 percent of all crime went unreported.[112] And research in the counties adjoining London confirms this incredible capacity of the accused to evade the criminal justice system.[113] In the second place, those who entered the criminal justice system were easily lost along the way or bargained their way out, for several reasons: constables and witnesses' neglect in prosecuting offenders, grand juries' dismissals of charges, trial juries' high acquittal rates, the technicalities of legal procedures, the system of pardons, and legal loopholes such as benefit of clergy. These need amplification.

The criminal justice system proceeded in distinct stages. At the outset, a constable had to apprehend and examine criminals, and there are strong reasons to doubt the effectiveness of everyday police enforcement in London. But even when constables succeeded in rounding up suspects the reluctance of victims and witnesses to testify in person and the necessity of having the justice of the peace who initially conducted the preliminary examination be present at later hearings meant that many suspects avoided trial.[114] Many escaped "by proclamation" because legal officials, plaintiffs, and collaborators were absent. According to Samaha's study of Elizabethan Essex, "a full 33 percent of all persons imprisoned on suspicion of felony were freed . . . because no one came to court to prosecute."[115]

Attrition continued when a defendant finally came to trial. Juries at all levels of the criminal justice system—the hundred, the grand, and the petty sessions—were reluctant to return guilty verdicts. The hundred jury decided, if sufficient evidence existed, to indict criminals and passed them on to the grand jury to be charged formally or freed from further legal action. If the grand jury favored an indictment, then a trial jury was convened to decide on the substance of the case. It is at the level of the hundred and grand juries that the influence and privilege of the wealthy were clearly visible. They easily exploited their power in the community, had indictments quashed before trial, intimidated their lessers to avoid prosecution, and directly defied the courts by refusing to attend trial procedures.

According to Samaha "fully 15% of all persons indicted for felony did not appear for trial."[116] Gentlemen were escaping trial "at the shocking high rate of 79% and nothing was done to stop it."[117] Furthermore, "between 1558 and 1568, 19% of the yeomen indicted never faced public trial; but by the closing years of Elizabeth's reign they were avoiding legal process at the rate of 43%."[118] This rate increased despite a decline in the total number of yeomen charged with crimes.

At the next stage the petty trial juries released many prospective criminals from death by acquitting those who had previously been indicted or by reducing the seriousness of the offense. Perhaps as many as one-third of all defendants were freed outright because their peers would not find against them.[119]

In addition, the law itself provided a considerable number of escape exits. The knowing invented and indulged in practices that reduced even further the likelihood of punishment or hanging. Pardons, jury by matron, and benefit of clergy, were legal loopholes that conferred special powers and affected court proceedings. Pardons were technical but two general types prevailed. The first was general, discretionary, not pleaded, and awarded directly by Parliament and the crown. The other was special, pleaded by the victim, and generally available to those who could pay for, draft, and plead them in court. Since they were a source of crown income they were encouraged; judges would often grant delays in due process until pardons could be procured.[120]

Pregnant women also had special prerogatives. A jury of matrons was convened if a woman found guilty by a jury claimed she was with child. Technically she was entitled to a temporary respite until the child was born, but in practice "pleading the belly" was akin to a general reprieve. Such women were put to bail and seldom reappeared for trial.[121] According to Samaha, one-fifth of all women in Essex convicted of felony during Elizabeth's reign went free through "advantage of their womb."[122]

Finally, benefit of clergy was still a major legal loophole. In the medieval era, all persons in holy orders and even inferior personnel could claim the right of royal arrest or trial in secular courts. Initially, special status was guaranteed by dress, by tonsure, and by the ability to read. But by the early fifteenth century literacy had become the primary proof, and thus the door was opened for wider lay use of clergy benefits. According to Firth, by the Elizabethan period, actual literacy had become a mere form. Even blind men escaped by memorizing and allegedly reading a "neck verse."[123] So routine had this privilege become that convicted men were allowed time to learn the verse if they failed on the first recitation. Thus, plea of clergy was a regular feature of criminal justice and convicted felons, instead of facing the rope, were turned over to church officials. Indeed, by the middle of Elizabeth's reign, convicted felons were released outright after plea of clergy, subject only to a discretionary one-year imprisonment.[124]

The power of benefit of clergy was most pronounced in the middle ages with the Tudors largely responsible for legislation restricting its use.[125] However, in fact the practice continued. As Samaha has noted,

> skillful use of legal technicalities in prescribed felonies was not the only value benefit of clergy bestowed on convicted felons, because in practice it was never limited to the crimes that statutes defined for it. Though most men employed it in simple theft, which the law definitely allowed, it was also pleaded in every other common law felony in existence from violent murder to highway robbery and horse stealing; all of which the law forbade. When statutes were not flouted outright, a kind of sixteenth century plea bargaining went on . . . In return for a guilty plea, murder was occasionally reduced to homicide, burglary to mere breaking and entering, and robbery to stealing, all of which changed the crime from a nonclergyable to a clergyable one, thus allowing judges to permit clergy and set the convicted man free.[126]

The manipulation of such a privilege both within and without statutory bounds was frequent. In one county, between 1558 and 1603 some 25 percent of all guilty defendants were freed as a result of benefit of clergy.[127]

The law, then, was open to varied implementation. Its consequences were unsure. The casual labor market and deviant and criminal populations were not easily monitored. Indeed the translation of law into everyday practices blurred the borders between propriety and impropriety. The administration of criminal law was a malleable, complex process in which conciliation, intrigue, and trading were central. Moreover, as I discuss later, policing was marginally effective, and criminality was territorially supported and routinely organized. Furthermore its definition was often open to negotiation.

The London Criminal "Underclass"

The mediation of law was most irregular, shaped by power and privilege, distorted by geographical peculiarities, and itself refracted by internal contingencies. This resulted in diverse possibilities for the existence of a multiplicity of outcast populations. As Hill has noted, "beneath the surface stability of rural England then . . . was the seething mobility of forest squatters, itinerant craftsmen and building labourers, unemployed men and women seeking work, strolling players and jugglers, peddlars and quack doctors, vagabonds, tramps: congregated especially in London and the big cities, but also with footholds wherever newly squatted areas escaped from the machinery of the parish or in old squatted areas where labour was in demand."[128]

It is important to stress the point that features of the labor market and of the administration of the law also combined to foster a specific criminal underclass. The organization of this underclass is the major, albeit controversial, concern of this study. Hill has claimed that the underworld of crime has been overpublicized and "was no doubt far less important than the world of dock labour, watermen, building labourers, and journeymen.[129] But this is a rather narrow view of crime and its organization. Indeed it threatens to dismiss it, and perhaps romanticize the reputation of the casual poor. More recent work has tended to minimize vagrant-related criminality and to doubt the existence of a criminal underclass.[130] But the mass of contemporary evidence, particularly for London, cannot be disregarded.

Contemporaries from all walks of life witnessed the evolution of a criminal underclass. According to one Elizabethan preacher it was a related yet separate strand of the poor: "As for our rogues and vagabonds, I exclude them out of the role and number of poore men . . . they do not labour they should not eate."[131] A similar sentiment was voiced by another writer. There were two varieties of poor: "God's poor and the Devil's."[132] Thomas Harman, who spent time interviewing and investigating wandering migrants, observed that a distinct criminal subclass coexisted. These "ragged rabblement of rakehells" in his view constituted a unique social network with ranks, rules, language, and customs of its own.[133] William Harrison observed in the 1570s that an underclass of roguery had grown from among the dispossessed. "It is not yet full threescore years since this trade began: but how it hath prospered since that time."[134] Privy counselors, members of Parliament, and justices of the peace alike regarded vagrant soldiers, paupers, and itinerant traders as potential criminals. Poverty, unemployment, and roguery were cut from the same cloth; taverns and gambling ordinaries were both resorts for the idle and "nurseries of naughtiness," "the cause of great misdemeanours and outrages," "the very stock and stay of our false thieves and vagabonds."[135]

Recent historical research similarly confirms the presence of a criminal underclass among the masterless population. A study of migrant populations in Kentish towns indicates that the "chances of the child of a subsistence migrant dragging the same path, perhaps into professional roguery was terrifyingly good."[136] A review of recognizance and indictment records for Essex, Surrey, and Hertfordshire suggested that persistent forms of thieving were common.[137] Jordan, in his study of London poor relief, claims that at the "very bottom of society" were a tribe of "disorderly rogues, vagabonds and criminals with their 'doxies.'[138] A report by the Corporation of the City of London in 1632 provides some figures. It indicated that 4,000 rogues had been rounded up and detained in the city and then sent to their native parishes.[139] Finally, City Bridewell records suggest that some children were full-time miscreants living by pilfering. Some were regular thieves by the age of twelve. For example, one Julius Loney "aged seven years and more" was defined as a dangerous London thief and beggar.[140]

The specific character of the London criminal underclass needs clarification. A distinction should be made between crime in the country and crime in urban areas. There is some evidence that in the country beggars' brotherhoods with diverse organized forms of begging existed. Criminal beggars were highly mobile and specialized in impostures of innumerable kinds; they also engaged in theft as a main source of gain. However, the organization of beggars fraternities was not geared to the development of criminal techniques— pickpocketing, robbery, or prostitution—but to the supervision and organization of specific acts of imposture.[141] The so-called secret companies and societies represent examples of begging sects with differing clothes, members, rules, and functions. The rufflers, for example, pretended to be invalid soldiers, and Abraham men pretended to be rustic idiots.[142] The organization of thieving was left to the initiative of each vagabond, for the essence of the vagabond's life was freedom, mobility, and the absence of controls. What organization did exist was possibly the obverse of the social order—the semblance of a loose antisociety disbelieving in marriage, religion, family life, and work practices. Indeed, it is likely that these fraternities occurred throughout Europe.[143]

The London criminal underworld, on the other hand, was more properly a confederation directed toward the rational organization of criminal acts. Its locales were more fixed. There was less mobility and the routinization of skills and deceptions more directly addressed specific criminal objectives. One should be suspicious of suggestions that elaborate criminal commonwealths existed among the criminal underclass of London. A counterpart to rural beggars' fraternities, with a systematic hierarchy of fixed roles, rituals, and rules is unlikely to have existed. The criminal underclass was not a criminal conspiracy. There is little reason for supposing the presence of an integrated and vast set of relationships.[144] Yet, as I argue later, the world of crime in London did constitute a differentiated social world possessing a particular argot, set of institutions, division of labor, and territory of operation. The London underworld was built around a comparatively fluid and negotiable set of relations which were not subject to detailed regulation. Insofar as the criminal populations were organized the relationships were working associations, some of a patron-client nature. Such configurations were local, loose, and contained. On the other hand, the conditions of decentralized social control contributed to the emergence of criminal power brokers capable of enforcing a degree of regulation over variegated criminal trades. This takes us to the specific details of criminal organization and, in particular, to its ecological basis.

4

CRIMINAL
AREAS

Introduction

This chapter examines the hitherto little-explored links between social ecology and criminal organization. It explores the peculiar pattern of geographic, demographic, and political relations that gave rise to differentiated criminal districts and to an irregular and uneven system of city social control. I discuss the character and significance of illegal crime areas, particularly in relation to the enforcement of law and the formation of criminal associations and networks. I begin by looking at the formation of criminal sanctuaries, then explore the social nature of the major criminal areas of the city. Finally, the implications of territoriality are assessed in terms of the capacities of state control.

The Formation of Criminal Sanctuaries

Most urban capitals of Europe contained inner areas of contrasting social character, and London was no exception. Ecologically, it developed as a myriad of diverse and distinctive geographical units. Enormous expansion between 1500 and 1650 increased its heterogeneity and fashioned a metropolis lacking in cohesion and overall organization. Outlying territories were acquired without the land being cleared, and new tenements were built around or on top of existing crumbling edifices.[1] In these peripheral city territories lived the pauper and the vagrant.[2] By the mid-sixteenth century, London was ringed by crowded deregulated districts, many of which possessed the character of medieval liberties.[3] The term liberty referred to certain regions of the city granted special privileges by virtue of their having been ecclesiastical franchises that, by charter or proscription, were independent of city and royal control. Some regions were exempt from specific taxes; others were private municipalities of particular crafts; still others were free zones immune from city policing and authority. The liberties of Fleet Prison and of Saint Martin Le Grand Chapel, for example, were guaranteed by statute and harbored lawbreakers, debtors, and felons. Liberties around prisons and churchyards were semiprivate regions which were farmed for profits.[4]

The status of liberties was further complicated by the traditional right to sanctuary. In the medieval era, any wanted person who took refuge in a consecrated setting had the right to claim sanctuary. This right to protection was guarded by custom and law, and residents of a sanctuary could not usually be arrested.[5] Sanctuary initially could be either temporary or permanent. The former was afforded for forty days, provided fugitives accepted the discipline of the area and agreed to leave the country. Temporary sanctuary was de facto abolished by the sixteenth century. Permanent forms, however, continued despite de jure abolition until the eighteenth century. Such sanctuaries were in effect entrenched protectorates. As Thornley has observed, such domains were segregated from traditional forms of authority with "new oaths of allegiance" and new customary rules.[6]

The power and autonomy of sanctuaries were most pronounced during the medieval period. The closing of the monasteries and the absorption of church lands by the late Tudors altered many traditional rights and obligations. Legislation in 1604, 1606, 1623, and 1693 weakened the legality of such territories.[7] However, in fact the practice continued, and the Elizabethan and Stuart states lacked the means to eradicate many of the territorial principalities. Differentiated regions outside city and state control were maintained by a combination of customary right and outright defiance. Unauthorized sanctuaries took root in the shadow of ecclesiastical territorial privilege. church yards, hospital grounds, bedlams, and refuges for the poor became, in part, places of criminal asylum.[8] Indeed throughout the Elizabethan and Stuart periods, such social spaces extended their borders, absorbing wider sections of the city suburbs. As early as the fifteenth century there were thriving criminal zones in London.

> Unthrifts riot and run in debt upon the boldness of these places; yea and rich men run thither with poor men's goods, there they build, there they spend, and bill their creditors go whistle them. Men's wives run thither with their husband's plate and say they dare not abide with their husbands for beating. Thieves bring thither their stolen goods and live thereon. They devise their new robberies; nightly they steal out, they rob, they rave and kill, and come in again, as though these places gave them not only a safeguard for the harm they have done but a license also to do more.[9]

These same features were reproduced in nonmonastic liberties. Lay and royal franchises also intersected in the city landscape providing various forms of immunity.[10] Powerful elites possessed self-enclosed principalities which could not be entered without permission. The Inns of Court and Chancery, for example, were private enclaves outside local government control, and the Duchy of Lancaster in the Savoy was a segregated quarter ruled by manorial courts outside city authority.[11] Most important, London and the adjacent borough of Southwark were engaged in a constant struggle over the extent of London's jurisdiction. Many Bankside territories resisted incorporation as city wards and remained independent and unregulated deviant territories.[12] Outparishes located in the suburbs without the walls also contained swelling populations of debtors and criminals. Such regions were distant from city jurisdiction, and they constituted a second tier of unregulated territories. Denied liberty status, they nevertheless represented companion forms of sanctuary. Political conflicts between county, city, and central governments prevented the absorption of these outlying territories into a unified system of social control. The demands for casual labor and the desire of new competitive industries to escape guild and government supervision furthered centrifugal ecological patterns.[13] Regulatory policies and administrative unification were opposed within and without the city of London. For most of the period the outparishes were the expanding residential quarters of a growing rough and lawless population. They were "in many places no other but dark dens for adulterers, thieves, murderers, and every mischief worker."[14]

Regulations making it illegal to erect buildings on new foundations ensured that such districts were dense social worlds.[15] Covert construction in hidden courtyards and the subdivision of existing accommodation created networks of "clandestine hovels and shanties on lands of doubtful ownership."[16] The internal topography strengthened the segregation of criminal territory. Entire settlements contained labyrinths of tightly packed hidden lanes and alleys with buildings that provided "double, triple, even quadruple entrances and exits."[17] A survey of London households in 1638 observed that suburban parishes contained "alleys stuft with poor whom they maintain." Residents were "heaped up together and in a sort smothered with many families of children and servants in one house."[18]

Disparities between the city, liberties, and outlying parishes and suburbs were reinforced by the paucity and poor conditions of thoroughfares. Streets were narrow, close together, poorly lit, dirty, and inadequately maintained, a network of narrow, barely paved lanes, darkened by the overhanging fronts of houses. In some quarters streets were mere paths of "rutted soil soaked with the filth of centuries."[19] At night such roadways became ominous. Travel was hazardous. Piles of dung and heaps of building materials hindered movement. Primitive lanterns with discolored horn panes and guttering candles did little to illuminate the terrain. Seldom could watch and ward patrols provide adequate protection.[20]

The Criminal Areas

The nature and importance of illegality were in part defined by its social location. Different areas supported radically contrasting moral positions. Entire regions and communities gave widespread support to and participated in collective criminal projects, not just in London but elsewhere. Rule, Winslow, and Thompson have argued that rural crimes such as causing shipwrecks, smuggling, and poaching were also communally supported.[21] Similarly, urban palatines in Paris, Seville, and Rome underpinned distinctly criminal modes of operation and membership in criminal groups.[22] The following pages provide a preliminary analysis of the criminal areas of London from 1550 to 1700, dwelling on criminal practices and the implications of territoriality for the shaping of criminal organization.[23]

Probably the area of London with the most venerable reputation as a resort of criminality was Southwark in Bridge Ward Without. Justice Fleetwood characterized the entire district as an "admirable place . . . for conspiracies, a college of male counsel,"[24] and Fynes Moryson, a noted traveler, recorded that the area provided ample cheap entertainment and houses of pleasure, where thieving and cheating abounded.[25] Southwark was primarily a center of marginal occupations. Mobility was high, and populations of musicians, minstrels, actors, jugglers, and bearwards moved in and out of "diverse streets, ways and winding lanes, all full of buildings inhabited."[26] Bankside contained a half-mile stretch of tenements. Major streets were linked by networks of small alleyways. Gardens and courtyards were overcrowded with crumbling makeshift shelters. By 1600, land speculators had transformed the once splendid Bankside Gardens into a warren of sloping lanes. Eighteen alley paths running from Bankside to Maiden Lane crisscrossed narrower streets. A plethora of low tenements and disorderly structures cluttered the area and housed a growing and shifting population of masterless men and women. In addition to cheap "so and so's rents" (a string of tenements, usually run-down), the district was layered with gaming ordinaries, bowling alleys, taverns of ill repute, brothels, thieves' dens, and stalling kens for stolen property.[27]

Paris Garden and the liberties of the Clink and the Mint represented the geographical foci for crime in Southwark. The manor of Paris Garden was about a mile in circumference and was bordered on the east by the Clink liberty.[28] Like other extramural districts, it was the home of amusements and of pleasure. Bull and bear baiting were to be found there, as were the earliest theaters.[29] The pleasure gardens and entertainment institutions also attracted a large assortment of low-life occupations and criminals.[30] During the Elizabethan period some eighteen to twenty-two licensed brothels operated.[31] Adjoining many of these brothels were networks of low lodgings and bowling alleys.[32] The Barge, the Bull, and the Cock formed a brothel grouping that contained several slum lodgings. Smith's Rents near the Rose Theatre was composed of "7 pas-suages, 7 gardens and 1 wharf." Addison Rents, Maylands Rents near the Castle stewhouse, Tallow Chandlers Rents near Horse-shoe Alley, Griffins Rents, and Rockets Rents were slum quarters and contained a shifting population of beggars, thieves, and pros-titutes. Often stewhouses had adjoining tippling and gaming facilities. The Crossed Keys, the Three Tunnes, and the Golden Fleece, for example, were allegedly the resorts of gambling and confidence cheats.[33]

Next to Paris Garden and containing part of the Bankside stews was the liberty of the Clink. It was an area of about seventy acres ex-tending north to the Thames, west to Paris Garden, east to Saint Sa-viours Dock, and south to Saint George's parish.[34] Like the Paris Garden it harbored an array of stewhouses, slum tenements, and gaming establishments. The famous Holland's Leaguer, a house of ill-repute, was situated in what had once been the manor house of the domain. By 1609, the Clink harbored approximately 560 house-holders. Two hundred and one householders were classified as wherrymen (watermen) who transported people back and forth from Bankside to London. In addition, there were 100 handymen and 150 "poor people, widows and other." The remaining 20 per-cent of the inhabitants were composed of "others ready to take and not one of them fit to give."[35] In all likelihood the actual population of the area was higher, perhaps closer to 1,200, the bulk of whom were without work.[36] Moreover, the "Clinkmen" had entrenched traditions of collective rights. They guarded the boundaries of their precincts, provided refuge and assistance to pursued outlaws, and at times prevented the law from being enforced.[37]

To the south of the Clink, and opposite Saint George's Church stood the Mint sanctuary. Entrance into it was through guarded and semiconcealed gates, while escape was facilitated by passages that opened up into the adjoining Saint George's Fields.[38] The "Mint-men" like those inside the Clink liberty established collective life-styles and an organization that supported diverse marginal, deviant, and criminal activities. On major thoroughfares were to be found in-stitutions where criminals practiced their trade. Tumbledown Dick's, The Harrow, The Naked Boy, and the Old Bull were tippling houses where thieves and cutpurses allegedly resorted. Falcon Court was a large thieves' lodging complex, and May Pole Alley, opposite the Marshalsea Prison, was a sloping narrow corridor that served as living quarters for known dangerous felons.[39] The fields and marshes on the outskirts of the sanctuary were open areas attracting cockfighting, racing, and gambling, and with them dice cheats, gamesters, and confidence tricksters.[40]

The outlying village of Newington was similarly distant from regular official surveillance. A permanent criminal element dwelled there. The environs were the living quarters for highwaymen who worked the heaths and woodlands near Kingston, Croydon, and Lambeth. Gad's Hill on the road to Gravesend was "the high old robbing" hill and the resort of organized bands of thieves and robbers of "more than usual daring and violence."[41] James Clavell, a London thief, apparently acquired his skills on: "Gad's Hill and those Red Tops of Mountains where good people lose Their ill-kept purses."[42]

Southwark had a reputation for diverse forms of crime: prostitution, thieving, gambling, and cony-catching. But it was perhaps best known as a center for the merchandising of stolen property, particularly leather and metal wares.[43] Indeed, the entire district was a suburb of small dealers who housed thieves and pickpockets and tended to run the criminal marketplace. Kent Street was a permanent headquarters for city thieves. Laurence Pickering, a cutpurse, reputedly organized weekly meetings of thieves at his house in Kent Street where security, skills, and victims were discussed.[44]

A second well established criminal territory was to be found on the city's southeast boundary in the old ecclesiastical sanctuary of Whitefriars. The once fashionable area had been transformed by the late Elizabethan period into a large tenement slum, harboring a swelling population of casual laborers, debtors, and criminals. Known as Alsatia, it covered a large area extending from Fleet Street to the Thames River between the western side of Water Lane and the Temple.[45] The remains of a privileged liberty, it was only abolished by force in 1696. Poets, players, dancing masters, fencers, book sellers, and jugglers lived there as well as debtors, thieves, cheats, and gamblers.[46]

A mass of pennyrent lodgings covered the district. Great houses were subdivided, thus overcrowding the area. The mansion of Sir John Parker, for example, was "divided into twenty small tenements," and the household of Francis Pike, a victualler, was reorganized into no fewer than thirty-nine tenements.[47] The streets, lanes, alleyways, and courtyards of Alsatia were tightly packed together and inadequately lighted. Few were paved, and many were cluttered with laystalls and littered with sewage. The lanes jutting off the main arteries were narrow and rendered darker and smaller by overhanging stories and newly built sheds which almost met. Mitre Court, Fetter Lane, Ram Alley, Mitford Lane, and Water Lane, in particular, were zones of vice and crime. Drinking establishments, dram houses, and cookshops often concealed secret entrances and exits in and out of the sanctuary through which escaping criminals routinely and safely passed. The Mitre Tavern in Fleet Street had yards at the rear which opened up into the sanctuary, and fugitives had only to pass from Fleet Street through the tavern and into Alsatia.[48] Similarly the Widow Pondley had an establishment with back exits which she operated as a house for "receiving lewd women and playing at unlawful games."[49]

Ram Alley deserves special attention as it was perhaps the best-known center of criminal activity in Whitefriars. It was a long narrow passage, barely seven feet wide, running parallel with Mitre Court. The house fronts were dilapidated, the gutters broken, and the street unlit and poorly monitored. There was an assortment of unlicensed dram shops, small trades shops, and cookshops which supplied dinners to the neighboring taverns. The "widdys," so deemed by local courtesy, lodged over these shops and traded in sex. Ram Alley also housed a population of cooks, alemen, and laundresses as well as an assortment of bawds, whores, cheats, quacks, pimps, and thieves. Hanging Sword Alley was a companion criminal quarter housing Blood-Bowl House, a criminal institution where contacts between fences and thieves were routinely made. The alley was a long, very narrow, meandering walk. Entrances and exits were concealed by houses, and made difficult by steep steps that led up to other alleys. Indeed the whole of Alsatia was a maze of such climbing and sloping streets, intersected by irregular courts.[50] The many exits, entrances, and turns made surveillance, detection, and pursuit a difficult process.

The criminal groups of Alsatia, like those of the Mint and the Clink, were diverse. Prostitute-thieves and their male accomplices were apparently prominent. Crossbiting (the bullying or blackmailing of clients by prostitute teams) seems to have been a regular criminal practice. Alsatia also housed a large population of migrant mariners and vagrant soldiers. Skilled in warfare such men could form a bodyguard, offering considerable protection. Milford Lane, inside

Whitefriars, was an armed preserve of criminals. Constables and watchmen faced a rough beating or a spell at the water pump. Alsatia was also an entertainment center, and its theaters attracted low-life writers, dramatists, and actors and mixed crowds of wealthy gentlemen and gallants, as well as cheats, roarers, panderers, and cony-catchers.[51]

Alsatia was also known as a headquarters for the manufacture of counterfeit coins, and a center for dishonest lawyers, informers, and spies. As Shadwell remarked, here was many "a cheatly Sham-well, Hackum and Scapeall."[52] Its most prestigious street, ironically dubbed Lombard Street, was a major complex of thieves' dens and receiving houses. Moll Cutpurse (see Chapters Six and Eight), per-haps the most famous female criminal of the period, established and ran her clearinghouse for stolen property in Fleet Street on the bor-der of the santuary, thus giving her access to legitimate and crimi-nal marketplaces.[53]

A third, less developed area of crime was on the city's northeast-ern boundary, the Spitalfields-Whitechapel area. This quarter en-joyed the advantage of being just outside the city wall; thus thieves had easy access to the city's riches but could evade the ward watch-men, constables, and city marshalmen. It was an area on an arc from Bishopsgate in the north around to Aldgate in the south. These one-time suburban garden alleys had by Elizabethan times been cov-ered by dirty huts, bowling alleys, and tenter-yards.[54] It was an area of open prostitution and gambling. Houndsditch was the most famous quarter, housing braziers and dealers in old clothes, linen, and upholstery. It was the resort of ragmen—rag fairs were held there—and was also noted for its brokers and usurers. The Hounds-ditch environs were known as a district in which stolen goods could be disposed of easily. Traders, markets, and street stalls provided convenient covers for recycling stolen scarves, sheets, and various inexpensive trifles. Here, it was reported, "you shall not scarce find a dramme of honesty for a pound of craft."[55] The district was also a refuge for cutpurses and petty thieves who lived, worked, and traded in the run-down streets. Greene, in his descriptions of city crime, alleged that Houndsditch was for a time a headquarters for Elizabethan pickpockets.[56]

The Spitalfields-Whitechapel district was also composed of poor privy houses and tenement lodgings for which considerable rates were charged. It was not as built up as other areas of the city. Principal thoroughfares were few and major identifiable residences were lacking. The district was a rapidly expanding network of gardens, alleyways, and obscure corners with little uniform design (and cluttered with casual laborers and wanderers).[57] These expanding eastern city boundaries were developing brothel zones. Petticoat Lane and Rosemary Lane housed a population of women who "traded on their bottom."[58] George Whetstone, a London magistrate, noted that in this suburb, masterless men, needy shifters, unthrifty servants, as well as thieves, cutpurses, and prostitutes abounded.[59] Two hundred and fifty years later, Mayhew in his investigations of city crime characterized part of this area as "the worst place both as regards filth and immorality."[60]

To the south of Whitechapel and bordering the Thames was the Stepney area, center of shipbuilding and river trades. Mariners and sailors were to be seen there, as were shipwrights, anchor smiths, coal merchants, and other craftsmen associated with dock and naval activities.[61] During the period under investigation, Stepney was expanding to the east and incorporating outlying hamlets. Population soared and industry grew.[62] Perhaps the more important function the riverside areas served was as places of embarkation for traffic between the Southbank stews and the City proper. The wherrymen of Ratcliffe, Redriff, and Wapping transported beggar and thief, gallant and gamester, cony and cony-catcher, to and from the criminal sanctuaries of London.

A fourth region was composed of clusters of streets and lanes around the Newgate-Cripplegate area. This quarter bordered the city wall on the north and was the extension of the wards outside the city: Bishopsgate Without and Cripplegate Without. This district lay outside the power of the city. From early times it was the haunt of the traveler and was frequented by all types of people: barbers, surgeons, preachers, laundresses, jugglers, wrestlers, as well as political dissidents. Evelyn, the court diarist, noted that the area had an established reputation as a temporary refuge for the homeless. Extending several miles out from the city wall, it was a territory of "spotted tents, huts and hovels and portable accommodation."[63]

By 1605, Moorfields was transformed into a recreation ground, and according to the Reverend Mr. Denton, the area of Saint Giles Without Cripplegate, became a "riotous pleasure resort" catering to "the fashion as well as the riffraff . . . some for health, some for amusement and gambling, others for pocket picking."[64] Stow in his survey of London noted that the use of the area as a parade ground for archers had dwindled, "giving place to a number of bowling alleys and dicing houses."[65] Especially evident were songsters and ballad singers associated with "ribaldry, irreligiosity and immorality," who were known through their trades to attract crowds who were then set upon by collaborating cutpurses and pickpockets.[66] Moreover, petty chapmen and similar street sellers and barterers were convenient small-scale mobile fences.[67] Certainly Turnmill Street off Bell alley, outside the wall to the east of the Fleet Ditch, was a famous quarter of organized thieving. Here open houses of crime flourished, guarded by armed men who patrolled the streets.[68]

Equally important was the labyrinth of streets and alleys around Cockes Lane against Pie Corner near Newgate. This was the second largest brothel area in London, and the narrow side streets housed a large wedge of cheap bawdyhouses and hosts of wandering whores. Saffron Hill, the run-down foreigners' area between Holborn and Clerkenwell, was a densely inhabited slum and also had a reputation for housing prostitutes, receiving stolen property, and manufacturing false dice. According to Walker, the "Bird of Holborn" was the finest manufacturer of loaded dice in London.[69] Saffron Hill was also a thieves' sanctuary and a haunt of confidence cheats, and Shoe Lane and Fetters Lane, jutting off the hill, developed into haunts of a wandering prostitution trade.[70]

This survey does not exhaust the criminal quarters of Elizabethan and Stuart London. The area between the Strand and Holborn was taking the shape of a fifth criminal district. Lewkener's Lane and Drury Lane were acquiring reputations as zones of prostitution. In addition, the Strand on its north side contained a network of slum lodging houses. Many of these were the overcrowded resorts of thieves and prostitutes. Parts of Westminster harbored dubious populations. References to this side of its life are sparse, but "Thieving Lane" and the adjoining crowded and narrow streets were the domain of all types of foists (pick pockets) and lifts (thieves).[71] The Savoy liberty nightly lodged a veritable "noursery of rogues, thieves, and idle and drouken persons."[72] According to Lord Burghley, "almost every fourth house was an alehouse" harboring destitute and common "scalds."[73] Another section of London with a criminal reputation was a zone of small tenements in Dowgate Ward. This quarter was just outside city jurisdiction and was a sanctuary for beggars and wandering vagrants. Also, the precinct of

Saint Katherine by the Tower, famous for its breweries, was a low haunt of sailors and mariners and catered to the "whoring craft." The liberty of Saint Martin-le-Grand was an old ecclesiastical sanctuary that attracted a population of debtors, felons, thieves, murderers, and counterfeiters. It had an established reputation for the "manufacture of fabricated plate, jewels, beads, and other such Goldsmith's wares."[74] The thieves' sanctuary of Cold Harbour on the Thames River was a strategically located blind gaunt house (one that was difficult to see) at which criminals could hire boats to flee their pursuers.[75] Certain jurisdictions were fortified strongholds. Duke Humphrey's Rents near Blackfriars sanctuary, for example, was a territorial protectorate of considerable political strength. Strong walls, networks of bridges, and solid gates made it akin to a castle.[76] Confrontations with the authorities sometimes took on the character of resistance to a siege, and these areas at times became self-contained bastions similar to the greenlands and forests of bandits.[77] Highwaymen also had their rendezvous. They stationed themselves on the heaths and in the woodlands along the main arteries of travel. Newmarket Heath to the north of the city was a particularly well established domain of highway robbery, and by the end of the sixteenth century Shooters Hill and Hamstead Heath had achieved notoriety as bases of highway crime.[78]

To take stock, then, the city of London was spotted with thriving areas of thieves' quarters. These areas and various brothel districts persisted as distinct enclaves. Four major criminal territories were buttressed by the peculiarities of city ecology and by traditions of territorial custom. By deceit, privilege, and force, these criminal districts acquired a discrete territorial independence. Despite legal annulments of previous jurisdictions and privileges, these territories retained remarkable continuity throughout the Hanoverian period and up until the Victorian era. Both Mayhew and Binny, in their survey of criminal areas, found them congruent with earlier times.[79] And Beames in the 1850s remarked that the rookeries "still survive by their very isolation, and by their retention of past anomalies."[80]

Localism and the World of Crime

The concentration of the marginal, the deviant, and the criminal into specific geographic areas mirrored the spatial pattern of London social life. The city was divided into a plurality of social worlds. Occupational and work roles were dispersed into horizontally segregated communities. Districts often took on the character of the parishes and wards of specific guilds. Localism was common in the metropolis, and street communities certainly existed. Printers were associated with Fleet Street, and booksellers were located in Saint Paul's Churchyard. East Cheap was known for its cookshops and butchers; Bread and Milk streets and Goldsmith's Row indicated their inhabitants' vocation. Lothbury was the purlieu of founders, and haberdashers were located on London Bridge. The Houndsditch environs were the domain of clothes vendors. Living quarters were closely intertwined with work places.

Wealth also differentiated specific city regions. The river banks between the City and Westminster were the living quarters of the nobility. Their mansions were the hallmarks of their social status. The emerging merchant classes of London were housed in the old residences of the aristocracy. Such districts stood in marked contrast to the base tenement quarters.[81] Of course, there were mixed communities: the rich did live side by side with the poor, but most wards had a measure of social distinctiveness. London resembled a mosaic of segregated social zones. Geographical proximity did not restructure social habits. Social distance prevailed even though physical mobility was less hampered than it was in rural areas. Diverse social worlds coexisted within and just beyond the city gates. Aliens and foreigners were quartered in enclosed territories in outlying parishes. Community frontiers were not easily crossed. Studies of east end London parish records reveal that over half of the Stepney population was involved in shipbuilding and other marine industries.[82] The hamlets of Limehouse, Ratcliff, Shadwell, and Wapping had between 60 and 80 percent of their respective populations engaged in shipbuilding and other river and sea occupations. Similarly, adjoining communities were dominated by specific types of laborers or craftsmen. Middle-class trades in the eastern suburbs were notoriously lacking. Only 4 percent of the total population of Stepney was engaged in middle-class professions.[83] Some mixed occupational communities did exist, and the hamlet of Bethnal Green had an amalgam of land and marine occupations, with the professions accounting for 8 percent of the local population.[84]

Criminal sanctuaries, then, were geographical counterparts of citywide ecological developments. They paralleled the territorial ordering of respectable trades. Indeed, insofar as these regions were capable of defending and extending their privileges and their rights to jurisdiction and social space, they were perhaps analogous to the seigneurie collective of legitimate craft fraternities.[85] The seigneurie collective represented a de facto natural area. It was a jurisdictional territory regulated by craft members. Home and workshop were often located within its confines. Members formed relatively circumscribed communities and asserted control over much of their activities. Segregated from other crafts, they evolved specific occupational roles, rituals, and institutions. Guilds and their fraternity organizations were often competitors to centrally administered politics and law. They managed market outlets, developed trade technology and craftsmanship standards, established exclusivity and control over competitors, and protected the secret methods of their craft. Politically they operated as veto groups currying favor and dispensing patronage. They established their own legal and policing codes for regulating disputes. Fraternities neutralized the impact of public law and offered immunity and protection to member offenders. They also served important social and ideological functions. They operated as trusts in which social cohesion was forged. They set down rules, trained the novice, provided a community of colleagueship, kept out those who failed to maintain quality standards, and penalized the deviant. Common skills, problems, and practices were celebrated in special vocabularies and codes, all in a climate of secrecy.[86]

Guilds in London frequently engaged in struggles for space. These semiprivate jurisdictions were in an ambiguous relationship to the political center.[87] The guilds claimed the right to segregate themselves. Functioning as collective trade domains, they established elaborate codes of friendship, support, and exclusion.[88] The texture of everyday life in the sixteenth century was larded with such geographically based organizations. "In city or town or county village the whole municipal industrial and social life . . . moved in the circle of the gild."[89] George Unwin has described the close links between occupations and territory. Vast areas of social life were dominated by guildlike forms of social organization. "Kings and princes, barons and knights, cathedral canons, rectors of churches, curates, parish clerks, lawyers, wealthy merchants, comfortable shopkeepers, poor journeymen, peasants and football players were bound together for the pursuit of their class interests under similar social and religious forms and sanctions."[90]

Guilds, fraternities, and their unofficial ancillary associations underwent changes in the sixteenth and seventeenth centuries. Many of their powers were usurped by the emerging state structure, yet their organizational style was retained by many social groups. Indeed one scholar of such institutions has argued that the level of social ritual, pageantry, and splendor associated with guild collectivities increased in the sixteenth and seventeenth centuries.[91] Marginal groups of casual laborers and the begging poor, not just in England but throughout Europe, organized themselves into some version of fraternity association[92] in which forms of address and organization were based on military and craft models. Certainly criminal groups were described by contemporaries as if they constituted some type of illegitimate criminal dominion.[93]

Clearly the bastard sanctuaries could not offer the same measure of security, protection, and market advantages as the guilds. Confidence cheats, cutpurses, thieves, tricksters, and prostitutes seldom possessed elaborate guild arrangements. Undoubtedly contemporary chroniclers used convenient rhetorical devices to give criminal life shape and meaning. But it does seem reasonable to argue that a version of a seigneurie collective functioned as a model for criminals, debtors, and vagrants.[94] These illegitimate sanctuaries thus represented territorial protectorates that possessed a nucleus of armed strength which provided the world of crime with a measure of political authority. Like bandits and outlaws, criminals, debtors, and vagrants evolved a modus vivendi with the state and developed their own loose regulative functions.[95]

Certainly there were European parallels. The *cours de miracles* of sixteenth- and seventeenth-century Paris, which were densely populated regions in the heart of the slum quarters at the city's fringe,[96] approximated the sanctuaries of London. Indeed criminal districts and their undersocieties were to be found all over the Continent. As Henry Kamen has observed, criminal territoriality gave rise to a criminal organization that had

> its own rules and code of honour, but it was the honour of thieves, and the rule was to exploit others just as they, the poor, were exploited by the upper classes. Their morality was not that of society . . . they did not practise marriage, nor did they frequent the sacraments, and they only entered a church if it was to cut purses . . . Neither the norms nor the conduct of society then, were to be their guide. They were an anti-society,

organized against it, disbelieving in its ethics, dedicated to cheating and robbing it. They were separated from it by their own jargon, called *cant* in English, *Ratwalsch* in German, *argot* in French, *jerga de germania* (jargon of the Brotherhood) in Spanish.[97]

Moreover, the existence of autonomous districts of crime enhanced the stability and continuity of criminal practices. As Goubert has noted, many criminals "were not isolated adventurers but structured social groups whose combined strength could amount to several tens of thousands."[98] There are even marked resemblances between the criminal sanctuaries of early modern London and present-day crime areas of developing third world countries. Comparative research on South America, Asia, and Africa reveals that shantytowns and bidonvilles have emerged on the frontiers of new third world cities. These districts on the perimeter of social control have high rates of crime and possess geographically based organizations that provide shelter and immunity from arrest.[99]

Territorial Autonomy and the Implications for Crime

The major implications of autonomous territories for criminal organization were threefold: (i) they provided shelter and protection, (ii) they neutralized the law, and (iii) they fostered criminal middlemen.

Protection and Shelter

The most obvious function afforded by the criminal sanctuaries was access to shelter, protection, concealment, and escape. As has been shown, the crime areas were territorial protectorates. Specific pennyrent lodgings, cellars, taverns, and alehouses served as the sites of active agencies supporting escape, preventing arrest, seeking out and dissuading pursuers, bargaining for criminals, and providing living accommodation. Moreover, such establishments were also strategic bases of operation for the planning and execution of crime and for the concealment and distribution of stolen goods.

The internal design of these protectorates was often complex enough to discourage pursuit. The complex network of streets, courtyards, lanes, and tenter areas operated as helpful buffer areas through which criminals passed with impunity. According to one account, a regular strategy was to pass through a sanctuary to the outer fringe of the area, thus using the larger part of the crime area as a line of defense and protection against those joining the hue and cry.[100]

Sanctuary men also resided permanently within the borders of such domains. Alsatia and the Mint cultivated strong senses of loyalty and tradition, developing their own rules, oaths, customs, and codes of support and recognition. They had access to considerable means of violence and were only suppressed after military defeat. As Thompson has observed, "the Minters kept up an extreme loyalty [until 1722]—indeed, a whole ritual of solidarity—in defending each other from bailiffs."[101] Territoriality also functioned to underpin a material basis for a system of positional rules that demarcated ally from foe. Elaborate codes, signs, and passwords came to constitute a means of recognition and social identity. Canting—speaking in a criminal tongue—was a practical method of sorting out affinity-enmity relationships. As Thompson has observed, "from the 'sanctuary' at Southwark they [Minters] sent their emissaries, who were called 'Spirits,' out of the Mint in search of their antagonists. The Spirits were dressed . . . in long black gowns, which go over their heads, with holes made to see out at."[102] Sanctuary men had a sense of legitimacy about their institutions. They possessed their own rough justice and their own scale of ritualized punishments. They developed a vigilante enforcement force, a spy system, a hooded judiciary, and a humiliating penal code. Bailiffs, watchmen, and constables were unwelcome agents, and the sanctuary men organized councils that policed their boundaries, collected information, and warned of creditors, informers, and law officials.[103] Armed cutters and bullies were a type of street patrol. If the unwelcome were unwise enough to enter or be dragged into Alsatia or the Mint, they were subject to quick justice. Ritualistic insults and punishments were sometimes followed by injury.[104] Informers, after summary trial, were whipped, pumped, and ducked. According to the testimony (anonymous) of sanctuary men, bailiffs or informers were made to "utter blasphemies, to eat parchments, drink salt and water, or to be 'pumped.' 'Pumping,' with the head held under a street pump, could be extended to repeated ducking in foul sewers, until at length the filthy victim was forced to kiss a brick covered with human excrement and say: 'I am a Rogue, and a Rogue in Grain, And damn me, if ever I come into the Mint again.'"[105]

Protection and shelter were rendered more reliable by the ready availability of firearms. Control over the means of violence was diffuse. Private forms of violence were decentralized, often the prerogative of the powerful. Policing organization, as I demonstrate later, lacked the procedures, powers, competence, and control over military skills and equipment to eradicate competing private forms of violence. The spread of small, inexpensive, reliable, and easily maintained and concealed firearms further democratized the distribution and operation of violence. Criminal territories thus amassed considerable practical possibilities of force and aggression, capable not only of resistance but of opposition.[106] Certainly the sanctuary men of criminal areas were often described as armed with desperate weapons—a political factor that undoubtedly strengthened the areas' autonomy despite their legal abolition.

The Neutralization of Law

Territorial autonomy and geographical arrangements also affected the internal operation of the law. To begin with, practical enforcement of the law was splintered, tied to ward boundaries and not subject to overall regulation. In effect, there existed in London twenty-six locally administered social control forces with little central authority. The city was also governed by several other competing authorities: manorial courts, courts of city companies, crown courts, and chamberlains' courts.[107] Separate policing agencies tied to separate jurisdictions patrolled the same districts. Beadles, constables, and prison keepers and their assistants attempted to impose some regulation, but their work was difficult to coordinate and make effective. Furthermore, these disjointed groups were at the disposal of a number of authorities. Constables and watchmen could be called into service both by their aldermen and by the Privy Council. Legal control was a quagmire of ambiguous jurisdictions and authorities, privileged zones, and expanding and contradictory rules.[108]

The separation of criminal regions, moreover, radically checked the local enforcement of the law. Debtors, as well as felons, acquired immunity and remained protected. Decentralized coercive institutions seldom penetrated the territorial labyrinths surrounding the Clink, the Mint, or Alsatia. Here the practical face of the law was an intricately mediated artifice composed of secret informers, converted criminals, and extraordinary search and roundup patrols. Subterfuge, intrigue, diplomacy, and patronage were more common than outright coercion. The safety afforded by criminal territoriality and the weakness of city legal control meant that some version of institutionalized incorporation of criminal areas was likely. Not only were criminal structures tolerated in specific zones but the management of crime was entrepreneurial—a trading in "criminal skins." Just as pirates, outlaws, and smugglers were rescued from the gallows to serve as privateers, sheriffs, and revenue officials, so thieves were used as thief catchers. Such policies of cooptation often endowed a de facto legitimacy on areas of criminality.[109]

The exercise of the law was a blend of reputable and disreputable practices. The mediations of territorial custom and power meant that the city and the crown had to recruit the criminal as their own agents. A modus vivendi emerged that blurred the exercise of the law. A barter economy of justice resulted. Rewards, pardons, and patronage were manipulated and threaded together in an elaborate amalgam of compromise and exploitation, an arrangement that contributed to the legal and political ambiguity of the criminal districts. The modus vivendi was threefold: (1) A policy of tolerating crime areas developed. Criminal territories acquired an institutional autonomy as long as they were in the suburbs and the traditional ecclesiastical jurisdictions. Law enforcement was more a strategy of confinement than of coercion. (2) Territoriality ensured a degree of social closure; these regions were most effectively overseen by indirect strategies, which in turn enhanced the growth of criminal intermediaries. Powerful factions within these criminal districts negotiated the interplay between law, order, and crime. They tended to define the character of criminality, betraying the weak and the recalcitrant to the state and protecting the loyal. Thus the state to some extent relied on criminals to police criminal districts. (3) The organizational consequences for crime that resulted from territorial independence also contributed to the neutralization of the law. Working crews of thieves acquired the services of local middlemen: knights of the post, other false swearers, and what we would now call fixers, who forestalled or undermined the process of apprehension and arrest. Bribing, giving false information, and arranging deals with victim and enforcement agents, they provided a degree of immunity from the penal process.[110] The routine presence of these agents of corruption inside the world of crime was conducive to safety, and thus to organizational stability and continuity.

Criminal Organizational Rationality

Finally, the illegal sanctuaries copied the seigneuries collective by serving an important economic function: the regulation of a specific criminal market. The effective insulation of such territories spawned an array of criminal institutions that linked thieves to a local economy and to wider networks of trade and distribution. The criminal districts institutionalized arrangements to resell or return stolen property: such intermediaries were crucial to the organization of theft since by providing distribution outlets they provided a ready market for stolen goods. Receiving arrangements did feed into legitimate markets, but the segregation of criminal zones made the connection between theft and monetary reward more regular. By not self-fencing, thieves could minimize their risks. Intermediaries such as fences promoted relations between the underworld and the wider social order. Patron-fences coordinated client-thieves into a system that returned stolen articles (some of only personal value) to former owners. Rewards, informing, extortion, and thieving were often intricately intertwined in working practices that gave power to fences and rationalized criminal activities. Risks were reduced, competition curtailed, and a tendency toward market dominance established.[111]

The quasi-segregated nature of crime, when combined with weak policing, opened up a political role for such intermediaries. One means of market control was the threat to betray uncooperative thieves. This was rendered more feasible by the ecological limits of the criminal underworld. Fences colluded with informers and with the judiciary, and acquired a social usefulness which in turn protected them from prosecution. The autonomy of the illegitimate sanctuaries is perhaps most readily apparent in the political influence that accrued to such receivers of stolen property.

Political Authority and Decentralized Social Control

The development, strength, and permanence of territorial enclaves also reflected the internal arrangements and anomalies of city social control. The administration and jurisdiction of London were fissured and differentiated. The ward system, pivotal to city social organization, forged a radical decentralization of power and a system of virtual self-policing. London was a web of tenuously related local wards. It was an array of separate areas which were differentiated by wealth, occupation, privilege, and customary rights. Ward customs and authority were deeply rooted and exerted a major influence over daily life.[112] Allegiances and loyalties were tied to craft, parish, and ward institutions. Work, religion, politics, and social assistance revolved around local axes in a manner such that each ward tended to display an appreciable degree of political authority and independence, an autonomy that was defended and magnified by local interest groups. Wards, then, were urban microcosms of the county and the nation-state, overseen by their own parochial political structures. So powerful were ward customs and politics that attempts to centralize even limited social services such as sanitation and sewage were continually defeated.[113]

Policing in London was similarly fractured, reflecting the city's division into twenty-six wards. Each had its separate policing agency, further splintered into hundreds of precinct patrols. This meant that watchmen, constables, and beadles were organized according to customary procedures more befitting a rural and geographically static community. But whereas conventional policing based on ward boundaries and traditions of communal maintenance of order may have suited medieval town life, it faced severe strains when confronted with bands of footloose vagrants or the organization and skill of the persistent criminal. These numerous and competing authorities, jurisdictions, and ordinances hindered overall coordination of social control: crime management was fragmented, decentralized, and territorially bounded.[114] The watch system and constabulary represented street-level formal control with limited geographical powers of pursuit, detection, and arrest. Confined essentially to their ward quarters, they had little incentive or means to match the mobility of the vagrant or the presistent deviant.

This weakness of public agencies was accompanied by a considerable ambiguity surrounding the process of enforcement. The peculiar status of liberties and sanctuaries imposed constraints on central control activities. Certain territories within ward boundaries were self-policed principalities. Legally, ward officials had to call upon the king's justice and Privy Council to act in such domains. Fortified structures such as manor houses could be transformed into impregnable criminal bastions. Protected by walls, ditches, moats, and drawbridges, these strongholds could resist the arm of the law by force.[115] In other cases ambiguous areas between two or more wards could escape official regulation.

Ambiguity also characterized the organization of the law. Jurisdictional uncertainty contributed to the fissured nature of ward administration. Separate courts, policing agencies, and political authorities claimed similar mandates and patrolled overlapping jurisdictions. The watch and ward had many masters: the ward constables, the Privy Council, the city marshalcy, to name only a few. Competition, confusion, and conflict frequently resulted. Ecclesiastical courts, sheriff's courts, aldermanic courts, city corporations' courts, and magistrates' courts competed with one another. Beadles, constables, watchmen, marshalmen, Privy Council messengers, trained militias, aldermen and their assistants, and prison underkeepers attempted to develop some form of social coercion, but their efforts were seldom coordinated. More often they rivaled one another. Radically distinct organizations with competing institutional affiliations maintained separate objectives, personnel, jurisdictions, and means of punishment.

London was segmented into rival vectors of social control. The principal administration was in the hands of the cities of London and Westminster and the adjoining counties of Essex, Surrey, and Middlesex. However, with the increased growth of London between 1550 and 1650, frontiers were altered and city regulations were further fragmented. The structure of city administration then intermeshed with and bolstered the radical decentralization of social control. Constitutionally, London was governed by three councils or courts: the Court of Lord Mayor and Aldermen, the Court of Common Council, and the Court of Common Hall. In general, city government was an uneasy alliance of elected aldermen and common councilmen.[116] The Court of Common Hall, the largest and most popular of these assemblies, acted solely in an electoral capacity and possessed no deliberative powers. The Court of Aldermen was the executive governing body of the city. Aldermen acted as justices of the peace, a position that was tenable for life. Sitting as a body they framed citywide policy and were responsible for enforcement within ward boundaries.[117] The Court of Aldermen was assisted by the Court of Common Council which functioned as its legislative arm. Subject to Court of Aldermen control, the council met infrequently. While the Common Council had limited rights to control finances, assess municipal loans for royal and civic purposes, supervise transactions of municipal property, and independently make bylaws, its proceedings were fashioned by initiatives from the aldermen's council. An uncooperative Common Council could be administratively short-circuited. As Pearl has observed, "it was not unusual for the Lord Mayor and Aldermen to summon a hybrid assembly, on some occasions, which by-passed Common Council altogether and included themselves and the wealthiest commoners and liverymen of the city chosen at their discretion."[118]

The Court of Aldermen, then, enjoyed immense executive and judicial power. It exercised influence over legislative functions in the Court of Common Council. It acted as a judicial bench with judges of oyer and terminer and jail delivery, and as regular justices of the peace. Its responsibilities included the court of huskings, the sheriff's court, and the orphan's court. It regulated debt cases, monitored alehouse licenses, approved guild ordinances, managed the estates of minors, and directly petitioned the throne and the House of Commons. Procedures were chiefly initiated by petition, but deliberations were in secret. Patronage was concentrated in its hands. Important offices, over 140 by 1750, were farmed out for profits to favorites, and an informal oligarchy ruled at the center of London politics.[119]

The distribution of patronage, the secrecy of deliberations, lifelong membership, and the veto power and privilege of the Court of Aldermen incurred opposition from other interest groups. Quarrels between councils and internal disputes and conflicts fissured the administrative structure, making overall policies difficult to formulate and enforce.

Administrative uncertainties and conflicts were, however, evidence of a deeper political instability. Decentralization of formal social control was accompanied by fragmented political rule. Economically powerful guilds and corporations were at the center of city governance. They were often local competitors to centrally directed government. They advanced and defended their occupational and territorial claims. They sought influence over city judiciaries, commissions, and militias. Civil servants were frequently sponsored patrons, and city politics was an elevator of social and economic gain. Despite the number of city guilds and companies, by the mid-sixteenth century commerce in London was dominated by three major competing cartels: the clothier merchant companies, West and East India trading companies, and American colonial mercantile cartels. Each major grouping operated independently, and each vied for political power.[120] Little consensus existed, and city government was characterized by much conflict and radical shifts in political perspectives.

The pursuit of different economic objectives divided the ruling class. The traditional political leadership of the city had been wealthy, closely allied, and uniform in ethos. By the late Elizabethan period it had been overtaken by events. Its internal inflexibility was particularly evident in its incapacity to manage the growing social problems of ward life.[121] Traditionalism subjected it to the political authority of the crown. It frequently sided with the state on matters concerning customary charters, liberties, and outparishes. This meant that the city was incapable of incorporating such zones and asserting judicial control over them, since many of these districts were private, royal, or ecclesiastical enclaves. Conflicts between reform and traditional elements of the ruling city elites and the royal government ensued and further weakened the coherence of city politics.[122]

The judiciary and the Court of Common Council were battlegrounds, which witnessed regular purges and the formation of new alliances. Prestigious public offices were contested, usurped, and reconstituted. City militia commissions, naval administration and financial organizations all underwent dramatic transformations.[123] Ideological and religious differences within the city further contributed to a climate of change and conflict. Competition for ward seats and city offices sometimes took on the flavor of county feuds and underscored the extent to which power was local and shifting. Interested cartels operated as discrete entities wielding influence and expanding their private objectives. By the early seventeenth century political destabilization was severe. Links and alliances between the city and the royal government were collapsing. By the 1630s the problems caused by the lack of policy on anomalous territories came to a head: some of these areas became the headquarters of social and political rebellion, prompting Charles I's unsuccessful attempt to abolish them permanently.[124]

Conclusion

Whether one looks at city social ecology or at the character of government reactions to law and order, it should be clear that criminal areas were enduring protectorates. The growth and strength of criminal territoriality were closely related to the jurisdictional and administrative lacunae of city organization. While the implications for criminal organization have not yet been thoroughly drawn, it is nonetheless apparent that territoriality played a part in the formation of criminal associations, networks, and transactions. By affording shelter, protection, and immunity from the law, territoriality slowed down the penetration of social control and served to insulate criminal practices and organization.

5

COERCIVE
INSTITUTIONS

Community and Social Control

The nature of population settlements in England contributed to an uneven system of social control. Local topography exerted an influence on rural and urban policing. For example, coastal areas and the rugged north country achieved virtual autonomy from state supervision. Frequently such areas were unpatrolled and had recourse to their own legal and enforcement designs. Forest lands and common pastures harbored squatters and cottagers who formed self-contained communities outside official state regulation. Entire regions in the west country were isolated "dark corners of the land," and were havens for radicals, religious dissenters, and criminals.[1] The arm of secular justice could seldom penetrate certain feudal jurisdictional enclaves. The bishop of Ely's liberty and the territory lying at the northern end of the Welsh borders between the counties of the Oxford and northern court circuits represented "county palatines," immune from the king's itinerant justice, while the northern borders between England and Scotland were interstitial regions outside central political control.[2] Organized bands of criminals lived in these mountainous terrains and engaged in widespread criminal enterprises. Cockburn has observed that "despite [a] . . . special, reinforced system of border administrations, traditions of crime and justice by a 'well-tempered sword' remained strong throughout the seventeenth century."[3]

The difficulties of travel further increased the radical separation of districts. Many roads were "but small localized systems of narrow bridle paths" capable of handling the traffic of oxcarts, pack horses, and people on foot or on horseback but insufficient for transporting large numbers or heavy loads.[4] Highways were impassable at times, and certain segments were controlled by bands of highwaymen rather than by the state. In Essex the roads were frequently in need of repair, and adjoining shrubbery and ditches afforded the highway thief protection and concealment.[5] In Sussex the woodland areas outside London were noted regions of highway robbery.[6] Poor transport conditions frequently hindered the administration of itinerant justice, forcing delays and postponements in due process. Access, particularly for outlying circuit magistrates, was problematic. Journeys were difficult and tiring, and the movement of courts and militia was cumbersome. Immunity from common assault in court or on the road could seldom be guaranteed, and northern border judges traveled armed and with local escorts.[7]

The customs of local communities also bolstered the separation of shires. Social worlds were parochial and confined units. Traditions of oral communication and face-to-face relations were central. The village, parish, and town ward were the basic living units. Supraparochial institutions were by and large weak. Communities were self-supporting, visited only by small numbers of itinerant peddlars, carters, badgers, and merchant middlemen. As Everitt has argued, England was in large part an amalgamation of "independent shire-states, each with its own distinct ethos and loyalty."[8] Responsibility for maintaining the law often rested on local settlements or parish villages. Coastal districts, for example, possessed their own vigilante groups to guard their shores and settlements from pirates and wandering mariners.[9] Communal policing was a common practice of long standing. Even in large towns it was a decentralized and volunteer affair with local ward officials in command.[10]

Yet England was not a static society, and communal policing

proved inadequate to the changing needs of an increasingly mobile society. Although there was a hard core of people wedded to their native parishes "most men changed their abode at least once in the course of their lives, if only temporarily in some cases."[11] However, population movements were mostly confined to the neighboring parish or county.[12] London was the exception being a highly mobile and unsettled area. A study of parish depositions from London's east end, for example, suggests that over two-thirds of local inhabitants came from counties more than fifty miles from the city.[13] It has been estimated that perhaps one-sixth of the total population spent at least part of its lives in the metropolis. Moreover London grew at a dramatic rate and without coherent design or coordination.[14] By the mid-seventeenth century it had evolved into a loose metropolis of amalgamated hamlets, villages, parishes, and the old city, and was some ten to fifteen times the size of the largest provincial town.[15] City wards spilled over their borders, and nebulous neighborhoods of deviance, marginality, and crime formed on the fringes of the metropolis; these areas posed severe problems for policing. Surveillance and information gathering were problematic, and practical law enforcement was often a matter of subterfuge, intrigue, and maneuver. Seldom could formal agencies monitor the wayward or the criminal.[16]

The daily detailed supervision of social life was still exercised by forces drawn from the immediate community. The elementary forms of social control developed under Saxon and Norman law transformed the entire community into a posse comitatus and charged it with collectively pursuing and arresting an offender.[17] The hue and cry enjoined all male adults to take on the role of police constable. Communal policing units were responsible under pain of collective fine or punishment to seek out and apprehend wanted criminals. The preventive aspect of policing was handled by the watch at night and the ward officials by day, the repressive by collective hue and cry, and the punitive by presentments to courts against offenders.[18] The system of ward watching consolidated these principles, but also recognized a distinction between rural and urban policing in that it introduced watchmen as added assistants to local town constables. Watchmen guarded the gates of the town from sunset to sunrise. They had the powers of arrest during hours of darkness. In instances of hue and cry they were sworn to take up arms and pursue the call.[19]

By the mid-sixteenth century urbanization and the increased mobility of populations tended to make such local decentralized forces anachronistic. The security of the city, while still delegated to the entire population, came increasingly under the direction of the Privy Council and the city marshalcy. Watch and ward policing, however, remained the front-line force in law maintenance and crime control. Ward constables and volunteer watchmen were the pivot of city policing, and ancillary state control efforts and institutions were grafted onto the local ward policing organization. In the formal division of control work the city was policed by four major coercive institutions: the constable and watch, the Privy Council, the marshalcy, and the army and militias.

Watch and Ward Policing

By the mid-sixteenth century, the hue and cry was unable to manage a sustained policing response. Precinct watches and the citizens' constabulary were in decline. These essentially unpaid and volunteer offices were not being adequately serviced. The already heavy workloads of watchmen and constables were further compounded by the medley of contradictory charters, passports, edicts, orders, and privileges issued under the Elizabethan state. According to one historian of British policing, "the accession of Queen Elizabeth inaugurated a period of great activity for the police departments, . . . magistrates and constables were kept busy in administering the statutes dealing with apprentices, wages, disputes in service, hours of labour, and regulation of industrial trade, laws for the suppression of rogues and vagabonds and other enactments."[20] Constables at assizes had to be prepared for "inquiries into the activities of felons, vagrants, and recusants as also about the decay of houses and husbandry, the tillage of land, alm houses, engrossing and forestalling, molesters, the relief of the poor, sufficiency of petty constables, masters who had retained servants out of the justices; the erection of cottages, drunkenness, whoredoms and incontinency, discharging of servants, and thereby increasing rogues and idle persons, poulterers and purveyors who buy victuals, and resell at unreasonable rates and alehouses erected and maintained by any but . . . the person of the town."[21] In addition, the watch had to assist in keeping the peace, imprisoning offenders, guarding public morals, seizing and dismantling property, and admonishing and fining neighbors; while constables were also expected to make court presentments and oversee public punishments.[22]

Despite their numerous and cumbersome duties, constables were surprisingly restricted in their powers of arrest. In some precincts of their wards they had no jurisdiction. They could not enter, pursue, or arrest. In other places they needed official clearance. They seldom could leave the boundaries of their ward division except by agreement of the neighboring constabulary, Occupational hazards further restricted their activities. Constables were liable for wrongful arrests and for loss of prisoners in their custody. They could be penalized by having their property repossessed or by forfeiting their business to pay off court debts. They had to patrol unknown and sometimes hostile territories, cope with gangs of thieves and robbers, investigate the multitudes of base tenements, oversee the hidden and concealed lanes, alleys, and courtyards, and manage the severances of growing numbers of vagrants. Such duties placed the volunteer constables and watchmen at considerable physical risk, particularly in policing the criminal precincts where walled sanctuaries and traditions of defiance and force challenged the jurisdiction of watch and constable, and where the terrain made detection and apprehension highly problematic.[23] Amateur police personnel were easily outmaneuvered in the twisting lanes of the sanctuaries and in the interstices between ward jurisdictions.

The onerous workload was further complicated by the quagmire of ambiguous jurisdictions, privileged territories, and expanding and contradictory regulations and laws. In addition, these men were at the call not only of their aldermen but of the Privy Council as well. They were further obliged to obey the orders of provost marshals and later still the city marshalcy.[24] This overlap of authorities at times resulted in considerable conflict and hostility.

Policing, then, lacked a central command. The ward was the customary communal unit, so much so that by Stow's time (1598), it was already "more than four hundred years old."[25] In effect, the parochial institutional arrangement of London made it difficult to oversee. Twenty-six local ward policing units were responsible for law, order, and crime control. Centralizing schemes that took power away from local wards and institutions met with opposition,[26] and policing remained the responsibility of an amalgam of uncoordinated bodies with an array of heterogeneous rules. These separate parochial companies policed areas whose boundaries meant nothing to the criminal, and the policing agents lacked the communication and organizational scope to pursue criminals from ward to ward. At best, policing functions were organized around periodic forays intended to purge the city of problem populations.

Economic considerations also acted to discourage individuals from holding office and serving watch. The demands of bargaining, selling, buying, and maintaining the craft standards of the emerging capitalist commercial society left little time for fulfilling customary policing commitments. The compulsory tasks of serving as constables or even watchmen were unprofitable in themselves and directed valuable energy and time away from profit-making and income-earning ventures. Commitment waned and the recruitment and organization of policing suffered and became open to corruption.

The responsibilities associated with communal ward policing encouraged financially able citizens to find methods of exempting themselves from watch and constabulary functions. Increasingly over the century from 1550 to 1650, elected ward officials deputized their apprentices or domestics as replacements or hired substitute labor. A market in the speculation of policing offices and duties emerged. Gradually a body of regular full-time constables and watchmen, with widened discretionary powers, interposed themselves in a middleman's position. They were paid money to act as proxies or to hire alternative watchmen. Since there were no controls over wages, constables acquired considerable bargaining power. Because of their position in the nexus of communication and control, watch and ward officers could appropriate a secret wage. They negotiated fees for hiring substitutes and set the wages for hired watchmen. The two rates did not need to coincide, and a secret income was procured by ward officials.[27] Gradually the volunteer, unpaid watch acquired within it a wage-paid element. A pool of full-time substitute watchmen and a core of regular ward officials recruited from older men and the "baser sort" of London society emerged. The surplus supply of cheap labor came to staff growing sections of the city watch. These "Charlies," as they were later called, were frequently unfit for watch service. They were often old, in poor health, inadequately armed, nonuniformed, and lax in the performance of their duties. As Bacon noted "it was not the better sort of residents" who filled these offices.[28] Indeed, a more serious abuse emerged. Ward officials refused to hire substitute labor, and there were not enough policing agents. Evidence is limited, but some glimpse of the problem can be gleaned from surviving documents. The 1663 Act of Common Council set the number of watchmen in the City of London (21 of 26 wards) at 747; less than one-half were actually hired.[29] Constables pocketed "dead pay," understaffed the watch, sometimes neglected their stations, seldom enforced curfews, and did not police from ward to ward.[30]

The quality of police agents seldom compensated for failings of quantity. The local system of trading for offices and duties meant that those who eventually held stations were "of inferior, yea base condition which is a mere abuse."[31] Samuel Rid observed that the watch was irregular and reluctant in its surveillance: "what good rule is kept among your watch, how here one is drunk . . . there another asleep upon a bench complaining how his back aches with . . . burthens in the daytime . . . and . . . how you found this door left open by 'prentices either to let in their whores . . . or to purloin their masters goods to maintain their trulls; here to find a fit knave picking open a lock by the help of his art, . . . these and many more you might have busied your brain about."[32]

The city watch lacked passwords for communication and identification. They had little contact with and knowledge of adjoining ward policing. Criminals could view and time the patrols and regulate their crimes accordingly. Justice Burleigh noted: "for these watchmen stand so openly in clumps as no suspected person will come near them, and if they be no better instructed but to find three persons by one of them having a hooked nose they may miss thereof. And thus I thought good to advertise you, that the justice that had the charge, so I think, may use the matter more circumspectly."[33]

The Privy Council as a Policing Force

The inadequacies of watch and ward policing in London forced the state to bolster its social control forces more directly and formally through the offices of the Privy Council and through the creation of a specific city marshalcy. Privy Council policing consisted of an array of ad hoc temporary projects. It was not itself a policing organization. The Privy Council lacked the numbers, technology, and institutional competence to manage particular problems of law enforcement. It was a political council concerned among other things with problems of government, social unrest, and rebellion. It functioned more as a summoner of social control forces than as an actual agent in the field. Thus it was instrumental in raising fighting troops, dispensing coercive forces to trouble spots, and in case of an invasion, coordinating militias. However, it did concern itself with domestic problems, and in London and elsewhere evolved a series of special social control practices aimed at detecting and repressing crime.

The system of swearing parapolice constables and the use of secret organized searches and roundups were seen first as emergency measures to increase access to and information about outcast and marginal populations: their numbers, locales, habits, and organization. The council was concerned to achieve from above what ward policing could not effect at a local level.

The appointment of extra policemen or provost marshals with widened powers of search and arrest was a relatively common practice throughout Elizabeth's reign.[34] Typically, provost marshals were paid appointees of the Privy Council or the Corporation of London. Their mandates were temporary and usually included an entitlement to hire assistants.[35] Such officials were furnished "with numerous attendants on horseback, armed with pistols." They had the power to apprehend and to punish "sundry sorts of base people; some known apprentices, such as were the base manual occupations; some others, wandering idle persons of condition rogues and vagabonds; and some colouring their wandering by the name of soldiers."[36] Their sphere of action was wide, and they frequently engaged in systematic territorial searches of adjoining counties. Yet the office of the provost marshal was organizationally ill-equipped to perform work other than the suppression of periodic unrest, and even that work created friction. In the monitoring of mobile vagrants and the casual poor and in detecting crime it had a most oblique impact. It was circumscribed administratively and temporally. It represented little more than a temporary force dependent, in fact, on coordination with the local ward forces. With uncanny regularity extra constables were reappointed, but they were incapable of engaging in the commonplace business of monitoring and deterring crime. The Privy Council itself reviewed the appointments of provost marshals, and concluded that they failed in their objectives: "it is to be doubted that if by good order to be taken it be not prevented that many of them [masterless men] being driven from the city . . . and borough of Southwarke."[37] Masterless men "stealthily re-turn[ed] to the alehouses" from outside the city gates "in the night season."[38]

In conjunction with hiring extra policing officials the Privy Council evolved a system of mass searches and arrests. Prearranged round-ups of limited duration continued to be used until the Civil War.[39] Some "privy searches" lasted for twenty-four hours, some went on for weeks. Frequently they were undertaken under cover of dark-ness and were usually coordinated to take place throughout the en-tire city and the surrounding counties so as to prevent criminals fleeing over borders and escaping arrest. William Fleetwood, the city recorder, provided a description:

> I did the same night send warrants out into the said quarters and into Westminster and the Duchy; and in the morning I went abroad myself and I took that day seventy-four rogues, . . . and the same day toward night . . . took all the names of the rogues and sent them from the ses-sions house into Bridewell . . . Upon the twelfth day in the forenoon, the Master of the Rolls, myself and others received a charge before my Lords of the Council as touching rogues and masterless men and to have a privy search. The same day . . . I met the governors of Bridewell . . . we exam-ined all the said rogues and gave them substantial payment . . . Upon Sunday . . . I conferred order for Southwark, Lambeth, and Newington from whence I received a school of forty rogues, men and women, and above. I bestowed them in Bridewell. I did the same afternoon peruse Paul's where I took about twenty cloaked rogues . . . I placed them also in Bridewell . . . Upon Friday morning at the Justice Hall there brought in above a hundred lewd people taken in the privy search . . . Upon Friday last we sat at the Justice Hall from 7 in the morning until 7 at night, where were condemned certain horse-stealers, cutpurses and such like to the number of ten whereof nine were executed.[40]

Middlesex justices give similar evidence that such searches were akin to law and order campaigns lasting several months. In one ten-week mass search in 1589–1590 seventy-one persons were rounded up and sentenced for vagrancy-related offenses.[41]

The targets of the privy searches were the institutions and areas of crime: inns, alehouses, victualing places, stables, outhouses, bowl-ing alleys, low lodging houses, and certain market streets. The liber-ties, particularly in Southwark and Whitefriars, were the perceived regions of poverty, unrest, and crime.[42] The manhunts were designed to open up these worlds. Thus a day search for houses that received stolen property reported that it uncovered eighteen such "houses of entertainment" in London, Westminster, Southwark, and adjacent areas. In addition, it obtained a list of forty-five masterless men and women who were allegedly the "robbers of gentlemen's quarters and shops."[43]

Special sessions were organized to coordinate the mass roundups, and normal policing institutions were short-circuited in favor of special investigations with authority to apprehend suspects and to execute the law without delay. Such direct state manipulation of the enforcement process may have had some limited symbolic effect in bolstering the state's coercive capacities, but it also reveals the state's fragility. The effects of the roundups were short term at best. They temporarily alleviated street disorders, closed down some of the haunts and institutions, apprehended and punished a number of the outcasts, and dispersed the rest.[44] Privy Council policing proved capable of suppressing particular riots or crises, but it was ineffective in the commonplace business of routinely keeping the peace and detecting crime. It formed one of the buttresses against social and political unrest, but its influence lay in a defensive regulation of order. Evidence also suggests that ward constables themselves had little liking for the roundups, which added to their work load. They were required to take custody of and responsibility for the mass of prisoners. They were expected to inflict the harsh punishments of pilloring and whipping. They had to assist in dangerous pursuit and arrest campaigns, and they were liable to the authority of these overseers in their own territories. Frequently, the constables developed covert tactics of noncooperation. They minimized their appearances in public, sometimes evaded recognition by removing identifiable clothing and badges, and concealed their station and residence by removing their white staff of office from their doorways.[45]

Supervision over policing, then, was problematic even though central government initiatives and controls were now being fashioned. The Privy Council seemed incapable of systematically reorganizing, standardizing, and directing policing. Constables and their manhunts proved inadequate support for the legal order. Privy Council policing agents lacked familiarity with local ward affairs, and that unfamiliarity prevented routine peacekeeping and crime detection and control from taking root. Their numbers and stability were insufficient for them to function adequately as a crime control institution.

The City Marshalcy

The third arm of practical policing was the city marshalcy. The marshals and their assistants were the city's response to the need for a centrally directed policing force, and they attempted reform by superimposing a watchdog force on ward crime control. The model for this was the office of provost marshal. The Court of Aldermen regularized these duties and powers into an official policing office, and in 1603 appointed a permanent provost marshal for the City of London. Initially, the city marshalcy was composed of a marshal and two assistant marshalmen. These offices were originally filled by appointment or election, but toward the latter part of the seventeenth century they were contracted out to cover mounting city debts. The marshal was charged with five major tasks. He had to: (1) carry off rogues and vagrants to Bridewell, (2) see that due punishments were inflicted according to the law, (3) supervise the constables and the watch, (4) maintain supervision over ward officials to see that plague regulations were adhered to, and (5) attend to miscellaneous street activities such as licensing traders and sellers, and controlling the actions of fruiterers, hucksters, and other unlicensed itinerants.[46] The city marshal and his officers were paid officials, who wore uniforms and carried firearms. Their numbers increased from two in 1603 to four in 1617 and to six by 1626.[47]

Almost from its inception the city marshalcy faced serious difficulties. Though uniformed and armed, numerically it was too weak to have much impact on crime. In 1624, for example, the marshalmen were attacked and beaten by a crowd for escorting an apprentice who was being "cruelly whipped from Aldgate to Temple Bar."[48] Policing was weakest at the crucial level of detection and apprehension of crime. Not only were constables and watchmen unskilled, reluctant to do their job, and poorly organized, but communal support and cooperation were also lacking. Fear, lack of crime-reporting skills, the threat of counterprosecutions, the practical economic difficulties of framing and carrying out arrest indictments, and the lack of confidence in the judicial system distanced the citizen from the police and the courts.[49]

Proclamations and orders from all levels of government seem to point to an indifferent citizenry. A proclamation by the Lord Mayor in 1603 noted the "remissences and negligence" of enforcement personnel.[50] A king's proclamation in 1616 observed that many "robberies and felonies, burglaries, pilferies and other horrible crimes" were committed because of "want of good execution" of the law.[51] Five years later a royal proclamation stated that policing in London was poor and corruption widespread. Strangers of quality and wealth were daily being abused. Constables and aldermen were seldom at their posts, and "householders, citizens and inhabitants" were not diligent in watch, pursuit, or apprehension.[52] Tolerant passivity appears to have been the stance of the London citizen. Further admonitions in 1628, 1630, 1634, and 1642 confirm the same themes of street disorder, crime, and lax reporting and punishment of abuses.[53] So defective was policing and so uncooperative the citizenry that Parliament ordered that extra precautions be taken and extra personnel be deployed. The watch was given more arms, and the city was supplied with "expert guides capable of leading a hue and cry" and knowledgeable in the ways and locales of the "speedy flight of thieves and robbers." Stricter surveillance and security schemes were advocated to keep crime outside city boundaries, and local hostelers were required to monitor and report on travelers.[54]

Increasingly the state relied upon the self-interest of private groups. Citizens were exhorted and paid to transform themselves into agents of control. The management of crime was organized around a personal profit-making business. State rewards, albeit unsystematic, were offered for successful presentation of certain offenses. Money or payment in kind was offered to enterprising searchers. Neighbors and tradesmen were encouraged to spy and turn evidence on each other. "Goldsmith's merchants, and their factors, masters of ships, mariners, passengers" and other persons associated with "gold or silver in coyne, jewels, bullion plate or vessel" who discovered and convicted forgers or exporters of counterfeit gold articles were offered "one-half of gold or silver or of the value thereof being seized."[55] Searchers in port towns or in "havens along the coasts" who uncovered smuggling operations in valuable metals were rewarded "the fourth part of their labour, of as much as they should find so forfeited."[56] Private initiative in the business of crime control was also encouraged for robbery, theft, and burglary: "Such person or persons who shall . . . apprehend and bring in safe custody before any justice of the peace, or any other officer of justice, any person that has committed, or shall commit any burglary or robbery on the highway, or that has or shall break upon any dwelling or enter into any such house, . . . upon the conviction of such person apprehended, shall have a reward of ten pounds for every such person so apprehended and committed."[57]

Arrested suspects were similarly urged to inform on their accomplices in order to gain their own reprieve. Pardons or protection could be procured by suspected or convicted thieves and highwaymen if they made "any discovery of his or their accomplices, or other the like offenders."[58] The system was designed to give the criminal informer a limited or permanent immunity from legal prosecution and to create tension within the world of crime. Forgers and counterfeiters were set against each other. A person in custody or on the run from the law because of trading in false silver or gold objects could earn a free pardon for all similar crimes he might have committed if he informed on his confreres. He was also entitled "to such part of the [seized] forfeiture of the said other party to the same offense, as amply as any other informer or relator, not having offended might have done."[59] He thus could receive a reprieve and a share of the discovered goods. The tactic of using reprieves and rewards engendered a climate of suspicion and disunity. The threat of competitive accusations was designed to undermine working partnerships and solidarity, but it also made the boundaries between crime and legality ambiguous. Law and enforcement became negotiable. Indeed the constant use of reprieves may have acted as an impetus to commit crime.[60] For example, the thief who was not in custody could continue his illegal practices and earn a free pardon for all similar previous crimes if he informed on his colleagues.[61]

Offices in the formal state control apparatus were not shielded from such trading and selling. Prison administrators and officials, constables, beadles, and watchmen farmed their positions for private profit and advantage. Many officeholders routinely bought positions and sought personal returns on their investment. Incumbents tacitly expected to enrich themselves by means of influence peddling, bribery, and extortion.[62] One historian has observed that Elizabethan political patronage "lacked adequate safeguards against a free-for-all scramble for spoils."[63] Much private exploitation of political office created a vast black market in which opportunism and outright corruption flourished. this was particularly so for the city marshalcy. From 1627 to 1637, the city was without its appointed official. The officeholder farmed out his position for profit.[64] He continued to draw the marshal's salary and paid his hireling a percentage of his wage. From 1627 to 1632 his deputy worked on his behalf. Attempts to replace the original officeholder, Davis, failed when the crown intervened on his behalf. In 1632, the nominee marshal and the undermarshal were subjected to an investigation. Prisoners, common thieves, and felons were allegedly being released without due cause. For this and other unspecified misdemeanors Davis's deputy was dismissed from office and imprisoned. the original officeholder was enjoined to resume his office. Davis refused and again deputized a replacement who served from 1632 to 1637. Eventually after ten years' nonperformance of office, Davis was coerced by the crown into taking up his office. He served for six years until finally being dismissed for abuse of powers and incompetence.

Succeeding marshals appear more stable in holding office, although their supervision over constables, beadles, and the watch was problematic. A proclamation in 1655 criticized justices of the peace, constables, and "other officers" for "want of zeal, care and diligence" in executing the law,[65] and a proclamation by the Lord Mayor six months later complained of poor policing supervision, crime detection, and cooperation. Constables were enjoined to make themselves "better known and more readily found." They were further ordered to have their signs of office "set or fixed at their street doors" so all may "detect their dwelling place."[66] Weak and ineffective, the City marshalcy was unable to regulate policing activities.

The Army and the Militias

The weak and ineffective city policing agents were paralleled by equally inadequate military forces. The principal functions of the army and the militia were to fight foreign campaigns and to serve as reserve units in case of invasion.[67] The routine surveillance of vagrants and crime fell outside their range. Crime control—the detection, pursuit, and apprehension of lawbreakers—was thus an irregular part of their mandate and only sporadically undertaken. Moreover, the militias and trained bands were themselves parochial units and hesitant buttresses of social order.

England possessed little in the way of a centralized national citizens' army. Control over the means of violence was diffuse, and the military system was quasi-feudal in character. Organized violence was regionally based, and private centers competed with centrifugal political developments in the state.[68] The army and the militias were internally divided agencies linked at different times to divergent interest groups. Cohesiveness and solidarity were by many accounts weak. Most armies of the period lacked the regimental traditions to forge collective identities. There was little organizational unity. Loyalties seldom flowed to a central core but were tied to local patrons who had enlisted the bands of fighting men.[69] The English army was an ad hoc and loose agglomeration of professional mercenaries and local, politically sponsored and trained retainers. It was formed in time of war and disbanded in peacetime. Military power was entrenched at the regional level under the tutelage of powerful landholding elements or was in the hands of equally powerful brokers in the business of organized violence. Relations with the political center were weak. The state had to negotiate allegiances with powerful territorial interests to raise armies and quell rebellions.[70]

The state possessed no monopoly over the means of violence. Organized and private, violence was diffuse, and, despite the fact that some control over aristocratic uses of violence existed by the 1630s, England still resembled a mosaic of organized potentially violent groupings.[71] Men of property could command resources and technical knowledge that could be fashioned into fighting units. Violence in the streets of London was apparently common. The fields about the city and the arterial roads were continual scenes of upper-class feuds. Pitched battles regularly occurred in Fleet Street and on the Strand. Armed affrays involving feuding nobles supported by their retainers sometimes went on for days. Little protection could be offered by the city authorities.[72] Indeed, the distribution of the new means of violence was democratized during the period under study. The bow had been officially replaced as the chief weapon of war by 1595, and the use of firearms percolated down to all sectors of society.[73] William Harrison observed that most men carried a weapon:

> Our nobility wear commonly swords or rapiers with their daggers, as doth every common serving man also that followeth his lord and master. Some desperate cutters we have in like sort, which carry two daggers or two rapiers . . . wherein every drunken fray they are known to work

much mischief . . . I might here speak of the excessive staves which divers that travel by the way do carry upon their shoulders, whereof some are twelve or thirteen foot long. Beside the pike of twelve inches; but, as they are commonly suspected on honest men to be thieves and robbers, or at the least wise scarce true men which bear them, so by reason of this like suspicious weapons the honest travel he is now forced to ride with a case of dags [pistols] at his saddle-bow, or with some pretty short snapper, whereby he may deal with them further off in his own self-defence before he come within the danger of these weapons.[74]

The organization of the means of violence did not cohere into a rational state-controlled coercive institution.[75] England, because of the lack of land borders with the Continent, escaped the need for a full-time standing army. Indeed its insular independence and its growing mercantile empire favored naval forces and operations. National defense became a matter for the navy. As Hill has observed, "its mere existence protected trade; the expansion of the mercantile marine created a reserve of ships and seamen for the navy in a time of war."[76] Yet a maritime force was an uncertain agency for domestic control, and by the end of Elizabeth's reign the army "was in general a mere wretched militia."[77] As domestic policemen the army lacked administrative competence. Channels of communication between center and periphery were often cumbersome and detracted from organizational coherence. The sheer size of armies made them a burden on local populations. They were effective repressive forces in curbing territorial revolts. They could disperse and defeat riotous crowds, although dark corners of the country were not easily accessible even to such forceful agencies. Seldom could they monitor the everyday world of crime.

Coincident with the decline in the army was the rise of the trained bands and militias. These coercive institutions were, however, the armed forces of regional authorities. With the crises in the aristocracy and the rise of the gentry, the state attempted to increase its hold over patronage. It established a foothold over *douceurs* and appointments. Increasingly, London became the central matrix through which local magnates asserted their influence. The power of the gentry was realized in part in its capacity to obtain control over local appointments: sheriffs, justices of the peace, and commissioners. This it did in part by bartering support, staffing the civil service, and voting taxes for government schemes that reflected its own interests.[78] It replaced the overlords of the aristocracy, acquired control over the trained militias, and usurped legal and political power by serving as justices of the peace and deputy lieutenants. Indeed the creation of the office of lord lieutenant was a calculated compensation to local elites which provided them with pockets of political influence. Since these offices were staffed by members of the gentry, these landowners could "manipulate musters and war taxation to help friends and penalize enemies."[79] The state and the landed gentry were symbiotically connected. The crown could not rule without the support of the landed classes, and they, in turn, depended upon royal patronage to protect and expand their interests. While the state exerted a measure of control over the office of lord lieutenant and the militias by scrutinizing appointments and making them dependent on court favor, militias remained essentially a part of a decentralized system of social control in which recruitment was local and voluntary.

Militias, like other policing institutions, were also poorly equipped, financed, and coordinated. Musters were infrequently held and poorly attended. Weapons were old and defective and supervision was not standardized.[80] Local commanders were frequently deputized, and a growing slackness came to characterize the militia, particularly during the first half of the seventeenth century. Internal conflicts were widespread, and hostility and opposition were directed toward the militias and the deputy lieutenant.[81] As a policing agency the militias' role was ambiguous. Loyalties were divided and tied to parochial interests. Local politics and patronage networks exerted a strong hold over military alliances and strategies. Peripheral groupings could oppose or not carry out state directives. The regulation of the law was fraught with conflict. Feuding powerful families frequently flouted the law and tyrannized the county administration. Such congregations of armed men could fight against central state interests, as in the case of the Civil War when the authority of the crown was challenged by regional interest groups who attracted to their cause sections of the militia and various trained bands.[82] Furthermore, the militia was sometimes neutralized by those who sponsored and protected criminals. It could do little to restrain thieves and poachers if, with the support of powerful families, these lawbreakers received official immunity.[83] Patronage as a system of government was perhaps strongest at the regional level, and local communities guarded their own frontiers and were suspicious of outside militias. An overall military force with strategic central command was thus lacking, and private groups possessed considerable power. In Shropshire, Sir Thomas Cornwalle, for example, started and funded a gentlemen's voluntary company, and the Derbyshire and Cheshire gentry established private and freeholder companies as distinct from the militia and trained bands.[84] Domestic order was maintained by a quagmire of competing oligarchies. The means of violence was decentralized, and the state was unable to accumulate sufficient power to gain control over its exercise. Relationships within military organizations were fluid and indeterminate. Uneven and hesitant domestic surveillance resulted. Mutinies did occur, and the militias sometimes engaged in plunder, becoming themselves problems for social control.[85] The shire-state nature of coercive institutions circumscribed their role organizationally, and the volunteer nature of membership limited them temporally. Local customs merged with difficulties of travel and terrain to limit their striking radius. Their primary strength lay in their ability to control renegade populations. They could be mustered to police periodic crises, but even then the movement of troops was slow.[86] Rarely were the army or the militias deployed in patrolling crime. Fears of arming the citizenry slowed the spread of technical expertise. The services of the military were directed primarily at the treasonable and the politically suspect. The army, the militias, and the trained bands were a regionalized backup force. Their involvement in and impact on crime control were indirect.

In sum, the social importance of territoriality to the organization of crime was further bolstered by the precarious nature of the administration of justice. Decentralized state power and geographical contingencies mutually reinforced each other, encouraging diverse possibilities for crime. Yet if the importance of both are clear, the organizational effect is less so. Did a criminal underworld take root in these protectorates? What were the types of crime? What was the division of labor? What was the scope of criminal organization? Was there an infrastructure to thieving and prostitution? What were the power and market arrangements within organized crime? These questions are examined in the next two chapters.

6

THE CANTING
CREW

Introduction

This chapter reassembles and interprets focused features of criminal
craft practices. I concentrate primarily on (1) the criminal vocabulary
as historical data, (2) argot and criminal technique, (3) the formal organization of crime, (4) the infrastructure of crime, and (5) the merchandising arrangements in the criminal marketplace.

The recovery of past worlds of crime is problematic. Much was ta-
boo, secret, or undertaken in private circumstances. There is little
collective memory that can be probed. Court records, a major source
of information about deviance and crime, are for this period sparse
and in need of decoding. They are transmuted catalogues of offenses sealed from broader historical contexts. They reveal little of
the criminal act and less about the skills, experiences, and organization underpinning crime. Past worlds of deviance and crime
can, however, be reconstructed. The collective traces of legally
proscribed groups—thieves, confidence cheats, pickpockets,

prostitutes, and gamesters—are recoverable from surviving street ballads, broadsides, dramatists' descriptions, prison ordinaries' accounts, malefactors' dying confessions, criminal biographies, and criminal canting dictionaries.[1] Such materials remain a principal source of knowledge about crime. Many of them were anecdotal, bombastic "awful examples." As street literature, they were hawked in alehouses, cookshops, and taverns. Some were undoubtedly fabrications or exaggerations of literary imagination.[2] Yet it would be premature to ignore or dismiss these accounts as ephemera with little value to social science.[3] Presenting a discourse of the streets these documents contain vital clues to unofficial forms of social organization which are salient for criminological research.[4] They are short descriptive accounts explaining the skills of particular criminal crafts—the underlying technology and division of labor. These narratives, combined with surviving glossaries of criminal cant, provide an array of evidence about criminal organization.

Cant as Criminal Speech

Cant was a common feature of sixteenth- and seventeenth-century Europe. Closely allied to the rising tide of vagrancy, it was a vocabulary of international dimensions; essential terms were common to many Beggars' Brotherhoods.[5] Cant, Ratwalsh, and argot were deviant speech forms which indexed discreditable ways of life. Their significance is known through written accounts such as the *Liber Vagatorum* (1455), Harman's "A Caveat for Common Cursitors" (1566), B. E.'s *The Canting Crew* (1698), Captain Smith's "The Thieves' New Canting Dictionary" (1719), and the anonymous *A New Canting Dictionary* (1725). The origins of cant coincided with the arrival of gypsies in the fourteenth and fifteenth centuries, and some cant terms derived from gypsy lore and language.[6] However, by the mid-sixteenth century cant had become a criminal parlance. Justice Harman, a pioneer chronicler of criminal life, noted that it was a specialized vocabulary known only to beggars and rogues "whereby they buy and sell the common people as they pass."[7] Not knowing criminal language, he had to interrogate thieves to learn its meaning.[8] Cant, then, was not an informal deviant speech known by various sections of the population, but the language of outlawed deviant populations. Its specialized vocabulary covered techniques and structure of criminal practices, as well as what they meant to criminal populations. Greene noted: "consider as the carpenter hath many terms familiar enough to his 'prentices, that others understand not all, so have the cony-catchers."[9]

Cant was an expressive lexicon, and it referred primarily to methods and techniques. It should not be confused with other lexicons that indexed deviant mannerisms, or that used cant expressions as a type of low humor to satirize the moral decline of authority.[10] Rather, it represents a specific *parole parlante* and embodies a referential code of the past.[11]

Cant was a private code of identification and a social passport into hidden worlds and practices.[12] It served to delimit criminal groups and acted as a means of assessing trust and loyalty, of screening potential group members, and of linking disparate people into networks of criminal association. Argot terms were also designed to conceal criminal practices and confuse victims. It was a mask which operated to "shadow . . . villainy withal . . . that the ignorant may not espy what their [the criminal's] subtlety is"[13] Specialized language also served as a social support for an outlawed way of life, and is a sign that the types of activities chronicled then were not temporary phenomena or confined to isolated individuals. For as Maurer has demonstrated, criminal argots are group phenomena that occur to meet specific needs, techniques, and divisions of labor that may not be adequately transmitted in existing speech.[14] Knowing the cant of any period allows recovery of past criminal forms. The map of such forms lacks clear contours. However, a cautious use of cant writing allows us to prize out criminal structure from other social vocabularies.[15] To do so, however, it is necessary to determine the dispersion of argot terms, their authenticity and indexability, and their adequacy of meaning.

Since cant was born of oral language, in written form it is self-conscious and lacking in spontaneity. Although compilers explain argot terms, we have no way of assessing their actual use within historical criminal populations. Cant users limited the knowledge of it to members only. Its appearance in documents written for public consumption was slight. Court records are not likely to turn up argot terms since legal rules forbade the use of cant words, including, of course, cant terms for occupations.[16] The few references available in private correspondence confirm the validity of argot terms, but tell us little about when or how frequently they were used. However, the records and correspondence of prison personnel and the remnants of criminal biographies assist considerably. Written in collaboration with criminals, these biographies were filled with argot references, which indicates some degree of argot knowledge, use, and transmission. Apprehended criminals' usage of cant terms overlaps with the classifications and expressions found in cant glossaries and confirms the genuineness of dictionaries.[17] Moreover, the continuous reappearance of similar cant words suggests that their use was probably regular and their knowledge generationally communicated.

Canting dictionaries relied on earlier editions, and authors copied from previous glossaries. Errors and misprints were in some instances carelessly reprinted in later works. Plagiarism did occur. Skepticism is not unwarranted. Yet, despite the evidence of plagiarism, copying was, by and large, not excessive. The compilers of argot recorded existing criminal skills and behavior. Cross-checking with other historical sources confirms the accuracy of many of these glossaries. Deficiencies are minimal and have been identified.[18] The recorders of criminal life and cant were close to the world they chronicled. They had first-hand contact with the lexicon and with the activities they described. Some of these narratives may have been exaggerations, but they were stamped with the direct participation and observations of the transcribers. They were translations of foreign practices. Furthermore, the anonymity and dubious authenticity of some of these crime pamphlets are counterbalanced by the style of reporting found in the recording of argot. There is a concern for detail, a relish in describing criminal techniques and skills, and an irony of repentent tone, all of which suggest genuine contact with criminal life. Finally the canting dictionaries themselves are free of the deceptions found in Grub Street fabrication or in the fictional narratives criminals sold for ale before they were hung. They are direct transcriptions.

The problematic connections between spoken argot, classificatory glossaries, and lived historical experience are further complicted by the fact that speech and writing can give rise to relatively autonomous linguistic traditions. As Kwant has argued, language has the peculiar capacity to transcend experience. It need not necessarily index existing objects. It may be abstractly anchored in literary imagination, providing no recognizable relation to lived experience.[19] The world of crime has generated a shadow world of dubious authenticity. The literature of roguery does constitute, in part, a linguistic tradition; "an autonomous culture of the word," in which language acts back on itself generating its own independent streams of meaning.[20] On the surface some of these crime narratives are identical to fictional accounts. Indeed, they were written by literary professionals.[21] However, distinctions must be drawn between cant as low wit and cant as a genuine catalogue of references. In the former case, it is used as a linguistic convention, as a conscious application of criminal metaphors to convey the corruption of officialdom. These particular devices are lacking in the glossaries and in many of the crime narratives embroidered with cant terms. Despite spectacular titles, crime dictionaries and narratives are mainly mundane accounts. There is little embellishment of language, and meanings are specifically decoded by compilers. The underlying design is to fill in lived meaning and make it objective.

The anonymity of canting dictionaries and pamphlets makes interpretation difficult. There are few rules that decode the intended significance of authors and audience. There are no codes for assessing how meanings were carried and projected to the present. Reconstructions and displacements occurred, yet the mode of knowing them is unsure. Indeed, if the past is seen as a series of discrete periods, than the interpreter can have no grounds for knowing it. However, if the past is seen as an unfolding synthesis threaded by overlapping traditions such that past and present horizons constantly intersect, then it becomes possible to enter into the forms of life organized by predecessors.[22] Yet the process of making sense is not achieved at the level of the intentionality of subjects.[23] Rather, the significance of the texts is their ability to take on new meanings as connected items that are part of what Gadamer has termed "traditions of the past."[24] Their embeddedness in these cultural frames gives the texts a meaning outside individual intentionality. The foundations and forms of these traditions are alive in the here and now. The argot of crime represents a specific discourse into which one may enter. By moving back and forth—by living in the language itself fused by past terms and expressions—a degree of historical understanding is possible. The adequacy of meaning then addresses itself to delineating continuities within discourses, to demonstrating that the things accomplished through the medium of argot express a congruence over time. This does not imply that temporality must be abandoned for decontextualization.[25] The meaning of texts is also assessed by reference to other documents and forms of evidence which fill in the skeleton of criminal forms. Historical and present-day evidence also demonstrates the usefulness and meaning of cant terms.

Cant, Criminal Technique, and Group Organization

Cant terms reveal the skeletal forms of criminal organization. The surviving fragments of criminal language permit retrieval of both the internal and external features of the underworld: the craftlike configuration of crime—routine, small-scale, rational, and formal—and the more general infrastructure of crime—institutions, power, markets, and apprenticeship patterns.[26] I have rearranged contemporary thieving catalogues into the following division of criminal work roles:

1. nips and foins (pickpockets),
2. lifters, curbers, and dubbers (sneak thieves),
3. lifts, markers, and santars (shoplifters),
4. bobs and fences (receivers of stolen property).[27]

I also include an analysis of other criminal crafts: confidence cheating, dicing, and prostitution.

By the Elizabethan period, skilled pickpocketing and robbing were elaborate and routinized criminal projects. The foin and the nip were specialist criminal roles involving stealth and teamwork. The foin was a degree above the nip, using conversation, deception, and dexterity to remove a purse from a cully (victim). The nip was less sophisticated, usually slashing and palming a purse.[28] The entire theft was managed by a flexible unit of members with specific tasks. Although the criminal act varied in scope, technique, target, and take, most groups integrated a partnership of stall and snap into their setup. In a manner similar to that practiced by present-day pickpocket teams, the stall identified, isolated, and maneuvered a cully for the pickpocket to lift. The snap received the bung (purse) from the foin or lift, concealed it, and escaped with the valuables.[29] Knuckles (young pickpockets) were trained in approaching and jostling victims. For example, bulk the cull to the right was an instruction for a stall to hit a client on the right breast, so that when the client put his hand up to ease the pain, a pickpocket could lift the pocket on the left and pass the booty to his partner behind him.

Giving gammon was a deliberate strategy devised to keep the cully lodged between a stall and a foist to make it easier for the latter to nip his fob (remove his money).[30]

Differentiation within the ranks of pickpockets was considerable. Prestige was attached to a network of gentlemen foins who dressed well and lived the life of gallants. The "masters of the trade" "go so neat in apparel, so orderly in outward appearance, some like lawyers, clerks, others like serving men, that attended there about their masters' business that they are hardly smoked, versing upon all men with kind courtesies and fair words, and yet being so warily watchful"[31] They were recognized for their daring, deception, and legerdemain. They refused to carry a cuttle-bung (a knife with a curved blade) and were contemptuous of those who lacked the physical dexterity required to draw (pick a pocket).[32]

Pickpockets regularly worked with queens (female accomplices), often crossbiting their victims.[33] In a crossbite a trull (prostitute) might lure a simpler (client) into an alley or an alehouse where he was then robbed by a second party. Sophisticated versions involved pickpocket teams, armed with ingenious mechanical false fingers that allowed them to "dive deeply into a simpler's fob" (a victim's pocket), or blackmail, with the prostitute and her male accomplice threatening to reveal the compromised status of the victim to respectable society.[34] But crossbiting was also a low grade of criminal skill, often involving violence and little stealth.[35]

Not all forms of pickpocketing involved ingenuity. Forking was a primitive technique in which the foist thrust his fingers, held straight, stiff, and open deep into a pocket and then closed them, hooking and tearing what could be grasped. Similarly the bulk and file used a crude method in which the bulk deliberately bumped and angered the cully in order to distract him and enable the file to pick his pocket and escape.[36]

Elizabethan curbers or anglers who stole from windows, stalls, and hedgerows were also specialized by task. The curber was protected by the warp who functioned as a spotter and lookout. Curbers angled for the snappings (the take, here essentially linens and clothes) with a device six feet long, jointed like a fishing rod with a small hole bored through it about an inch from the top. Into this groove was inserted a portable hook designed to lift. Curbers also used figging boys (child thieves) in their organization, directing them to reconnoiter and enter premises and steal portable commodities.[37] The argot of burglary reveals that burglars formed a criminal unit often reliant upon dubbers who were armed with an array of gilks, ginnys, glims, and filchs. Most of these tools were picklocks, cudgels, or lanterns designed to open locks, remove window pins, pry loose shutters and stalls, pull out protective gratings, and light the way.[38] Codes of understanding linked budge and stand togethers. Touting the case and looking the glaze meant that thieves would spot, mark, and observe the premises to be robbed. Code words coordinated the theft itself: "tis all bob" was the sign that the coast was clear; "dub the gigger" was the go-ahead sign to flick the lock and enter; "bowman" signaled the budge (inside the house) to gather and pass the snappings to the waiting stand; "tomme" warned the budge to lie still and flat; and "brush your grig" was the signal to take to the streets.[39] Of course, not all house burglaries were well organized. Milling the gig and milling the ken were smash and grab tactics. Thieves broke windows and escaped with what they could carry. The faggot and storm was a low-skilled strategy involving considerable force: houses were opened up, occupants intimidated, and quarters robbed. Little scouting or skill was used.[40]

Shoplifters were also organized with a fixed division of role specialization. Attention was paid to choosing a target and planning the crime. Specific stations, signals, and functions were interlinked so as to conduct the lift quickly, efficiently, and without attracting notice. A lift and marker entered a tradesman's shop. The marker's task was to engage a shopkeeper's interest, asking him to display valuables, while the lift removed items, passing them to a santar, who was stationed outside the tradesman's entrance as a lookout and runner. The garbage (stolen goods) was then concealed and fenced by the santar who never came within the shop. Should the shopkeeper smoke (suspect and accuse) the thieves, the incriminating evidence was removed from the scene of the theft.[41]

The same type of division of labor occurred in cony-catching and dice, bowl, and card cheating. Confidence tricksters performed highly skilled cons, working quickly and using little violence. The taker and the verser formed a partnership responsible for spotting and luring a customer into the orbit of a confidence game. The taker-up was dressed as a gentleman and feigned the appearance of a man of culture. By means of conversation he engaged the interest of a cousin (victim) and led him to a prearranged site, usually a nearby tavern. There the verser, also dressed as a man of wealth, joined the taker and cousin in drink and congenial conversation. After a period of drinking and becoming acquainted, they were joined by a third party to the setup, the barnard. During the conversation he would spread his money about buying drinks and attempting to create a climate of trust. Cards or dice were brought out, and all at the table were persuaded to join in. The taker and the verser subtly convinced the victim to take advantage of the barnard's innocence and dupe him of his money. Wagers gradually increased and the victim was allowed to win. However, as the game proceeded the taker, verser, and cousin lost to the barnard and by means of conspiracy, false cards, or loaded dice the victim was fleeced of his purse. In case the cousin should smoke the confidence cheats there was often a fourth party, a rutter, whose role was to bing the bill (bully the victim) and allow the cheats to escape. The four later divided the winnings.[42] This form of confidence game has a long history. Some 200 years after Greene wrote his description, it was known as the drop and was performed in the manner described above, except that the taker-up, the verser, and the barnard were known as the picker-up, the kid, and the cap.[43]

Dice frauds also involved enticing a customer into a gambling house and then manipulating the game so as to cheat him. The cole, or shifter, was charged with the role of persuading or taking up a customer into a gambling ordinary. Once there, the knap of the case introduced the client to a game of dice. Gradually the stakes were increased, and through a subtle interplay of verbal skills, betting, and manipulation the victim was duped into making higher and wilder bets.[44] Indeed, some gaming ordinaries employed gull gropers, who served as bankers advancing loans to players. Then, by means of false dice they fleeced him of his wealth.[45]

The roles, techniques, and artifacts of cozenage were on the whole quite elementary. By using subtle, nonviolent methods, deceptions, stealth, and salesmanship, playing on the avarice and gullibility of the victim, designing ingenious fake dice and cards, accepting limited takes, and neutralizing risk by using public places and the threat of force, the cozening crews showed a remarkable capacity for persistence and innovation.[46] The argot is particularly revealing about the criminal techniques of dice cheating. Langrets, barred cater treys, flat fullams, gourds, bristle dice, and contraries were types of loaded or marked dice,[47] while palming, trapping, slurring, knapping, and stabbing were various sleight-of-hand techniques.[48] Palming, for example, involved the cheat placing "one dye into the box [used to cast the dice] and keeping the other in the hallow of his little finger; which, noting what is uppermost when he takes him thus, the same shall be when he throws the other dye, which runs doubtfully, any cast. Observe this—that the bottom and top of all dice are seven, so that if the four be above, it must be a three at bottom; so five and two, six and one."[49] Stabbing required that the gambling cheat drop the dice into the box so that one dye lay upon another: "So that turning up the box, the dice never tumble, if a smooth box, if true but little; by which means you have bottoms according to the tops you put in . . . So that if two five be a top, you know you will obtain two two's."[50]

Criminal argot also reveals much about the actual artifacts. The making of false dice and cards and the forging of licenses, passports, seals, personal papers, and property contracts were major counterfeiting activities.[51] Counterfeit seals for travel were often poor replications and were carved "with the point of a knife upon a stick's end."[52] Counterfeiting had a primitive technology, and most fake gybes (documents) failed in replicating details. Yet some counterfeiters were relatively skilled. The trade in the manufacturing of artificial sores and wounds involved a considerable degree of ingenuity and an elementary grasp of chemistry.[53]

Forgery consisted partly in altering the words of documents, but primarily entailed attaching false seals, which were equivalent to signatures. Thus counterfeiters were experts in dividing the wax and lead seal as to expose the ribbon that passed through it, and then reattaching the divided sections so that they enclosed the ribbon fastened to the false document. Of course complete documents were also forged.[54] Richard Farr developed a system of exploiting the dying and the deceased. He would forge documents making himself a principal creditor and thus heir to their properties. In addition, he traded in forged leases and credit contracts, gaining thereby land, personal effects, and cash.[55] The minting of counterfeit coins certainly involved an elementary knowledge of chemistry and metallurgy. During the Elizabethan and Stuart periods coin debasement was common. Metal money suffered from wear and tear, and a regular trade was carried out in holding back unworn coins and circulating lighter ones. Illicit profits were derived by paring down and scraping the edges, thus allowing removed metal to become a base for new coins.[56]

Pickpocketing, burglary, shoplifting, confidence cheating, and the underworld of gambling were guided by codes of action and material techniques that supported a craft specialization designed to expropriate money and property rationally. Working criminal teams were small in size; they exhibited foresight, planning, and skill in their choice of targets, the management of theft, and the avoidance of detection by social control agents. Criminal crews had their regular places of assembly outside the apparatus of state surveillance and control. An elaborate infrastructure of crime took shape within the sanctuaries which afforded not only refuge and protection, but opportunities for rational crime planning, marketing of illegal merchandise, and wider criminal associations.

Criminal Institutions

Contemporaries noted the importance of criminal territoriality and stressed the organizational consequences. Greene observed that the sanctuaries had arranged quarters where nips and foists "conferred on weighty matters touching their workmanship," and where methods of operation and escape were devised.[57] Criminal areas, according to Whetstone, "had set hands to filch, heads to deceive and friends to receive."[58] The official reports from government search and arrest campaigns verify the existence of fencing kens. In one raid alone, city justices uncovered seven such institutions in London, "six more in Westminster, three more in the suburbs, and two in Southwark."[59] Criminal brokers, as the Lord Mayor of London reported, "are nowe [1601] of late grown so many and so dispersed into privileged and exempt places in and near unto the city of every purpose to avoid the entry into the Register of such parcels of goods as they buy or take or pawn: By means whereof many times such goods are stolen are never found"[60] Entire streets were noted for their bousing kens (alehouses) and for their chandlers' shops, green stalls, and metal and leather dealers which were used as depositories by thieves. The city suburbs, "about . . . the town' end" harbored "travelling brokers" of illegal wares.[61] "And being abroad they all in general use receivers of stolen things that are portable as namely the Tinker in his Budgett, the peddlar in his hamper, the glassman in his basket and the lewd proctors which carry the Broad Seale and Green Seale in their bags. Covers infinite numbers of felonies in such sort as the tenth felony cometh not to light for he hath his receiver at hand in every alehouse in every Bush, and these last rabble are very Nurseries of rogues."[62]

The marketing of stolen property was stratified, with some bobs better able to handle more diverse types and greater amounts of merchandise. The lowest grade was associated with the smaller stalls and mobile dealers. The higher grade of fence was more habitual in his operations. According to Greene, these shops were convenient drops at which incriminating evidence could be disposed of immediately, thereby minimizing risk and encouraging the perpetuation of crime.[63] Some receivers even specialized in high-value goods and directed fencing operations that extended to the Continent. "Brokers seek by all possible means to abet by selling the stolen goods unto Dutchmen, Scots and French Brokers: who secretly convey the same beyond the seas to the great hurte and prejudice of Her Majesty's subjects."[64]

Although much receiving was local, the brokers of these fencing kens acquired influence over some aspects of crime. Lifts and cutpurses "lived in" at the houses of notorious brokers, and receivers, "through their alluring speeches and their secret counsellings," stimulated the operations of thieving.[65] The fence provided economic assistance to thieves, accepting merchandise as payment for lodgings and services. Other fences were contact sources who received payment for making arrangements to dispose of the booty. Many accepted linens, woolens, plate, and jewels, made out bills of sale in false names, protected their sources, and fostered the regularity of thieving practices. Market handling was rationalized and supply and demand could be calculated. "Thus are these brokers and bawds, as it were efficient causes of the lifters villany . . . the lift for want of receivers would be fain to take a new course of life, or else be continually driven into great extremes for selling his garbage."[66] In Dekker's phrase receivers' shops were "academies of thieving": "for how could thieves bestow cloaks, sheets, shirts and other garments, being stolen, if they had not stalling kens to receive them?"[67] So advanced were some stalling kens that they had doors to delay intruders, false fronts to conceal operations, and hiding closets, sliding panels, trap doors, and intricate corridors by which thieves could make their escape.[68]

The strategic merchandiser's role had organizational consequences.[69] Bousing kens were criminal employment bureaus providing counseling services and information on tips, working partners, targets, and techniques.[70] Increased security in the form of
shelter and alibis was also afforded. Harman observed: "Yea, if it is
fortune any of these upright men to be taken, either suspected, or
charged with felony or petty bribery, done at such a time or such a
place, he will say he was in his host's house. And if the man or wife
of that house be examined by an officer, they boldly vouch, that
they lodged him such a time whereby the truth cannot appear."[71]

The fence was in a structurally prominent position. Similar to a
patron, he mediated the world of crime, protecting, advising, and
coordinating. Indeed some receivers acquired considerable power,
organized theft on demand, and herded trained "gangs of night
thieves" under their command. They thus enhanced the organization of crime, providing market skills, security, economic benefits,
and shelter. "The house [fencing establishment] with an apt porter
to it, stands ready for them [thieves] all hours of the night . . . Without the fence, [the thieves] can do nothing."[72]

Bousing kens also aided in the training of criminal apprentices.
One must, however, be cautious about conveying the wrong image:
much training was informal, passed on by relatives, friends, and casual acquaintances. Pickpockets learned by observation how to lift,
stall, cut, and identify likely victims.[73] Burglars developed the tactics of sneaking, picking locks, and breaking and entering on the
job.[74] Cony-catchers and dice cheats also acquired their skills gradually and in a climate of deliberate secrecy. Trial and error, combined
with a strategy of releasing technical knowledge as trust was established between expert and novice, was the model.[75] An important
part of their apprenticeship was to learn timing and the way to produce an impression appropriate to "fleecing a cully." Reginald Scot
observed that "their stock in trade . . . was the ability to make the
conies think they [the cheats] were conies themselves, and to lead
them on by playing on their vanity."[76]

A limited tutelage did, however, intersect with informal methods.
Pickpockets sometimes trained in alehouses and used dummies as
learning guides. As one city official observed, "amongst our travels
. . . there was a schoolhouse set up to learn young boys to cut
purses. The pocket had in it certain counters and was hung about
eight hawks' bells and over the top did hang a little scaring bell, and

he that could take out a counter without any noise was allowed to be a *public foister*, and he that could take a piece of silver out of the purse without the noise of any of the bells, he was adjudged a *judicial nipper.*"[77] Novices were taught to "spie . . . foyste, nyppe, lyft, shave and spare not."[78] Jack Cottington, a pickpocket, communicated his skills by providing demonstrations in select kens about the city.[79]

Criminal practices and organizations flourished in other institutional contexts. Pennyrent or low lodging houses, for example, spotted the criminal areas, forming small allied neighborhoods. Quarters were minute, pushed together, and linked by narrow passageways and connecting sheds and yards. They were the milieu for socialization into crime. Some were open brothel areas or thieves' dens. A section of the criminal population was thus born into thieving and schooled in its lore and language. Parents apprenticed their children to rob and steal, as their parents in turn had done. The criminal argot reveals the existence of age-specific roles. Figging boys were child sneak thieves, knuckles were novice pickpockets, and dubs were youthful picklocks. These criminal roles had their adult counterparts in the organization of thieving and were essentially supportive in nature: luring, stealing and looking out.[80] City Bridewell records, for example, suggest that street beggars and child thieves were sometimes career deviants by the age of twelve.[81]

Surviving life histories of criminals also suggest that careers spanned a number of thieving crafts. Moll Cutpurse was a pickpocket turned fence.[82] Mulled Sack was a highway robber and street thief before becoming an accomplished pickpocket.[83] Richard Farr had an uneven criminal career which included thieving, fencing, and wheedling (swindling).[84] Taylor, the water poet, observed:

> "Some thieves are like a Hornboake, and begin
> Their A.B.C. of fielding with a pin;
> Their primer is a point, and then their pralter
> May pick a pocket . . .
> Then with long practice in these rudiments,
> To break a house may be his accidence.[85]

Accomplished criminals had to: "play the foist, the nip, the stall, the stand, the snap, the curb, the crossbite, warpe and lifte, decoye, prig and cheat."[86]

Attached to criminal roles and practices, it would seem, were various beliefs that received some degree of communal support. For example, thieving and confidence cheating were justified, in part, as practices related to a world of increasing material aggrandisement. Greene observed: "The two ends I aim at are gain and ease . . . you know that few men can live uprightly unless he have some pretty way, more than the world is witness to, to help him withal. Think you some lawyers could be such purchasers, if all their pleas were short, and their proceedings justice and conscience; that offices would be so dearly bought, and the buyers so enriched, if they counted not pillage as honest kind of purchase; or do you think commodities without falsehood, when so many of them are become daily purchasers? Nay."[87] Thieving, in particular, was legitimated as the mirror reflection of the values of the merchant middleman, the shopkeeper, and the judiciary. A condemnation of the condemners resulted. For example, an immoral status was attributed to magistrates, prison keepers, and other legal officials. Members of criminal organizations were able to accuse those in the legal world of corruption and criminality. As one street observer of crime put it, "for the occasion of the most mischief, of greatest nipping and foisting and of all villainies, comes through the extorting bribery of some cozening and counterfeit keepers and companions that carry unlawful warrants about them to take up men."[88]

Organizational collaboration, coherence, and permanence were also assisted by networks of criminal haunts: bowling alleys, gaming ordinaries, sporting establishments, and playhouses. As the Lord Mayor of London recorded, "besides, to these places resorted the light and lewd disposed persons, as harlots, cutpurses, cozeners, pilferers, etc., who, under colour of hearing plays, devised divers evil and ungodly matches, confederacies, and conspiracies which could not be prevented."[89]

Brothels, in particular, were important haunts. Many were segregated in the Bankside sanctuaries and had strong traditions of deviance and criminality.[90] Some doubled as low lodging houses for thieves. Others were more directly the gathering place of pickpocket teams, receivers, prostitutes, and confidence cheats.[91]

Prisons were also important as criminal institutions. According to Fennor, jailers lodged thieves and prostitutes on a daily and full-time basis.[92] Indeed, the Rules areas of city prisons were residential sectors akin to territorial sanctuaries. Here were lodged "official" prisoners who enjoyed considerable freedom and mobility.[93] Not surprisingly, prisons were considered colleges of ill repute. Gambling cheats procured their loaded and false dice at Newgate. Prostitutes and pickpockets found working partners, and cony-catchers broadened their contacts and their techniques.

> A prison, as upon records is seen,
> For lodgings and for bowling, there a large space . . .
> Old Newgate I perceive a thievish den,
> But yet there's lodging for good honest men . . .
> Bridewell unto my memory comes next.
> . . . for vagabonds and runagates,
> For whores and idle knaves and such like mates,
> 'Tis better than a fail to those,
> Where they chop chalk for meat and drink and blows.[94]

The prison environs also harbored, on its fringes, an array of dubious representatives of the criminal justice system. Cheating solicitors and knights of the post were but two types of arrangers who routinely bribed legal officials, persuaded victims to accept restitution in lieu of pressing charges, and hired "swearers" who perjured on behalf of arrested thieves.[95] Thus the organization of crime extended "beyond acquisition of the manual and social skills necessary for organized execution of the crime itself."[96] The availability of ancillary criminal roles provided seventeenth-century thieves with "prior political preparation for evading detection and for evading punishment in the case of detection."[97] Pickpockets, for example, regularly procured the services of go-betweens who provided the equivalent of the fix. "For they [nips and foists] are provident in that every one of them hath some trusty friend whom he called his treasurer, and with him he lays up some rateable portion of every purse he draws, that when need requires and he is brought in danger he may have money to make composition with the party."[98]

In sum, the London underworld was a fluid ensemble of working associations, ancillary institutions, criminal networks. New opportunities for crime, city geography, tradition, and stigma routinized and enlarged the scope of criminal practices. Criminal vocabulary, intricate in form, preserved some of the trappings of organization: an elementary division of labor and technology; codes of selection, coordination, and protection; an embryonic apprenticeship system; and rational operations. The focal unit was the canting crew, the small (three or four member), craft-specific, and loosely confeder-ated, criminal team in which informal patterns of tutelage and au-thority prevailed. However, the organization of crime consisted of more than a formal allocation and integration of criminal roles. As a social configuration it included an informal grouping of social sup-port, legitimacy, and organizational rationality. The working crews were elements of a more complex criminal structure. There was a power base to criminal practices, and it revolved around the strate-gic merchandiser's role of fencing. But did the division of labor be-tween criminal work groups and fencing establishments form a com-mon unified structure? Did the fence achieve a monopoly of the organization of crime? What was the nature of power and markets in the world of organized crime?

Power and Markets in Organized Crime

The surviving argot of crime provides us with few clues about the quality of power and control. What evidence we have, however, suggests that fence–criminal team relationships rarely congealed into a uniform organization. Like present-day receivers, the fence operated more as a patron-sponsor, overseeing and directing vari-ous forms of crime.[99] Although fences strove to achieve a monopoly of the market, such a power relationship did not lead to administra-tive dominance. Relations between criminal teams and fencing inter-mediaries were characterized by tension and mistrust. Betrayals fanned by rewards, pardons, and the profits to be made from in-forming, and the plethora of informers and spies vitiated tendencies toward centralized criminal organization. Centralized control, in the sense of an integrated and efficiently functioning organization oper-ating with impunity, was absent. Operations were for the most part decentralized, and links between pickpockets, prostitutes, burglars, shoplifters, and fences were fluid and negotiable.[100] Yet the fence did exercise power over thieving crews. But this domination resem-bled a system of clientage in the precise sense of the term. Fencing establishments were not firms, but rather a locus to which criminal groups were attracted. Receivers dominated an elastic system in which they operated as advisers and go-betweens. Although they acquired influence over criminal crews, they seldom integrated them into a single, enduring crime cabal.[101]

Fencing arrangements did acquire political importance, particularly when fencing was combined with informing and thief-taking. For much of the period policing was, as we have seen, inadequate. Watch and ward, constabulary, city marshalcy, and the Privy Council were incapable of surveying and detecting crime or apprehending criminals. Policing was amateur, volunteer, and reluctantly performed. Social control was decentralized, anachronistic, and uncertain. It was undertaken by an unpaid, overworked, divided, geographically circumscribed, and bureaucratically uncoordinated and unsupported force. A lack of uniformity characterized the supervision and subordination of criminal groups. Since entire regions of the city were virtually independent of formal crime control, their regulation was often mediated and indirect, and involved the brokerage of power. Receivers in particular were structurally crucial in the world of crime. They were in a position to serve as valuable police agents. At the center of market merchandising and information control, they achieved considerable discretionary power over the fate of criminal groups. They took charge of, protected, and betrayed specific groups of criminals. Intimately acquainted with criminal structures, they opened up the relatively sealed world of crime. Criminality was thus often negotiated rather than determined by law. The more powerful within the organization of thieving acted as middlemen playing equivocal roles.

The implications for social control were considerable. The state recruited the deviant and the criminal as its own agents. Official institutions hired brigands, smugglers, poachers, and thieves as enforcement agents. These agents defined the operation of the law. An intricate barter economy grew up around the justice system. Political immunity was offered the favored, and rough justice handed the recalcitrant. The state indirectly contributed to a considerable commerce in crime, and the fence served as both predator and herdsman. He turned in the marginal, the novice, and the unaligned, and culled the steady criminal, integrating him into a more coherent and disciplined arrangement.[102] Moreover, this clandestine apparatus of the state had the effect of confusing and blurring the boundaries between legality and illegality. Elaborate patterns of collusion, betrayal, and conflict led to an economy of power that undercut the organizational integrity of the law and its enforcement.[103] The implications for the organization of crime were also profound. The growth of criminal intermediaries fueled a tendency toward a more hierarchical and coordinated criminal organization. It concentrated more and more power in the hands of receivers, increased the vulnerability of criminal crafts, and encouraged more dependence of crews on fences. The wholesale trafficking between criminals, middlemen, and the state provided receivers with a legitimate vocation which further bolstered organizational innovation in crime. Not only did bobs and fences tutor thieving crews, they industriously cultivated and expanded the opportunities for and the practices associated with theft.

The case of Moll Cutpurse is exemplary.[104] She acquired some control over the organization of thieving in London in the 1620s and 1630s, and established a warehouse for handling stolen property. Her subordinates were paid higher than the going rate and worked mainly for her; she in turn returned the goods to their former owners. Her influence as a receiver and thieftaker was institutionalized. She had informers and accomplices who kept her advised about robbers and pickpockets and who advertised her reputation. Pickpockets, shoplifters, prostitutes, cheats, and house burglars were herded under her authority. She cultivated specific areas of illegal activity, initiating a lucrative trade in stealing and returning shopbooks and account ledgers that had value only to their owners. She fashioned a "brokery" in high-value items such as personal jewels, rings, and watches. Her influence in the organization of thieving reflected an accumulation of power attributable to her intermediary function as defender of the public interest. After a theft, she guaranteed the recovery of the stolen property. Her role as an insurance broker was tacitly acknowledged by state officials. Commercial interests, government, and the public at large recognized her authority, and the open trade in pardons and rewards linked the judiciary to private retrieval and thief-taking schemes.

Her "lost property house" was not a single, unified organization, but a loose establishment to which thieving crews were attracted. As a patron of crime, she did provide shape and discipline to internal thieving arrangements, and she expanded the frontiers of theft. However, her authority was seldom that of a boss. As a broker of crime, she was successful in cornering specific provinces of theft activities but she was unable to translate market dominance into administrative control. Wide areas of thieving remained outside her influence. Criminal competitors, other fences, informers, and low-level prison officials ran parallel rackets.[105]

Despite considerable changes in property relations and forms of social control, present-day forms of theft and confidence cheating
overlap to a striking extent those of the sixteenth and seventeenth
centuries.[106] The sanctuaries and liberties discussed above are akin
to contemporary bidonvilles and barrios in emerging third world cities with their different patterns of association and autonomy. A
study of crime in West Africa reveals that youth gangs are prominent, thieving in teams of two or three, and a study of female
offenders in Ghana argues that nine-tenths of those involved in theft
and prostitution were "directed by group associations, even though
many committed their offenses alone and were arrested alone."[107]
Scivostata, in his work on crime in urban centers in Asia, has described the functions of juvenile thieves in terms that would be ap-
plicable to sixteenth-century London. "They [juveniles] are . . . better suited for certain types of activities for instance . . . small thefts
as they can manage to escape easily . . . the majority of . . . 'cat burglaries' are committed by juveniles who are especially trained for the
purposes and act according to the instructions of their seniors. They
have easy access to places generally out of bounds for adults . . .
They are adept at removing clothes and articles . . . often they are
let off without punishment . . . Partnership with juveniles means
more profits to the adults as . . . [the juveniles] usually get the minimum share."[108] Similarly, criminal knowledge and technology are
generationally communicated. In the 1930s professional criminals in
India were taught how to steal stealthily, conceal stolen property,
and protect, support, and defend associates,[109] and in Mexico segregated criminal districts have resulted in a culture of crime in which
the old tutor and control the young.[110]

Particular linguistic codes, rituals, and apparel mark off rank and
criminal craft. For example, the criminal societies of Malaysia who
robbed, kidnapped, and ransomed developed specialized parlance
and rites which shielded their practices and identified membership
and station.[111] Perhaps the relationship between social ecology, differential association, and group organized crime is best shown in
the criminal tribes of India. Segregated at the borders of village and
town life, they have for centuries lived by dishonest means. Over
generations, a diverse thieving order has evolved. Criminal tribes,
like Elizabethan criminal organizations, possess specialized argots to
identify victims, strategists, division of roles, and agents of control.

"In the commission of crimes each caste and tribe had its own rituals, omens, taboos, methodology and peculiarities. Some tribes committed only dacoities, some only highway robberies, some were expert in burglary, some committed petty thefts . . . some only picked pockets, some were shoplifters, some counterfeited coins and some were confidence tricksters."[112] Unmonitored, many of these criminal crafts and regions have developed arcane and elaborate social forms. In particular, and paralleling European experiences, alehouses and taverns serve as the focus for criminal operations and networks.[113] Finally, the structural prominence and claims to power of fences in sixteenth- and seventeenth-century London are not unlike those of the Calabrian and Sicilian mafioso networks which operate parallel brokerage systems between a weak, decentralized system of social control and autonomous criminal processes.[114] Indeed, the present debate on how organized organized crime is, would find useful the distinction between market monopoly and administrative dominance as a way of conceptualizing the scope and substance of criminal organization.

Such a catalogue of comparative examples could be amplified and suggests that what are sometimes thought of as unique criminal structures are probably more general in form: my analysis and these comparisions stress the centrality of work crews, territoriality, criminal opportunity structures, a particular kind of social control, and the informal underworld. A caveat is, however, called for. These notions must be used with care and separated from the implications of the moral judgments of ruling authorities. Historians have not always been that cautious. Some have accepted the universality with which these terms were applied and in so doing wildly exaggerated the size, scope, cohesiveness, and hierarchy of criminal organization.[115] On the other hand, recent research is denigrating the importance of criminal organization entirely. In the randomness of legal case files, an equally fatal bias is being introduced. The absence of evidence in legal records is taken to mean that in all probability professional roguery did not exist.[116] But there is a break here between premise and conclusion. Aside from the consideration that court records are only marginally reliable sources of data about persistent crime and criminal structures, it does not follow that the silence of criminal voices means that no organized crime existed. Archival materials rightly warn us to be skeptical about the existence of organized criminal gangs operating over vast areas. But criminal organization, as I have argued and as has been demonstrated in comparative research, is not a mere matter of large numbers. It is very specifically the receivers, the houses they and the thieves frequent, the brothels and other haunts, the cant vocabulary, and the characteristic skills transmitted in bousing kens and prisons.[117]

7

INFAMOUS
COMMERCE

Introduction

In this chapter, I expand the survey and analysis of criminal organization. Particular attention is paid to the world of prostitution: its
scope, diversity, and infrastructure. Prostitution warrants focused
attention for three reasons. First, like other criminal crafts it was
an endemic feature of London life during the sixteenth and seventeenth centuries. Contemporaries remarked on "hospitals of tenne
times a day dishonest strumpets," who cloistered together in alehouses and taverns.[1] Platter, a traveler in many European countries,
observed of London that "great swarms of these women haunt . . .
in taverns and playhouses,"[2] while Phillip Stubbes catalogued the
"horrible vice of whoredom" as the major social problem.[3] Court
records confirm this. On one day in August 1620, at a session of the
Middlesex Court of Quarter Sessions, true bills were found against
nineteen women for brothel keeping; sixteen of them were located
in one area of the city at Cowcross. Saffron Hill was a notorious

district of common prostitutes "who customarily solicit from the doors of their lodgings." Four years later, in the same court, true bills were found against thirty-two persons for brothel keeping, and a further thirty-two convictions were found against persons "receiving inmates against the law."[4] An anonymous pamphlet printed in 1642 lists twelve segregated districts of bawdyhouses, and by 1660 the number of zones had apparently increased to twenty-two.[5] Petitions and proclamations also record that brothels were numerous and the sites of companion forms of crime where "bodies are poxt and pockets are pick't."[6] Street songs frequently gave citizens rhymed advice to "forsake lewd company, cards, dice, and queenes."[7]

> Therefore in railing sort,
> She thrust him out the door
> Which is the just reward of those
> Who spend upon a whore.[8]

So regular was prostitution that one contemporary writer remarked, "whores we spurne and spit, and hisse as they passe."[9]

The study of prostitution also affords insight into many aspects of female criminality. Women were well represented in the criminal underworld, operating especially as thieves, confidence cheats, receivers of stolen property, and prostitutes. They were also important as accomplices. They teamed up with men and children.[10] They acted as lookouts, and as transporters of incriminating evidence, stolen goods, and criminal technology. Some, like Moll Cutpurse, were directors of thieving rings. Many who were prostitutes acted as trapaners, drawing victims into situations in which they could easily be robbed or blackmailed.[11]

Some women formed associations of their own. There existed female gangs of shoplifters and house burglars,[12] and counterfeiting seems to have attracted female apprentices.[13] Pickpocket teams were often composed of two or three women fronting as prostitutes. June Harmon and Nan Robinson, for example, were two notorious prostitutes who worked in league with a doorkeeper at a pimp house and who routinely robbed clients, leaving them drunk and unclothed.[14] Others robbed their victims while servicing them; "purses and pockets they will dive into and pick even when they are dallying with them."[15] Some women worked alone. Emma Robinson of Saint Botolph's Without Aldgate was a well-known "common queene" who "sitteth up at the door til XI or XII o'clock in the night to entertain lewd persons that resort to her,"[16] and Mildred Wilkinson of Bethnal Green was described as an "occasional queen" who entertained "certayne men at her house unknowne."[17] An examination of prostitution not only indicates the centrality of women to the underworld of crime, it further elucidates the methods and organization of theft.

Finally, the world of prostitution deserves our attention for the light it throws on later forms of prostitution. As with theft, there are remarkable continuities of style and organization. By a reconstruction of earlier criminal organization, it is possible to show the persistence of diverse organizational configurations surrounding the various types of prostitution. Although there was a close association between prostitution and habitual theft, this link was not inevitable. There is a distinction to be made between those who used prostitution as an opportunity for robbery and those who earned a living through the sale of sex. Like other criminal practices, prostitution was a complex of skills and relationships.[18]

In piecing together the world of prostitution I have relied for the most part on broadsides, ballads and companion forms of street literature. Canting glossaries helped me determine forms of thieving, but there are few argot terms that reflect criminal process and structure as they relate to prostitution. As with the organization of thieving, what results is a somewhat static presentation, a snapshot perspective of organized prostitution.

The Organization of Prostitution in London

English towns were not the only places favorable to the development of prostitution. The great cycles of poverty in the late sixteenth and early seventeenth centuries forced increasing numbers of women to sell themselves along roadsides and hedgerows. Prostitutes roamed the countryside adjusting their itineraries to the calendar of fairs, markets, and other seasonal events.[19] However, prostitution developed most fully in an urban milieu where it acquired elaborate forms and was institutionalized. For centuries, London had public stewhouses, owned by and run for royal, ecclesiastical, and municipal authorities. Brothels were usually owned by persons of wealth but leased to keepers who were responsible for making profits. Keepers were managers: they recruited and trained prostitutes, maintained house and community order, provided lodging, food, and services, and disciplined the unruly.[20] Medieval London also had several houses of toleration, which were bathhouses that were resorts of prostitutes or headquarters for procuring and for making assignations.[21] Finally, prostitution was also practiced as an individual craft, outside closed quarters. Independents were usually overseen by procuresses who sponsored and circulated prostitutes to prospective clients, in effect, acting as go-betweens, recruiting, arranging, and mediating the world of prostitution.[22]

Constructing a typology of prostitution for sixteenth- and seventeenth-century London is difficult. However, by eliminating amateur and clandestine prostitution, about which little is known, and basing my ordering principle on evidence of habitual and routinized patterns of commercial sex, I can specify three forms of prostitution.

The most prominent type was the prostitute who rented herself out as a private mistress to men of wealth. There were tongue pad whores who "worked their way into acquaintances," established rapport, and over time deceived gentlemen of property and wealth, and pad strumpets who advertsied themselves as women in search of companions.[23] More accomplished were the "commonwealth of ladies" who leased themselves out, often on long terms, to prestigious clients.[24] They were organized into a loose consortium and held regular meetings, advertised their skills, discussed techniques of trapping wealthy clients, and actively sought out and trained recruits to behave as proper consorts.[25] Converted manor houses and newly established inns were the settings for contacts with such costly prostitutes. Fish Pond House, for example, a late Tudor building with elaborate decor, had impressive gateways, ponds, and strolling gardens in which courtiers and courtesans made one another's acquaintance.[26] Many "night gown ladies" also worked in Pall Mall, Hatton Garden, and Saint James Street. The more fashionable had maids and lived in private dwellings.[27] They had procurers who negotiated arrangements and bullies for enforcement.[28]

Prostitutes of this general type relied upon a limited but wealthy and tactful clientele. They advertised discreetly and within select circles. They avoided conduct that might reveal their vocation, and they kept clear of resorts of common prostitutes. In all likelihood they were well paid. Some had private go-betweens who spread their reputations.[29] Not all prostitutes operated independently and from private establishments. Dancing schools and brothels functioned as consortiums, openly advertising their trade but restricting the type of client. Brittanica Hollandia's establishment, an old converted manor house, was perhaps the most celebrated in London. Her brothel was located within the liberty of Old Paris Garden and was in turn further protected by networks of ditches, with bridges and gates. Nearby taverns, theaters, bowling alleys, and bear-baiting rings attracted a regular gentry clientele. The women who worked there were for the most part permanent residents paying room and board and receiving regular employment and immunity from the law.[30]

In addition to these pleasure houses, located mostly in Bankside, there were private brothels and rental bureaus operated by city madams. These procurers were seasoned prostitutes who acted as employment agents putting clients in touch with prostitutes of "fine habit and manners."[31] Less discreet, but also catering to high-class clients, were the prostitutes of Hatton Gardens, the Exchange, and Covent Garden. Dressed in elaborate clothes they were easily identifiable, and they advertised their skills by a touch of the arm, a squeeze of the elbow, and in some instances written communication. Many functioned as independents or worked out of private dwellings, usually in league with lodging keepers who doubled as enforcers.[32]

Prostitution was tied to the leisure habits of the rich. Islington was a favorite rendezvous. An elaborate social life was organized around its walks, gardens, and wells. The underside of its seasonal activity was the throng of confidence cheats, pickpockets, gamblers, and fake physicians selling fertility waters and elixirs.[33] Part-time prostitutes frequented the district, setting up seasonal establishments in the suburbs of the wealthy.[34] The more expensive brothel keepers, for example, had a ready supply of ape-gentlewomen (part-time prostitutes) who discreetly concealed their profession but who were on the rolls of particular brothels.[35] Moreover, the open market conditions, the surplus of casual labor, and low wages encouraged servant maids, seamstresses, nurses, midwives, glasswomen, and traders to become involved in prostitution, either as procurers or as casual night walkers. John Dunton reported that families sometimes engaged in prostitution with husbands procuring clients for wives.[36] Amateur prostitution had a base in the wealthier suburbs as well. The equivalent of Victorian suburban whores was a variety of "pensionary misses," women who solicited their clients at expensive locales, but lived at a distance from the centers of prostitution and were marginal to the profession.[37]

One trade that linked part-time and independent prostitution into a wider social network was the procuring business, usually controlled by bawds. In this arrangement an experienced prostitute acted as an agent placing customers with desired women; the procuress collected a fee from both parties, and if she kept a lodging house, she also collected rent and fees for drink, food, and other services.[38] The better-off brothels had a staff of permanent prostitutes as well as a pool of circulating women. Often procurers were male accomplices who set up matches between young heirs to estates and prostitute partners. The "art of wheedling" was designed to cheat gullible gentlemen of their money and property, either by encouraging false loans and investments or by planning elaborate robberties.[39] The procuring business, then, involved using prostitution as a means to achieve a more elaborate criminal project: the confidence cheat.

This "Commonwealth of ladies," played for high stakes. These women had coaches, good lodgings, and an array of fineries. They were likely to be better educated than other types of prostitutes, and their time and labor were monopolized by free-spending favorites. The pinnacle of success for them was to appear at costly gaming ordinaries or in the boxes of quality at theaters dressed in glittering clothes.[40] Not surprisingly, their links to the "legitimate" world were close. Their use of language mirrored that of respectable society. Professionals were termed "ladies," and often used as aliases the names of real noblewomen. The more experienced apparently earned the title of "countesses of the trade."[41] Moreover, they were sought after by the politically and economically powerful and could often obtain for themselves or their houses sponsorship by a wealthy clientele and protection from the law.[42]

A second and equally heterogeneous class of prostitutes was known as the "wandering whores." They were a world away from the better-paid women of London. Some were sailors' strumpets haunting the dockside and Ratcliffe highway. Others, running bawds, common queenes and trulls, worked the fairs, corners, alleys, and streets.[43] Some had access to night houses and were in league with tapsters and keepers of taverns. Others were part of a brothel mob under the direction of a controlling bawd. Still others were part of small working crews such as the "aunt and niece," where young apprentices joined up with experienced prostitutes who provided lodgings, practical training, access to clients, and a degree of protection. So common was the aunt and niece gambit that a circulating directory existed. Anonymous street pamphlets suggest that bawds and procurers formed working alliances whereby they "change young women with another and cheat the cullies as if they were first ones newly come from the country."[44] Wandering whores seldom established the long-term client relationship prominent among high-class prostitutes. Wages were tied to volume, and whereas courtesans and pensionary misses tended to establish their exchange value on the assumption that their relationships would be regular and extend over time, common prostitutes earned their wages on a mass production basis.[45] Not surprisingly, there was a demand for cheap, mobile labor. Aunts exchanged their nieces and urged procurers to recruit new labor. Brothel keepers circulated members of their houses and selected a pool of amateur trulls to manage problems of undue familiarity with staff. The "whores exchange" extended vertically throughout the world of prostitution and was graded socially according to class of customer.

Although the world of night walkers and common prostitutes was characterized by transiency, stable sites and social bonds certainly existed. Identifiable institutions such as "Mrs. Beagley in Butlers Alley," "Castle Tavern," "The Turks Head," and "The Ladies Regent at the Bell and Falcon," for example, were stable links in the fluid chain of relations that characterized much of the social life of prostitution.[46] Such locales were agencies of discipline for amorphous populations of women on the move. They were the nurseries of lore and language, and the institutions of an alternative moral system. Here the fledglings were initiated and incorporated into wayward forums of ideas, alliances, and roles. A tract exposing a famous bawdy house in London describes them as the obverse of the morally reputable: "devils churches where cheating nunnery" was learned and practiced.[47]

Brothels were a regular feature of some city wards. Richard Holland and John Knight, for example, kept several brothels in East Smithfield, Tower of London, and Aldgate areas. Frequent complaints by the church officials and parishioners of Saint Andrew-by-the-Wardgate in the liberty of Baynards Castle led to a Privy Council petition condemning Richard and Amy Holland for "keepe[ing] and maintain[ing] a lewde disordered and infamous bawdy house . . . [where] many fights and outrages in the night time are committed, divers many hurt and in danger to be slain."[48] Mrs. Cresswell was also a famous lena (brothel mistress or manager) whose houses were community institutions. She ran well-advertised brothels around mobile prostitutes in the Saint Bartholomews area, in Shoreditch, and eventually in Lewkenor's Lane.[49] These places of assignation were the training grounds for sexual practices, theft, and confidence tricks.

A level below the brothel queens and mobile nieces was a further collection of wayward street prostitutes. Some were associated with cheap slum lodgings and alehouse keepers; others plied their trade on the streets and in the alleys. These "poor pitiful whores" represented the diverse but distinctly lowest order of prostitution.[50] Some worked singly or in teams out of rented accommodation houses picking up men in the streets of the suburbs or in alehouses; others were tenement prostitutes who led a group existence centered around a landlady's pennyrent lodging.[51] Nominally independent, they went out into the streets to solicit their clients, bringing them back to the houses where they lived. Finally, the lowest grade were street dwellers for whom the alleyways were home and work place.[52]

The women who worked this trade picked up their clients in the warrens of windy streets, rather than in gaming ordinaries, playhouses, or other haunts, but the wandering trade was not confined solely to the poorer suburbs. There was an intermingling of "cracks" and "night gown ladies."[53] Listed as places for finding "poor whores" were Cornhill, Leaden Hall, and Bloomsbury as well as the traditional criminal sanctuaries of Turnbull Street, Moorfields, and Dog and Bitch Yard. Burford has noted that much prostitution existed outside the more regular houses of prostitution and was spread unevenly over the city and parishes.[54] This trade at the lowest level represented the last degree for prostitutes who had previously worked in licensed or private brothels. Denied a roof, and institutional supports in the form of food, clothing, primitive contraceptives, midwives, and protection, such women had little recourse except to become servants to other prostitutes, or worse, waste away on the streets or in jail where they served prisoners and officials who could afford to pay in money or favors.[55]

124

A variety of locations served as permanent links to the street haunters. "Pennyrent whores" lived in broken-down tenements that housed anywhere from three or four to perhaps dozens of prostitutes in their parlors and kitchens.[56] Inns and bousing kens offered a variety of accommodations, usually temporary, but sometimes permanent. Rooms in the slums abounded, and street walkers found refuge in outlying barns or in the tenter yards and shed houses that grew up around the squalid alleys and squares of the outparishes.[57] But these must have been weak and unstable foci for the mobile lower orders of prostitution. Little safety could be guaranteed. Health and sanitation were poor. Elementary medical services were lacking, and peace had to be made individually with local control agents.

Nevertheless, a sense of a common trade and of collective morale seems to have taken root, partly in response to the swarms of clandestine and part-time prostitutes and partly out of a need to establish craft control and rules. Street pamphlets confirm that the wandering trade constituted a loose community of occupations organized around an informal hierarchy of roles.[58] A prostitutes' census reveals rudimentary rules of membership and rank. Despite the rivalry, exploitation, patron abuse, individual nature of the act, and lack of stable work patterns, an embryonic organization stressing the separate nature and status of the trade emerged with a regular but nontechnical vocabulary, training systems, and a varied degree of craft pride.[59] Since an unknown but reputedly considerable volume of prostitution merged with other criminal crafts, it is not surprising that the argot of prostitution reveals a general use of thieves' cant. Yet surviving broadsides, pamphlets, and fly sheets also reveal a scattered prostitutes' terminology indicating a unique division of labor and classification of patrons and clients.[60]

There are some revealing continuities between mid-seventeenth- and mid-nineteenth-century descriptions of London prostitution. The activities of independent milliners, equestriennes, and Chelsea ladies of the late nineteenth century resemble those of the pensionary misses and nightgown ladies of Stuart times.[61] Perhaps even more remarkable are the overlaps to be found among the lower orders of prostitution. The levels used by Acton and Mayhew to catalogue prostitution, for example, could be applied to the seventeenth century as well. It would seem that the wandering whores and poor pitiful whores had their counterparts in the night-house tarts, dollymops, and sailors' whores of Victorian London.[62]

Accounts of prostitute-thieves and their partners abound in early nineteenth-century London. For example, Patrick Colquhoun remarked to the Select Committee on Police in 1816 that prostitution was a regular pretext for robbery: "The major part of them [prostitutes] . . . are associated with thieves, who actually live with them, and who follow them in the streets, not only to tutor them in the way they are able to commit robberies, by pulling out watches, money, etc. etc. but also are near at hand, ready to attend them . . . in order to receive the booty and run off."[63] Similarly, Beames and Mayhew noted that prostitution survived by virtue of its segregation in criminal areas.[64] Indeed one of Mayhew's collaborators comes close to describing what in the sixteenth and seventeenth centuries was known as crossbiting and in the eighteenth as buttock and twang. As noted, this was a low-grade criminal gambit organized around a small team of two or three. A trull or buttock (woman prostitute) was the lure entrapping a client in a tavern or alleyway. By arrangement a second party, the crossbiter or twang, then intruded, bullied, and robbed the victim. "Picking up" also combined prostitution, bullying, and theft: "The woman looks out for a 'mug' . . . She then stops him in the street, talks to him, and pays particular attention to his jewellery, watch, and every thing of that sort, of which she attempts to rob him. If he offers any resistance, or makes a noise, one of her bullies comes up, and either knocks him down by a blow under the ear, or exclaims: 'What are you talking to my wife for?' and that is how the thing is done, sir."[65]

Ellen Reece echoed the accounts of prostitution in the mid-seventeenth century in her autobiographical revelations of 1837: "I have lived entirely by prostitution and plunder. Seven times as much by robbery as the hire of prostitution. None of the girls think so much of prostitution but it furnishes opportunities for robbing men."[66] According to her testimony, prostitutes robbed by violence. Their targets were frequently drunken men. Their tactics varied from using the skills of the pickpocket and the confidence cheat to using the terror of thuggery. The link between prostitution and theft continued throughout nineteenth-century London. As Pike remarked in the 1870s, "prostitutes . . . especially of the lowest class . . . are associated by indissoluble bonds with the habitual criminals of the male sex."[67] Thus, not only did criminal areas, institutions, and thieving practices acquire an independence of form and considerable continuity, so too did the types, relationships, and practices of prostitution retain a distinct and stable character.[68]

The Infrastructure of Prostitution

Prostitution tended to take shape around one material necessity: accommodation in which to practice the trade. The most sharply defined type of prostitutes' accommodation was the closed brothel household such as existed in the Southwark stews. Southwark had long been a segregated area of brothel life. But during the Elizabethan and particularly the Stuart period, the brothel areas expanded. Manor houses were converted into high-class brothels that catered to the conspicuous consumption demands of the gentry. Inns were rebuilt or newly fashioned as prestigious houses to accommodate traveling wealthy gentlemen. Older establishments were subdivided into private whorehouses. Taverns and alehouses attached lodging house-brothels and secret passageways for the more discreet clients.[69] In all probability such establishments accommodated only a small section of the entire population of prostitutes. The more ostentatious combined pleasure and business. Reception rooms adjoined spacious courtyards, there was often an assortment of dining and entertainment facilities, and the prostitutes' chambers were frequently upstairs and of varying sizes and tastes to accommodate the status of the client. Holland's Leaguer, a famous house of obscenity, had a complex system of payments, in which clients paid fees for chatting privileges, garden rights, food and wine, access to gaming facilities, and the prostitute herself.[70]

At a lower level the closed brothels were more functional. The quality of services was lower and the turnover quicker. Time was more clearly money; prostitutes had to ensure the maximum number of customers in a working day. In the lowest class of brothel, there was little decor or entertainment. Working conditions were more demanding and labor untrained. An aspect of this is summed up in the "Poor Whores Complaint to the Apprentices of London":

> Our rents are great, our clients go apace
> And we forsaken are in ev'ry place.
> None pities us nor hearkens to our moane
> But ev'ry shag-bag casts at us a stone . . .
> Besides all this with hot encounter, we
> Too many of us, scab'd and mangy be.[71]

Brothel household arrangements, however stratified, had certain features in common. First, the prostitute tended to be a permanent employee as long as her economic drawing power lasted. She resided on a full-time basis. Brothel keepers thus exerted considerable influence over these women and their earnings. Food, clothing, rent, and sundry service charges were deducted from their earnings. Discipline was strict, extortion was common, the hours were long, and the career span was probably short. In exchange for their labor, prostitutes received shelter, regular work, and protection from the law.

Second, the brothel household gave rise to a cluster of elaborate ancillary roles and middlemen.[72] The lena typically was the strategic planner who decided the location of the establishment, fixed rules of conduct and behavior, recruited the labor force, and developed clients through discreet policies. The lena also served as fixer, currying favor and establishing contacts with influential legal officials, gathering important information on possible actions, and bribing marshals, constables, and beadles. Few brothel organizations actually set up regular positions for arrangers or corrupters, but the lena, through careful selection of area, and by sponsorship and negotiation, engaged in prior political preparation to maintain immunity from arrest, prosecution, and punishment. Where necessary, she or a delegated appointee handled such delicate matters, paying in kind as well as in cash. The use of bullies (enforcers) to maintain the rules of the house also helped ensure the continuity of household brothels. The bullies screened clients, kept order, and controlled members, and were assisted by apple-squires (checkers) who kept count of clients and charges. In addition to those holding formal positions within the brothel household, there were often a number of panderers who worked directly for a lena, or functioned independently as tactical guides, assembling and recruiting potential prostitutes, advertising specific houses and favorites, and steering customers to specific establishments.

Several consequences flow from this division of labor: (1) the occupational specialization reveals a degree of organizational rationality. Prostitution entailed a formal arrangement in which the positions of strategist, enforcer, and assembler were coordinated by rules and loose understandings that supported the allocation of roles. (2) Organizational structure was simple and local in scale. However, the prevalence of criminal sanctuaries and weak policing made such a simple structure adequate to achieve objectives successfully and consistently. (3) Various kinds of talent were required to fill the specialized roles. It was necessary to be adept at business, acting, sexual techniques, hustling, the use of defensive violence, and often the techniques of pickpocketing. The lena, in addition to managing the brothel, was also skilled in the disposal of stolen property. She either had a list of client-purchasers or access to a network of intermediary receivers.[73] The work of the prostitute was technical in the sense that it overlapped with other criminal ventures. It embodied the organization and argot of thieving. The prostitute learned dress, manners, hygiene, salesmanship, and techniques of bodily pleasure. However, these skill were not reflected in a developed vocabulary of technique; rather, much of the parlance of prostitutes was hybrid —a combination of thieves' argot and vulgar colloquialisms.

A third common feature of the brothel household, related to its support of occupational divisions, was that it spawned networks of loose and transitory alliances. They incorporated "aged but experienced prostitutes who as "cooke wenches" and "girlie scullions" remained in the trade as domestic workers, musicians, dancers and entertainers, midwives and quack doctors, and sots and sparks who were regular clients and who, among other things, advertised and introduced new clients to the house.[74] Although the lena exerted influence over her hired workers, these looser alliances lacked hierarchical structures of control and authority and were not crucial to the rational conduct of prostitution. The turnover of laundry lasses, charwomen, maids, waitresses, and cooks was apparently considerable. Midwives and surgeons were seldom on the permanent staff of brothels but functioned on a consulting basis. Similarly, entertainers had fleeting contacts with the trade, as did scores of part-time prostitutes. It is doubtful if such brothel households generated strong group solidarity. What integrated structure there was tended to be on the level of brothel ownership, seldom that of management, or resulted from the cohesiveness of working prostitute teams.

Yet a wider system of activities seems to have been tied to the brothel household. While the specifically criminal practices were conducted in small, reasonably coordinated groups, unconnected with any wider criminal organization, prostitutes also attracted and shared a complex of relationships over a wider institutional area which would suggest a loose community of life style. The brothel was an organizational focus not only of infamous commerce but also of related criminal projects. As one customary piece of drollery put it: "cheaters and bawds [went] together like washing and wringing."[75] What emerged was organization only in the broadest

sense—an enduring but fluid structure that linked patron, prostitutes, clients, allies, and other criminal groups together, irrespective
of occupational skill. Recruits were put in touch with the experienced, the retiring and downwardly mobile learned of employment
as domestics, crimes were conceived and planned, working associations were formed, technical information was exchanged, diverse
criminal trades were linked together, and access to markets in which
goods could be converted into cash was provided. The network,
then, was a wider functioning totality, a loose assemblage of criminals and criminal working teams. Although the formal organization
of prostitution in a brothel household overlapped with the informal
network, tied to, but not of, the brothel household, they were essentially different kinds of organizations. The former was more
clearly a criminal organization rationally designed for the purpose of
making profits through the illegal sale of sex. The latter was the
supportive background, not itself geared to committing crime in the
technical sense. Its raison d'être was less the achievement of collective goals than the mediation of criminal practices and standards of
conduct, the forging of different collective life styles.

There was a sense in which prostitutes, their allies, and their regular associates and clients were an identifiable social grouping.
Dress was perhaps their most distinctive feature. They indulged
themselves with decoration: some with periwigs and powder, others
with dye and paints, colored veils, and vizored masks.

> Rustling in most brave attire
> With hood and silken gown
> A handkerchief she had
> All wrought with silk and gold.[76]

Even the poorest in the trade wore "gawdy apparel" and were
dressed in cheap paint, perfumed clothes, and scarves.[77] The virtu-
ous woman was advised to eschew cosmetics, masks, ornamented
clothes and jewelry lest she be mistaken for those "who sell their
flesh."[78] Similarly, others closely associated with the world of high-
class brothels dressed flashily. Dunton provided a portrait: "Hat
cock't up, long wigs powdered, flannel shoulder cloak powdered,
beau muff, perfumed gloves, sparkling rings." Thus dressed did
wits, gallants, and beaus engage in their search for pleasure.[79] They
were a cut above the street gangs of roaring boys (street delin-

quents), who engaged in delinquent adventures bombashing (attacking and mocking) prostitutes, scouring the watch, and frightening the citizenry. They appear to have been governed by sets of rules that mocked conventional mores, and they openly displayed their alternative values in a lexicon of bragging and swaggering which stressed dress and manners, combined with an antagonism toward the family, marriage, and law and order.[80]

A distinctive language emerged around the world of prostitution born of the bravado of its patrons and supporters, the involvement and overlap with organized thieving, and the internal organization of the trade. This was not a secret argot, but more properly a vulgar slang, composed of trite swear words, discarded argot from other criminal crafts, and a few terms classifying technical specialties, work roles, and patrons.

The terms diving, foyling, and lifting, for example, were cant terms which referred to pickpocketing and stealing, and were prominent in identifying types of prostitution. Thus a Mrs. Carter and her daughter were foylers; "savoy birds" were expert "divers . . . well skilled in confidence and the depth of pockets"; and wandering prostitutes were versed in "tipping bungs and gulling cullies of their nab" (picking their pockets). Aliases abounded and included the vulgar as well as the high toned. Among the common whores were found names such as "Mother Cunny," "Butter and Eggs," and "Fair Rosamund sugar cunt."[81] The groomed posed as ladies. Thus, among the "ladies of the commonwealth" were "Lady Shrewsbury" and "Lady Salisbury."[82] Clients were referred to interchangeably and uncomplimentarily as rumpers and dicks, roughly equivalent to square johns. Thus, clustered around dress, manners, aliases, second-hand argot, and general slang there was a rudimentary artificial language which suggests a degree of stability and continuity in these practices, relationships, and life styles.

A second form of accommodation, distinct from the closed household brothel, was the pennyrent lodgings. Dunton noted that lodging houses catered to "pensionary misses", and "night gown ladies" as well as "common cracks and trulls." Accommodation varied from well furnished rooms with attendants and amenities, discreet hideaways, and escape exits to cheap bare rooms with few services.[83] Such establishments were the regular work places and living quarters of a variety of prostitutes. The women in these houses recruited their clients on the streets or in taverns, gaming houses, and other haunts, bringing them back to lodging houses, which gave them a degree of independence denied their brothel counterparts. In the poorer districts these lodgings were traditionally presided over by experienced prostitutes, often in conjunction with alehouse keepers or victuallers who were capable of controlling a houseful of rough prostitutes and extracting a considerable share of their earnings.[84] Such "blind taverns" managed to operate a legitimate business on the same premises.

Pennyrent prostitutes generally led a loose team existence around a bawd's house, an alehouse, or a chain of taverns. As in the household brothel, prostitutes could live in on a regular basis, paying a high rent and being under the tutelage of a bawd or keeper. In return they obtained the advantages of the house, in particular the protection of a strong-arm bully. But much of their environment was less stable. Working arrangements were transitory, with prostitutes apt to change lodgings or to frequent several places at the same time.

The relationship between bawdyhouse keepers and their prostitute lodgers was rife with tension. Both lived in fear of being defrauded. More independent than her brothel counterpart, the pennyrent prostitute was frequently on the defensive. She attempted to secure payment in advance for herself and as much credit as feasible from her keeper. She was on guard against her rivals and her customers. Lodging keepers customarily attempted to keep their prostitutes in debt so as to maintain leverage over them; too large an indebtedness could, however, lead to default and the loss of their investment.[85] A street ballad captures the sense of this conflict:

> The usurer consumes those youthes
> The priest decoye doth bringe
> To usurers; and whores consume
> The priest with filthie lust;
> The bawd eates up the gagninge whore
> Who putteth her in truste;
> The taverner beggars the bawde
> And next is swallowed up.[86]

Although little in the way of a formal division of criminal roles existed around this form of prostitution, clustered around the lodging house were loose webs of alliances not all directly tied to the act of prostitution. The houses were centers for teams of pickpockets and thieves. Lupton observed that in his city tracts, brothels served as residences for armed toughs,[87] and countless street sheets equated lodging houses and poorer alehouses with the dens of forgers, false witnesses, robbers, and embezzlers.[88]

The exact relation of such criminal groupings to the world of prostitution is difficult to specify. Some of the thieves and other criminals may have operated in the sex trade as "bullies, hectors and pimps," or functioned as go-betweens in a wider chain of intermediaries ending up in a receiver's house. Some were direct accomplices, "moneysuckers" engaged in frauds and thefts of small amounts from large numbers of clients.[89] Others were suspects on the run seeking refuge from the law. A ballad recounted this function of the whorehouse as follows:

> For without money/A man is but a beast
> But bringing money, thou shalt be
> Always my welcome guest.[90]

Some of the comments of justices of the peace and Privy Council officials would indicate that some of the alliances between prostitute lodging houses and criminal teams were more cohesive than I have suggested. Some lodging house brothels were tightly run enterprises taking skillful advantage of the stigma attached to consorting with prostitutes. "Cheating nunnery" was a criminal gambit in which the threat of exposing a cully to his neighbors or to the law was made. Here bawds, whores, and confidence cheats were allied in a routine criminal racket: blackmail and extortion.[91] Yet the impression I have is that the world of prostitution at this level was very mobile. The pennyrent lodgings offered shelter for impermanent populations and imposed a limited shape on these amorphous groups of women. As institutions anchored within ecologically distinct territories, they represented vital transformers of norms and traditions. Such establishments were, despite the unenduring nature of teams and relationships, nurseries of lore, language, and technique.[92]

Prostitutes had recourse to a third place of assignation: the night house. Prostitutes did not live in these places; they simply frequented them with their pickups and hired a room for a limited period.[93] Pensionary misses, for example, often had discreet arrangements with night-house mistresses. Some formed regular connections with such establishments, acquiring a degree of security while maintaining autonomy from keepers. Some had their own private establishments in the suburbs, while others formed temporary alliances with lodging keepers and tavern owners to exploit a seasonal trade.[94] the period of accommodation was variable, contingent upon purse and inclination. In the better-off areas around Hatton Garden, Pall Mall, and Covent Garden there were fashionable music houses and coffee places which contained concealed interiors with private rooms, parlors, and secret passageways that led into gardens and arbors.[95]

More common than night houses were the slum rooms rented by lodging and alehouse keepers. Here "wandering whores" and "poor pitiful whores" did most of their business. They worked regular beats, picked up their clients, and made use of local accommodation houses—usually a rendezvous at a tavern. Rooms were hired on a pro rata basis for quick servicing.[96] Similarly, coffee houses and cheap eating places with back passages leading to private rooms served as temporary bed chambers.[97] These tenements were strung together in a hidden mazelike fashion and contained multiple entrances and exits. As Whetstone observed, in such "blind houses" for "forty shillings or better," a young man might procure "a pattle or two of wine, the embracement of a painted strumpet and the French welcome."[98]

> In Whitecross Street and Golden Lane
> Do strapping lasses dwell
> And so there do in every street
> 'Twixt that and Clerkenwell.
> At Cowcross and at Smithfield
> I have much pleasure found
> Where wenches like to fairies
> Did often trace the ground.[99]

These transient places of assignation were also the haunts of crossbiters and thieves. As Greene noted, they "are resident in London and the suburbs . . . but basely minded, who, living in want, as their last refuge, fall unto their crossbiting law," where they swindle, rob, and blackmail.[100] In all likelihood relationships here were short-lived and uncertain.

The organization of prostitution underwent some transformation in the following centuries. By the late Victorian period the conspicuous high-class houses of prostitution and the closed brothels were seldom to be found. Mayhew, Binny, and Acton claimed that by then the most prominent form of prostitution was the independent who "sailed on her own bottom."[101] Chesney, in his examination of the Victorian underworld, found that "from the West End to the Ratcliffe Highway, the vested interests of prostitution were mainly concerned with cashing-in on the ranging prostitute."[102] Yet much about prostitution remained the same. Tobias observed that nineteenth-century prostitution was confined to streets and quarters that had strong traditions of sin and theft.[103] The entire pattern of Victorian prostitution was directly descended from that of the Elizabethan period. In particular, the mobility of prostitutes continued, and many of their activities remained only marginally organized.[104] Moreover, the close links between pickpocketing, robbery, and prostitution, although weakened by Victorian times, did not dissolve entirely. While many prostitutes "could earn more out of straight prostitution than as a thief's accomplice," the lower and more numerous orders of prostitutes maintained their connections with criminals.[105] Mayhew noted that sailor whores around the dockside and prostitutes in Saint Giles rookery, in league with rampsmen (bullies), frequently ambushed, coshed, plundered, and stripped clients.[106] There were, of course, less violent techniques. "If a well-dressed man went into an immoral house in Spitalfields, Whitechapel, or Shadwell, he would assuredly be robbed, but not maltreated to any greater extent than was absolutely requisite to obtain his money, and other valuables."[107] As in the sixteenth-century underworld, prostitution in Victorian London was mediated by competing networks of bawds, procurers, introducers, and plug-uglies.

Other institutions were equally important to the prostitution underworld. In particular, coffee shops and cookshops were the resorts of prostitutes and other criminal types.[108] Bousing kens were the gathering places for the wandering trade. As with other criminal crafts they served as the work places as well as providing shelter, information, companionship, and immunity from the law.[109] Since among the poorer sorts in the trade, thieving and prostitution were more closely linked and organizational rationality was rudimentary, the prostitute had either to fence stolen valuables herself or to pass them on to an intermediary. Bousing kens were convenient broker-age shops. Dunton observed that tapsters and keepers would accept swords, jackets, and wigs in pawn as payment for room and board.[110] The more regular prostitutes received short-term credit and loans.[111] Also significant were the so-called academies, some of which overlapped with lodging accommodation houses. From the little evidence at hand, it would seem that they were fronts to en-trap cullies, places at which contacts between wealthy clients and willing and "trained ladies" could be forged, and nurseries of the trade, in which younger prostitues were apprenticed to the more ex-perienced.[112] It would appear that the full-time prostitute, whether street walker, house prostitute, or independent, was taught basic sexual techniques and rules of the occupation. Panderers and brothel madams were active recruiters of prostitutes. As in the pres-ent day, street level and independent (call girl) forms of prostitution possessed rudimentary apprenticeship systems. These prostitutes were tutored indirectly and acquired most sexual techniques by ob-servation and trial and error on the job.[113]

The training of house prostitutes also seems similar to present-day procedures. Brothel madams in sixteenth- and seventeenth-century London had elaborate tutelage systems. They turned out prostitutes in the sense of directly transmitting craft techniques and rules. The training covered physical skills and strategies, verbal skills for han-dling clients, personal hygiene and presentation of self, and work values and establishment norms.[114] The first category stressed how to perform certain sexual acts, and instruction in techniques for managing certain types of clients and their sexual demands. In-cluded were tactics on how to deal with difficult clients and escape from troublesome encounters. House prostitutes were also tutored in hustling. This included learning the verbal skills necessary to con-vince the client to spend more on the amenities of the brothel: food, drink, gambling, music, and chatting privileges, as well as sex.[115] Among the more prestigious brothels, the maximization of gain did not include stealing or cheating. In the decidedly lower-class houses verbal skills could include confidence cheating and setting the client up for either theft or blackmail. Novices were schooled too in dress, grooming, hygiene, birth control, cosmetics, and personal demea-nor. They were advised on appropriate manners and body lan-guage, and on house morals. Finally, the apprenticeship included the teaching of values and rules. Although the major stress was on

maximizing earnings while minimizing effort, there was also training in honesty and loyalty. House rules included fidelity to a madam
and fairness to other prostitutes. In particular, prostitutes were
warned against stealing from the house or from colleagues, holding back on earnings, providing sexual extras without charging ad-
ditional fees, and neglecting to encourage the use of house activities and facilities.[116] Brothels and dancing academies were crucial to
the socialization of prostitutes and were clearly functional to the
overall structure of the craft.[117]

The playhouses were also "seminaries of vice" where the fascination of sex complemented the fascination of art.[118]

> The Play house punks, who in a loose undress,
> Each night receive some cullies soft address;
> Reduc'd perhaps to the last poor half crown,
> A trundrey gown and petticoat put on
> Go to the House, where they demurely sit
> Angling for Bubbles in the noisy pit . . .
> And better known, then is the dawdry crack
> By Vizor-Mask, and Rigging on her back
> The play house is their place of Traffick, where
> Nightly they sit, to sell their Potten Ware.[119]

The stage productions were a hurly-burly of activities and attracted
a variety of prostitutes. In the boxes and the pit were to be found the
best of the profession: the vizards and tongue pads. In the galleries
the bulkers or common trulls trafficked. The galleries were noted for
their roaring and brawling; there an assortment of bullies, sharpers,
and sots advertised their women, sought out clients, and staged
thefts and confidence cheats.[120] A regular feature was the orange
girls who operated as intermediaries negotiating discreet acquaintances between male admirers and actresses and prostitutes.[121]

> The Doughty Bullies enter bloody Drunk
> Invade and grubble one another's punk
> They cater maul and make a dismal Rout
> Call sons of whores, and strike but ne'er lugg out:
> Thus, while for Poultry Punk they roar and stickle,
> They make it Bawdier than a conventicle.[122]

Stage plays and interludes, in particular, were singled out by London authorities as places at which bad values were learned. Theaters

served as recruiting grounds for prostitutes and cozeners, and the plays themselves provided moral competition to the prevailing wisdom. They turned the world upside down. Young unescorted women were avid playgoers, and many received their sex education through stage anecdotes and jokes. The language of the criminal and the vulgar slang of "loose and mean people" were used as a type of low wit to mock the powerful and wealthy. Politicians and magistrates were turned into criminals, and prostitutes and criminals were romanticized.[123] The heroine of Middleton and Dekker's *The Roaring Girle* whose name was Moll Cutpurse, was celebrated for her independence. She breached all social codes: she wore men's clothes, fought with a sword, outswore and outswaggered her underworld associates, and ruled them with iron discipline.[124] Certainly the Lord Mayor and aldermen were consistently concerned over the "inveiling and alluring of maids" by the theaters.[125]

Gaming ordinaries and bowling alleys were also specific rendezvous for prostitutes. Here independent prostitutes rented themselves out as personal escorts. Procurers and bawds worked the "strumpet and brat" in which they blackmailed gentlemen for allegedly making a prostitute pregnant;[126] they also extorted funds and property from wealthy clients by cheating at gambling,[127] or made the pickups for their prostitutes. Here was "a general market of bawdry . . . but that every wanton and his paramour, every man and his mistress, every John and his Joan, every knave and his queen, are there first acquainted and cheapon [bargain for] the merchandise in that place, which they pay for elsewhere as they can agree."[128] The status of these institutions within ambiguous jurisdictions made regular enforcement difficult. Appeals to close down and remove licenses were often ignored. The city and the royal government could not agree on a common policy, and such places continued openly as criminal refuges and working places.

Owners, Keepers, and Procurers:
Markets and Control in the Prostitution Underworld

While patterns of association in the world of prostitution were diverse, local, fluid, and tied to distinct ecological areas, the Bankside stews were under a measure of central control. Surviving property deeds indicate that brothel consortiums were under the control of prominent merchants and businessmen. The Castle, the Bullhead, the Antilope, the Swanne, and the Gonne were a group of brothels owned by Sir John Bodley, Sir Mathew Brand, and Hilaire Mempris, haberdashers of London, who farmed these houses for much of the early Stuart period.[129] The Crane brothel was a possession of the Tallow Chandlers Company from 1504 to 1633, when it was converted into a soap factory,[130] and the Unicorne, the Bell, the Barge, and the Lock were a quartet of stewhouses under the directorship of the prominent Philip Henslowe.[131] Hugh Bowker, notary of London, owned the Cardinal's Hatte brothel in 1579, leasing it out until 1615. He also acquired the manor house in Paris Gardens which he leased as the famous Holland's League brothel.[132]

The court records also suggest that a Holland mobb (a prostitute family or organization) may have existed. John Holland of the Hog Lane, Aldgate, and his wife Amy owned and maintained "a well-known disorderly house." Richard Holland and a partner kept several brothels in East Smithfield, another Richard Holland near Paris Garden was known to the courts as a brothel manager, and Roger Holland was a keeper of a male prostitutes' house in Hoxton. Finally, an establishment in Clerkenwell was reported as a stew controlled by a Holland, and a third Richard Holland and his wife "maintained a lewde disordered and infamous Bawdy House" in the liberty of Baynard Castle near Blackfriars.[133] Although not much is known about the connections between the various Hollands, it is clear that some of them were related and that there were exchanges of capital and labor.[134] One chronicler of prostitution in Bankside has speculated that the famous Dame Hollandia probably had many aliases and managed an elaborate network of brothel lodging houses.[135] This was certainly so for Edward Alleyn, an actor and man of property, who owned and operated three brothels. Indeed, at the time of his second wife's death he paid out a bawds rent as a form of charity to the worthy poor.[136]

The pattern of ownership suggests that the owners were less a tight gang than a loose consortium. There is little evidence for assuming that relationships between such holdings were integrated. Brothel ownership was part of a wider pattern of property ownership. It was probably a lucrative investment. There are cases of businesses and factories closing shop and reopening as bawdyhouses.

Although they were not tightly integrated, these contained complexes could assert domination, albeit of a fragmented nature, over some aspects of recruitment, working conditions, and wages.

There was of course a political payoff associated with such prominent ownership: protection. Wealthy owners could provide an umbrella of immunity, but more commonly their role was defensive: reducing punishments, taking care of imprisoned prostitutes, facilitating quick processing of legal cases, bribing high officials for favors, and perhaps paying fines.[137] Some establishments were patronized by the reputable: Holland's Leaguer, for example, was the reputed "queen of the bawdy houses" and catered exclusively to courtiers and the gentry. Such a combination of prominent proprietors and clients represented a formidable locus of powerful contacts and support which undoubtedly afforded guarantees of operation. Capital, labor, and patronage could be procured and called on in times of emergency.[138]

Relations with the law, however, were by no means certain. Powerful sponsorship did not ensure smooth relationships with social control agents. Brothel owning and keeping were hazardous trades. Keepers were accorded the major role of corrupter and handled the routine bribery of marshals, constables, and watchmen and their deputized assistants.[139] Behind the brothel's usual business, there existed a hard world of management. Provisions, cleaning, laundering, repairs, medical inspections, labor problems, and difficulties with clients, as well as recruitment and training, had to be attended to. The territorial proximity and segregation of brothels suggest that a network of brothel keepers was likely. The existence of a prostitute blacklist, at least among the more prominent places, also indicates some communication between locales.[140] But competition and rivalry mitigated against any integrated network of brothel owners and keepers. At most, brothel keepers had localized working relations with other keepers. Cliques and mobbs could effect a craft discipline, but seldom did this amount to administrative control.

Another central feature of the organization of prostitution was the "conveniency of spunges"—pimps, panderers, and bullies who lived in a profitable relationship to the trade.[141] Some worked in league with prostitutes, blackmailing those who resorted to brothels. Others were more properly procurers, establishing relationships and linking together client and whore. Many—for example, drawers and glassmen in bars, midwives, hawkers, and travelers—were in strategic positions. They represented a news network, and for a share of the gains they served as invaluable go-betweens.[142] As Burford has noted, brothel keepers had to "cope with bully boys running protection rackets."[143] It is difficult to sort out who these intermediaries were. Some undoubtedly mixed trapaning and pimping with other criminal ventures. Others were employees of specific houses of prostitution and subservient to the overall influence of the lena. Many, however, capitalized on the system of rewards and reprieves offered for information. Informing and blackmailing could thus be used against the prostitute as well as the victim. The power to betray gave such intermediaries a hold over segments of infamous commerce. Influence was not institutionalized; rather it was shifting and renewable. Nevertheless, the climate of betrayal and reprieve fostered by the state did allow for a large trade of informers to exploit the interstices between weak policing and prostitution. A ballad provides a worm's-eye view:

> Some atturnies, and some that solicite law cases
> That at the vacation in the country plods
> They like King James, can use double faces
> And bribe to set neighbour with neighbour at odds;
> Now hither they come, with their bags full of law,
> But the profits they all to themselves do confirm.[144]

Court records also reveal the workings of informers. In brothels congregated "men of the basest condition . . . panderers [who] lived by sharking and oppressing." Such small-time thieves and blackmailers earned money by threatening to betray bawds and prostitutes. Amy Holland, a notorious prostitute of Blackfriars, was at least twice informed upon, once by a neighbor and then by a panderer.[145] Informing could be motivated by a number of factors: self-protection, the desire for personal vengeance, social disapproval, and of course profits.[146] While informers were plentiful and important buttresses to the maintenance of social order, they themselves were often drawn from the world they policed. Informing shaded into corruption and forms of protection brokerage.[147] Within the world of prostitution this strengthened the role and influence of a parasitical stratum of hangers on. An "exposé of bullies and setters" claims that intermediaries lived off the earnings of prostitutes, "eating their bread . . . fighting their battles . . . and gathering their contributions."[148] On the fringes of the criminal underworld, these go-betweens betrayed as well as selecting and gathering. They thus acquired formidable influence over the craft of prostitution, attaching women to themselves as clients. Dependencies were, however, contained. The existence of elaborate integrated rings of pimps and protectors, with large numbers of prostitutes working for them, appears unlikely. Nevertheless, sponging operated at all levels of the prostitution underworld. Unlike receiving and variants of thief taking, it does not appear to have contributed to the economic rationality of crime. Rather, the relationship of pimp to prostitute was more properly a parasitical one based on coercion or the threat of violence in an economy of social control designed to encourage private entrepreneurship and betrayal as a mechanism of crime control.

8

THE MEDIATION
OF CRIME

Introduction

In previous chapters, I noted the growth of intermediaries. The state relied increasingly on middlemen who reported breaches of law for private profit. State rewards were offered for information leading to the successful prosecution of certain offenses. Proclamations and orders from king and Parliament offered money or commodities to enterprising searchers. Neighbors and tradesmen were encouraged to spy and turn evidence on each other. Forgers, thieves, robbers, highwaymen, and burglars were, from time to time, the subjects of specific legislation. Arrested suspects were urged to inform on their accomplices in return for a pardon or protection.[1] The system was designed to give the informer partial or permanent immunity from legal penalties, and to create fissures within the world of crime. In particular, the fence was in a structural position to betray thieves and prostitutes. Law and enforcement were negotiable, and the maintenance of domestic order was characterized by perplexing ambiguity and contradiction.

State Power, Patronage, and Law

The state possessed neither control over the means of violence nor the infrastructure to coordinate effective power. State power was a mosaic of concessions, collusion, tutelage, and arbitration. It should be thought of in terms of political process, as a matter of delicate balance and intrigue. Networks of powerful cliques were woven into a rudimentary system ordered by access to court favors, positions, and influence. Loyalty was commercialized, purchased with services and material benefits. Calculated barter and maneuver lay at the foundation of Elizabethan and Stuart rule. An economy of power existed that was a mixture of both weaknesses and excesses.[2] The coverage of the law, in particular, was defined by the moral status of those in a position to dispense patronage. The concentration of power at certain privileged points meant that law functioned according to mechanisms that were irregular, inconstant, and uncertain in their effects. The law was a contrivance shaped by local powerful elements, who bargained over its principles, altered rules, and arranged outcomes. Law, then, operated in a discontinuous manner that rendered it open to purchase and direct favoritism.

The patronage system of the sixteenth and seventeenth centuries was unlike its successor in the Hanoverian period. The latter was designed to forge a working political relationship between the crown and select political factions. The Tudor and Stuart situation was both grander and more closely monitored: "It was a patronage which aimed not at the adherence of a party or a faction but at the good will and confidence of a whole class."[3] The class involved was numerically small and socially close. Peers, prominent gentry, aspiring lesser gentry, and political careerists were integrated into a subtle system of rewards and favors, the most valuable of which was public office.[4] Yet patronage was pervasive as a system of government. The state's continuing fiscal crises fed its reliance on the monetary resources of independent powerful groupings. Political order was effectively mediated by elaborate webs of affiliation and parochial hierarchies that developed around semiautonomous centers of influence. These networks were seldom institutionalized, and state rule was a matter of shifting diplomacy and favoritism.[5] The system of patronage, moreover, was horizontally vast and vertically pervasive. Court, central administration, regional government, military and naval service, land administration, and the judiciary were tied to elaborate networks of office speculation and influence peddling.[6] How did the distribution of patronage work? What were its implications for the mediation of law and crime?

Perhaps most important, the distribution of patronage, the management of patron-client linkages, was often difficult to supervise. Despite attempts to monitor the selling and trading of perquisites, the central crown government found it difficult to maintain scrutiny.[7] In particular, the sale of office and its associated web of gratuities and reciprocal favors lacked safeguards. Unchecked, the procurement and sale of public position at all levels of bureaucracy, city, county, and crown, resembled a competitive market. Indeed, offices were defined as personal domains to be farmed for maximum profits and favors.[8] This appropriation of private benefits from public service had important consequences for the mediation of law and crime.

First, patronage predicated on arrangements with powerful families and patrons produced a collection of populations with effective immunity from the very laws they were to enforce. The political influence of patrons was normally sufficient to guarantee selective law enforcement, the neutralization of definitions, processes, and agencies of legal order, obvious and widespread bargaining, and frequent abrogation of specific regulations.[9] As J. H. Plumb has noted, members of the gentry "played ducks and drakes with the law when it suited them, breaking with impunity what they were supposed to maintain."[10]

Second, the direct manipulation of law by private principals affected the formal organization of the state. Patrimonial bureaucracy, particularly in its social control capacity, was liable to abuse. As McCaffrey observed,

the . . . prizes . . . were, first of all too small; too few offices provided adequate salaries, and the incumbent was driven to increase his income by any means open to him. Second, the terms of appointments were in many cases ill defined; the fees and profits attached to an office were all too often only hazily known, either to Crown or to patentie, and this encouraged the office-holder to exploit his opportunities, often to the detriment of both Crown and subject. Third, the private exploitation of political advantage created a vast "black market" in which political influence and favour were increasingly bought and sold. . . . Lastly, the poverty of the Crown drove it to make unwise concessions to suitors for favour or place. . . . But grants of this speculative type encouraged the recipient to more and more unabashed exploitation of its possibilities.[11]

Incumbents speculated in their offices with a degree of official sponsorship. Tolerance was high and questionable practices were indulged in with impunity. Patronage was central to city administration, a feature of most levels of the social control process. Justices of the peace, prison administrators, and city marshals, for example, frequently acquired their posts through sponsorship, and a system of tutelage linked underkeepers to keepers and to prison overseers.[12] Officeholders, however, did possess discretionary autonomy. Within their private domains of public service, they easily arranged legal outcomes. For example, in one year alone, out of a total of 1,651 prisoners discharged, 285 were released by direct bribery.[13] The monitoring of crime was persistently mediated by strategies of arbitration rather than by direct coercion. Third, the centrality of the sale of offices to social control processes and its easy abuse made the meaning of criminality unsure. Lawbreaking within the legal machinery acquired a level of protection and legitimacy that made collusion with criminals a possibility. Such strategies of protection, immunity, and betrayal endowed aspects of criminal activities with a de facto legitimacy. With the state regularly recruiting deviants as its own employees, the boundaries between legal and illegal became blurred.[14]

The crystallization of patronage in operation is best illustrated by government treatment of piracy. The waters around England were not easily patrolled. Uneasy alliances were carved out between powerful government officials and influential pirates. Piracy was rendered manageable by recruiting pirates to police the waters. In return, they were implicitly entitled to booty as payment for their service to the state. Thus, certain forms of criminality were protected in order to suppress others. Indeed piracy shaded into privateering and with official state support such forces were useful allies in military campaigns. They exploited their ambiguous situation, operating as fighting men, private plunderers, and paid officials of more powerful patrons. The management of piracy, then, involved a complicated combination of subtle alliances, realliances, and betrayals.[15] Much the same type of policing governed the treatment of highwaymen, and this process carried over into the surveying and suppression of urban crime.

Informing and the Brokerage of Power

In situations of rudimentary government structures, weak policing, and active criminal processes, middlemen thrive. Anton Blok has demonstrated that in Sicily mafioso networks emerged to fill the gaps left by decentralized and inept law enforcement.[16] Banditry and outlawry similarly have thrived in the interstices of distant central law administration and weak communal policing.[17] The management of urban criminal structures in early modern London was also subject to complicated processes of mediation. In particular, the system of patronage fostered the use of clandestine agents.[18] So involved was this business in sixteenth- and seventeenth-century London that informing was a nationwide profession.[19] Like the criminal structures it preyed on, informing had an established pedigree. It was an important component in policing activities during the Reformation,[20] and by the Elizabethan period represented the mainstay of the enforcement of economic legislation and tax collection.[21] Nor was the spread of this form of brokerage odd for it was part of a wider blooming of middlemen businesses.[22]

The Elizabethan and Stuart states were particularly reliant on informers for the mediation of law. These agents were drawn from a number of sources. Many were regular members of craft organizations who informed on a part-time basis. Others were licensed agents of the state enjoined to form working groups of inspectors on a career basis.[23] Some acquired enforcement monopolies in specific territories or businesses. Elton has recorded how one professional informer developed a detective agency involving at least six accomplices and covering the coast of England from Norfolk to Somerset.[24] Still other informers worked alone as promoters or in small, unspecialized teams.[25] Professional informers were frequently drawn from the world they were to supervise. Many, as in the case of economic and apprenticeship regulation, were drawn from the lower middle class of petty tradesmen and artisans and had inside knowledge.[26] Some informers were mobile, handling cases in adjoining regions, while others possessed permanent networks with agents spread across the country.[27]

Clandestine operators reaped most of their rewards directly from the accused. When sanctioned by the state, informers were entitled to a share of the fine or a portion of the forfeited property. Often they had to fight for their fees. Settlements were reached by bargaining and often came to less than the expected rate of payment.[28] The scope of action of private informers appears to have been limited to cases of nonindictable offenses, or misdemeanors punishable by economic sanctions. Serious crimes—felonies—were usually outside their domain, but the trade in free pardons was designed to foster chains of accusations. Thus informing in itself does not seem to have been a high-profit enterprise. It involved considerable economic, social, and physical risks, unless one could obtain official sponsorship.[29] Yet common informers could capitalize on another market, the *personal* rewards offered by victims of the crime or by other private agencies. Information leading to the arrest and conviction of offenders was often a matter for private specialists.[30] Furthermore, informing easily shaded into corrupt practices, with the informer playing both sides against the middle. Beresford has noted that clandestine agents were often "an army of contact men, informers, and other parasites who batten on the innocent—and the avaricious." Undercover guardians of the state regularly "dissolved into first class members of the criminal classes."[31] Davies has argued that the legal context encouraged this drift. "The prolonged expenses of taking prosecution through to trial, and the risk of costly upset thereafter, strongly tempted informers to make illegal use of the first entry of an information and the writ issued thereupon."[32] Settlements out of court were more profitable. Expenses were reduced and more money was squeezed from the accused. Illegal charges took several forms: (1) licensed compositions, but at inflated rates, (2) unlicensed charges on actual evidence, (3) money extorted by forged or pretended information, (4) fees from defendants for false information to prevent the entering of valid prosecutions, and (5) a miscellany of modes of extortion.[33]

Criminal groups were also regulated by means of suborning and the brokerage of power. Informers and thief catchers were recruited from criminal networks and sent back to oversee them. The use of pardons transformed accused persons into temporary spies and betrayers. An array of blackmailers, false accusers, and framers of evidence and trials emerged around the world of crime.[34] One broadside portrays them as sham-plotters (man catchers), their whole "cargo and stock being only a stock of impudence, lies and oaths." Sumners, jailers, and a variety of go-betweens "lived upon the sins of the people," and with ample rewards, played double roles acting as middlemen of crime.[35] Schooled as they were in the practices, lore, and language of crime, they easily won the confidence and penetrated the institutions of the criminal underclass. Imprisoned thieves or pickpockets were regularly recruited as prison underkeepers. For example, in 1580, Thomas Taylor "a common cutpurse" and a condemned felon was made an underkeeper of Newgate Prison.[36] Luke Hutton, a prisoner of Newgate, related that condemned prisoners were serving as custodians of the prison keys.[37] Underkeepers thus had a function in the exercise of the law; they operated as thief takers.[38] Similarly poachers, smugglers, and highwaymen were co-opted from their criminal worlds and sent back to monitor them. They brought to the task a knowledge of criminal persons, networks, and institutions acquired over the years that few local ward constables or marshals possessed.[39]

Common informing also was practiced as a sideline to other interests or activities, particularly when economic difficulties were severe. Other criminals turned informer under pressure, because of obligations, and for personal vengeance. Much informing was discontinuous—a checkered side occupation. Yet, the full-time informer was not a rare phenomenon.[40] However, the relationship between informers and state agencies was an informal one. The patronage setup established and enhanced a trade in the private monitoring of suspect worlds; yet, there is little evidence of central control of informer systems. Indeed the careers of professional informers were sometimes intertwined with sponsoring and directing criminal projects.

The "Black Dog" System and Crime Control

Important to the development of criminal entrepreneurship were the activities of the "black dog" system. These thief takers came to prominence with the introduction of the general warrant as a means for checking theft. Not much is known about these general warrants other than that they authorized arrest on *suspicion* of crime and served initially to force apprehended criminals to confess, inform, return stolen articles, or face a far more expensive and unpleasant stay in prison.[41] These general warrants could be secured by injured parties from justices of the peace and members of the Privy Council and used to force thieves to make good the loss suffered. One contemporary writer provided an example of its use: "But of late a great scourge has fallen among them [cutpurse and pickpockets] for now if a purse be drawn of any great value straight the party maketh friends . . . and they send out warrants, if they cannot learn who the foist is, to the keepers of Newgate, that take up all the nips and foists about the city, and at them be there while the money be re-answered "into the party, so that some pay three pound, nay five pound at a time, according as the some loss did amount unto, which doth greatly impoverish their trade."[42] Prison keepers both controlled the prisoners within jails, and went *outside* armed with warrants to search and arrest. Their role as executors of the law was enhanced as communal forms of coercion and control waned or were ineffectual and as a state-created market in general warrants, rewards, came more prominent. Keepers and their hirelings emerged as criminal entrepreneurs, manipulating legal procedures and playing dual roles as policemen and as sponsors of crime.[43] As prison officials they were largely unpaid employees and like many city officials relied on fees, as well as bribery and illegal charges, to earn a living. Since the keeper of the prison appointed, maintained, and dismissed the underkeepers himself, the controlling authorities seldom intervened in the activities of the underkeepers. Thus prison keepers and their associates came to control the interface between the reputable and the deviant.[44]

Cliques of thief catchers, with an intimate acquaintance of deviant ways, thus trafficked in crime. They also doubled as receivers, although seldom did they have to take possession of stolen property. Their legitimate calling was a convenient cover for dealing in stolen property. Such thief takers challenged the traditional role of receivers. In organizational terms, the thief takers impinged upon the thieves' power; as the thief takers' financial stake became more promising, they found it in their interests to manipulate and dominate thieves.[45] Thief takers established an elaborate system of playing both ends against the middle. They had scouts and spies who haunted the criminal areas and institutions. They obtained information on what crimes were committed and by whom. Like other receivers they returned stolen property to the rightful owners.[46] They had touts who advertised their skills and reputations. Once a client had been confirmed, they used their legitimate office and their knowledge of contacts to track down criminals. Usually it was the thief catchers who sought out the victim and offered their services, though Newgate Prison was probably a known headquarters of thief-taking rings. Thief catchers accepted an initial deposit from the offended party as a searcher's fee. Then, through their intelligence networks and under the guise of being law enforcers, they rounded up thieves, prostitutes, and pickpockets, extorting money and information as protection from imprisonment. The fear of jail and the cost of being out of circulation were often sufficient to guarantee payment. The real thief was quickly discovered, though he was not apprehended immediately. The main idea of the black dog system was to prolong the possibilities of intermediary payoffs from thieves and to amass intelligence.

Pickpockets appear to have been susceptible to thief taking, and it reportedly led them to increase their security precautions. Particularly notable was the emergence of the role of a treasurer to whom a sum was delivered: "To the use that whensoever by some misadventure any of them happen to be taken and laid in prison, this common stock may serve to satisfy the party grieved, and to make friends to save them from hanging."[47]

Thief takers nurtured as well as betrayed, and they gained increasing influence over the organization of thieving.[48] They received compensation from prison keepers for arresting malefactors, and they reaped profits from blackmail and from receiving and returning stolen property. It was thus often in their interest to encourage crime. Fennor reported that prison sergeants routinely extorted money from wanted criminals. For a price they would warn thieves of imminent arrest. Some lodged known thieves and prostitutes on their premises.[49] Hutton related how thief takers, after having criminals arrested, would then arrange for their release by buying them out of prison or by arranging that witnesses not appear: "Yet upon entreaty made by the cutpurse, the cony catcher [thief taker] promiseth for his part he will do him any good he can, wishing the cutpurse, as he is wise enough, so it were good for him to hold his own, and confess nothing to the justice, what proof soever come against him, and in so doing it may lie in his power to do him good, telling him further, that the man who lost the money . . . will partly be ruled by him."[50]

Within the world of crime, thief takers became politically more important and, when they combined this occupation with receiving, they asserted command over the criminal crafts. But competition was rife. Informers, cheating solicitors, and professional false witnesses were sometimes allied to fences and thief takers. They framed evidence, gathered information, traced the evasive, and disciplined the recalcitrant. They served a political role mediating the world of crime and enjoying influence with criminal intermediaries.

The Mediation of Criminal Organization

The growth of this form of criminal entrepreneurship strengthened a tendency toward market dominance. Enjoying a practical immunity from prosecution and strengthened by the cloak of officialdom, thief-taker–fences increased their organizational prominence. The combination of the market merchandiser role and the legitimate state-endorsed enforcement role provided intermediaries with considerable power. They formed a strategic front which fostered dependency relations and limited the working autonomy of criminal crews. They thus rearranged criminal relationships into a more integrated and coordinated underworld.

As a result of their acquaintance with criminal structures and their involvement in police work, they acquired influence over the fate of criminals. They could thus defend and protect certain forms of crime and groups of criminals, particularly those who accepted their supervisory role. Immunity from the law was afforded the favored. Indeed, the thief takers' powers extended to life and death.[51] The middlemen's official role in routine enforcement operations provided them with a powerful leverage over certain criminal crafts. In particular, they organized the activities of thieving teams. Private entrepreneurship in crime control led thief takers and fences to direct as well as protect and to act as advisers for criminal projects. They constituted an active agency of social control and criminal overseers at the same time.[52] Paradoxically, they functioned as a criminal elite in the London underworld. Dressed in the trappings of legitimate authority they went about the business of betraying the marginal and restructuring the diverse thieving trades.

The growth of these intermediaries further regularized relations within the criminal underworld. The power of informers and thief takers merged with that of the fence and represented the major locus of exchange between criminal, victim, and weak state control. On the border between legality and illegality, they cultivated a public role that enabled them to exercise considerable influence. The thief-taker–fence arrangement was set up to return stolen property while at the same time herding and protecting the original robbers.[53] The thief takers thus sponsored forms of crime and enhanced the stability, routinization, and continuity of criminal practices.

Thief taking also fueled a tendency toward centralization within the organization of thieving. Small-scale fencing establishments were put at risk. The political prominence of the receivers' role affected the internal design of the London underworld. A tightening of segmented associations seems to have occurred. The new discipline of the criminal go-betweens strengthened and extended the organization of crime. The thief taker's authority became recognized by commercial interests, government, and the public at large. Justices of the peace encouraged victims to seek out intermediaries to recover their rightful property. The state's free trade in warrants and general warrants linked the judiciary to private thief-taking enterprises. A more coherent design for the underworld was fashioned. Working teams of pickpockets, prostitutes, cheats, and thieves evolved ancillary organizational roles to protect themselves from being informed on, pursued, or arrested, and formed wider alliances as clients to receiver patrons in order to be afforded a limited protection.[54]

Earlier I specified the market importance of the fence. Although it seems doubtful that the organization of crime formed a cohesive configuration, the fence did strive to establish a monopoly over criminal crews. The fence's authority, however, could be better described as akin to power brokerage. Seldom was market advantage transformed into administrative control.[55] The question then is, Did the combination of thief taking and fencing lead to a more unified organizational system? Thief taking did transform the fundamental situation of thieves, threading closer links between a segmented criminal underworld and thief-sponsors, even to the point where victims routinely paid for recovery of their property. The black dog operations, and the lost property warehouse of Moll Cutpurse approximated such an elaborate form. Rarely, however, were the thief takers the architects or organizers of crime. Even when they appeared to exert command over thieves—expecting them to steal on demand—they did so only temporarily. For example, Moll Cutpurse's operation, the antecedent of Jonathan Wild's thief-taking system, lasted for less than a decade and was in essence a working method: an elastic network in which she operated as an agent, counselor, and director.[56] Indeed, what little is known suggests that intermediaries seldom had advance knowledge of crimes. Rather they got in touch with the thieves after the event. There is little to support the view of a criminal conspiracy with a mastermind exercising central control, or to suppose that stealing, betraying, and returning operated as a regular system of extortion.[57] Thief-taker–fences could help their own thieves, but they could not guarantee protection from others. According to Howson, the real problem for seventeenth- and eighteenth-century thief takers was to "keep the underworld divided for easier control without permitting it to fall apart."[58] This they managed by dominating the market relations with thieves; they threatened to inform on thieves who took business to competitors, and they provided assistance to reliable thieves. But this did not lead to an arrangement whereby thief-taker–fences exerted administrative authority over thieves. Perhaps the reason for this is grounded in the hostility that thieves feel for the buyers on whom they rely, a hostility as evident in the twentieth century as it was in the sixteenth.[59]

9
CONTINUITY
AND CHANGE

I have argued in this book that for the Elizabethan and Stuart periods criminal organization was neither absent nor a unified subculture of large, centrally controlled gangs. Rather, in London the criminal underworld was a fluid grouping of formal work teams and informal ancillary institutions and networks supporting criminal activities. Nor can the particular form of criminal organization be considered unique to these periods. There are remarkable continuities over time, as well as crucial differences.[1] The methods of crime control and certain features of the legal order show broad parallels between the medieval and modern periods. Earlier law enforcement has frequently been portrayed as decentralized and personal, and a recent study of seventeenth- and eighteenth-century law and crime shows the judicial system to be amateur, divided, and ad hoc. As Brewer and Styles have observed, "the entire legal fabric, from prosecution to punishment, was shot through with discretion. In consequence it was not difficult for office-holders to employ their position for their own private ends (including that of making money from the law), or for citizens to use the law. . . to legitimate some particular end such as commercial profit."[2]

Likewise, the use of the judicial process as an instrument of domination has considerable longevity. As early as the fourteenth century "the criminal justice system and the social system of the villages were bound closely together," and "manipulation of the judicial system through jury service gave the village oligarchs . . . a powerful weapon for dominating their villages."[3] This pattern continued well into the seventeenth century with village elites becoming even more manipulative in using the courts to force a new social discipline and order upon the so-called rough and meaner sort of folk.[4] Indeed, by the Hanoverian period, criminal law in particular was a highly articulated artifice, which was used subtly to effect class domination and control. Flexible, selective, and tailored to individual offenders, it represented a powerful societal ideology that combined justice with mercy, majesty, and a delicate circumspection. As Hay has observed, "the private manipulation of the law by the wealthy and powerful was in truth a ruling class conspiracy, in the most exact meaning of the world. The King, judges, magistrates, and gentry used private, extra-legal dealings among themselves to bend statute and common law to their own purposes."[5]

The same kind of continuity can be found in crime patterns. Research on criminal archives from the fourteenth to the nineteenth centuries indicates that crime was essentially individualized and small scale, consisting primarily of robberies, burglaries, and assaults, with small amounts being stolen.[6] Few and far between were the spectacular projects involving large teams and careful advance preparation, with large amounts being taken. Similarly, the territorial bases of crime have durable lineages: the "jago" area of Edwardian London, for example, is a successor of the illegitimate sanctuaries of Elizabethan times.[7] Not surprisingly, these districts have strong traditions bolstering certain forms of crime, and professional crime and criminal businesses, in turn, have relatively stable and continuous forms. The organization of thieving, for example, has certainly been transformed as more sophisticated means of protecting private property have evolved, yet earlier elementary craft forms of theft coexist with more elaborate and modern ones, still underpinning many aspects of present-day pickpocketing, burglary, and confidence cheating.

There are, however, crucial differences in crime and criminality that need to be noted. Indeed, the century and a half from 1500 to 1650 has been termed an age of transition, a time of revolution, and a period of seismic upheaval. Social, political, economic, and ideological changes were dramatic, shaping not only the character of education, religion, business, and science but the properties of crime as well. I believe that certain specific features of organized crime during this period demarcate it from earlier and later centuries. Opportunities for crime, in particular, mirrored the growth and expansion of commercial capitalism. Not only did London have a magnetic pull on capital, commerce, trade, industry, labor, the professions, and consumer goods production and consumption, it was also a beehive of illegal opportunity providing easier access to plentiful targets than ever before and supportive of a permanent thieving underworld. At the same time, the power of the absolutist state was on the wane, so it was increasingly unable to coordinate a systematic response to crime control. Although there was a selective application and manipulation of the law, an orchestrated "criminalization" of the poor, and a sustained effort at disciplining the so-called idle, formal law enforcement was exceedingly personal, amateur, and laggard. Gaps abounded, central authority was lacking, and the dubious and sometimes corrupt effects of patronage were woven into the fabric of communal and state social control institutions. Populations of masterless men and women, some resorting to crime, lived in the interstices of the changing social relations brought on by transformations in the underlying organization of production, and the relatively weak decentralized policing apparatus. Here they established as never before their rational work teams, networks, institutions, and techniques *for* crime.

Criminal sanctuaries, with their curious blend of the customary and the stigmatized, played an important role in providing refuge, protection, opportunities for criminal careers, crime planning, and the merchandizing of stolen property—just as they had in the fourteenth and fifteenth centuries and would in the eighteenth and nineteenth.[8] But unlike the situation in earlier periods, in late sixteenth- and seventeenth-century London, the city's dramatic size, diversity, density, mobility, and anonymity encouraged the growth of criminal territories. Criminal areas came to possess an elaborate yet unofficial social world with its own criminal vocabulary, criminal technology, division of labor, apprenticeship system, criminal haunts, and style of collective life. These groupings and institutions were more plentiful, stable, and coherent than they had been in the medieval under-world. The steady surplus population available for criminal ventures meant that by the late sixteenth century the professional criminal population was more numerous, more diverse, better able to make a steady dishonest wage from crime, and more tightly organized.[9] Yet the isolation, closure, and social homogeneity of criminal zones and institutions were not as complete as in later periods.[10]

Underworld leadership and authority were less centralized in the sixteenth and seventeenth centuries than in the eighteenth. By the Elizabethan period, crime was taking on the aspect of other forms of entrepreneurship, involving increasing amounts of capital (stolen goods), new markets for investment (the city), and a criminal elite who functioned as market patrons.[11] This development provided a marked contrast to the large, violent, and loosely organized noble and outlaw gangs of the feudal period, in which leaders seldom carved out new and lucrative areas for crime, but instead exploited the power that their positions as members of the declining social order gave them or acted as entrepreneurs of violence, working either for or against the peasantry.[12] The nature of criminal teams and networks in the London underworld and their relation to the social order changed over the centuries. Medieval criminal groupings tended to overlap directly with existing social organizations based on family or social rank. Hanawalt has noted of fourteenth-century crime that "the family was a natural social unit to act as an organizational basis for a criminal association, for it had within its structure all necessary elements. It already had established leadership roles, rules of conduct for its members, established procedures for division of labour and profits, and experience working together."[13] However, by the sixteenth century, and especially in London, family units were weaker, and as criminal affiliations expanded, criminals relied less on existing social organization and became more innovative in fashioning specifically criminal forms of association: the "underworld of masterless men and women." There was considerable competition for criminal skills and recruits, with thieves, confidence cheats, and prostitutes being multitalented, mobile, and tied to several criminal groupings. Mistrust and betrayal, fanned by informing, pardons, and patronage, ensured a fluid and somewhat diffuse situation. Of course the system of reprieves and rewards, later to become more effective crime control strategies, was undeveloped. The marketing of stolen property in the sixteenth and seventeenth centuries was open and competitive, more the work of a *confederation* of criminal units than an administratively centered system. As late as the 1680s, "there were hundreds of warehouses and repositories where thieves could sell their booty, within minutes of stealing it."[14] It was only in the eighteenth century that authority and control within the underworld became more uniform and centralized as thief takers controlled not just the market but enforcement work and therefore the fate of the criminals under their control.[15]

GLOSSARY

Abram or Abraham man. *Real or pretended ex-inmate of Bedlam.*
Alsatia. *A notorious criminal quarter of London.*
Angler. *One who uses hooks to steal from windows.*
Ape-gentlewomen. *Part-time prostitutes.*
Apple-squire. *Pimp, servant in brothel.*
Aunt and niece. *Team of prostitutes.*
Barnard. *Cony-catcher who comes in, apparently by chance, when game is already in progress.*
Barred cater trays. *False dice designed to seldom show a three or four.*
Bawds. *Common prostitutes.*
Beau. *A regular frequenter of prostitutes.*
Bell-brow. *Alehouse.*
Bellman. *Watchman.*
Bene faker of gibes. *Skilled forger of licenses, etc.*
Bing the bill. *Bully the victim.*
Bing the cull on the poll. *Attack unexpected intruders.*
Black art. *Picking locks.*
Blind. *Obscure, remote.*
Bob. *Fence (of stolen property).*
Bousing ken. *Alehouse.*
Bowman. *The sign for a housebreaker to pass the snappings out of the house.*
Boxman. *Man who controls the placement of the dice.*
Bristle dice. *Dice with a short bristle attached to one edge.*
Broker (or brogger). *Middleman; receiver of stolen goods.*
Brush upon the sneak. *A warning to move quietly.*
Brush your grig. *Get out of here and take to the streets.*
Budge. *A sneak thief or house burglar.*
Bulk and file. *A pickpocket team.*

Glossary

Bulk the cull. *An instruction to distract the victim of a pickpocket.*
Bullies. *Enforcers and accomplices to prostitutes.*
Bung. *Purse, pocket.*
Buttock and twang. *Eighteenth-century version of crossbiting.*
Cant. *Criminal language.*
Cap. *A mid-eighteenth-century version of the barnard.*
Cheating nunnery. *Threatening to expose a cully to his neighbors or the law.*
Cloy. *Steal.*
Cloyers of snaps. *Double-crossing pickpockets who betray and run protection gambits.*
Cog. *Cheat, especially at dice or cards.*
Cole. *First of a group of gambling cheats to strike up acquaintance with a prospective client.*
Common queens. *Common prostitutes.*
Confidence cheat. *Someone who cheats victims out of their money or property by taking them into his confidence.*
Contraries. *False dice with an opposite tendency to those in play.*
Cony. *Dupe, victim (literally rabbit).*
Cony-catching. *Trickery, especially at cards.*
Counterfeit crank. *Pretended epileptic.*
Courtesy-man. *A sophisticated and artful pickpocket.*
Cousin. *Dupe.*
Crossbiting. *Swindling, blackmailing, etc., associated with prostitution.*
Cully. *A victim of crime.*
Curb. *Hook used to steal from open windows.*
Curber. *One who uses hooks to steal from windows.*
Curbing. *Stealing through open windows.*
Cursitor. *A tramp.*
Cutters. *Hit men or hired killers.*
Cuttle-bung. *Cutpurse's knife.*
Decoying. *Luring under false pretenses.*
Dick. *A prostitute's client.*
Diver. *One who steals by employing a small boy to wriggle into rooms through small spaces.*
Draw. *Pick a pocket.*
Drop. *A mid-eighteenth-century version of cony-catching.*
Dub a gigger. *Open a lock.*
Dubbers. *Picklocks who work for thieving teams.*
Dubs. *Young picklocks learning the trade.*
Faggot and storm. *A violent form of house burglary.*
Fakers of loges. *A manufacturer of false passports.*
Figging boys. *Child thieves.*
File. *Pickpocket.*

File the cly of the tatler. *Steal pocket watches.*

Flash cases. *The Victorian equivalent of bousing kens.*

Fob. *Purse or pocket.*

Foin. *Pickpocket.*

Foist. *Pickpocket; the act of picking pockets.*

Forking. *A primitive hooking pickpocket technique.*

Foyl'd cloys. *Picked pockets.*

Fullams. *Weighted dice designed to throw up the side farthest from the weight.*

Garbage. *Stolen goods.*

Gentlemen foins. *Class pickpockets.*

Gilks. *Skeleton keys.*

Ginnys and filchs. *Criminal tools designed to open windows and doors.*

Giving gammon. *Shouldering a victim to allow a pickpocket easy access.*

Glims. *Dark lanterns for housebreakers.*

Gourds. *Dice hollowed near one face to produce a contrived result.*

Gull gropers. *Bankers who advanced loans to gamblers.*

Gullying cullies of their nab. *Picking pockets.*

Gybe. *False license; any document.*

Gybed jarkeds. *Sealed passports.*

Kid. *A mid-eighteenth-century version of the verser.*

Kinchin mort. *Vagrant girl.*

Knap of the case. *The head of a dice fraud team.*

Knapping. *A dice-cheating technique involving sleight of hand.*

Knight of the post. *Witness hired to attest to person's respectability; professional perjurer.*

Knuckles. *Juvenile pickpockets.*

Langrets. *False dice with greater length along one axis.*

Lift. *Rob.*

Lifter. *One who robs shops or houses.*

Lifting law. *Art of stealing from shops.*

Lena. *A female keeper of a brothel.*

Looking the glaze. *Observing a premise to be robbed.*

Madams. *Managers of prostitutes.*

Marker. *Accomplice of one who robs shops.*

Milling the gig (or milling the ken). *Breaking the window and stealing what you can.*

Mobb. *A prostitute family or gang.*

Mort. *Woman.*

Night walkers. *Street prostitutes.*

Nip. *Cutpurse.*

Nip a bung. *Cut a purse.*

Pad strumpets. *Prostitutes who practiced confidence games.*

Palming. *A dice-cheating technique involving sleight of hand.*

Glossary

Palming a purse. *Cut and grab technique of lifting a purse.*

Picker-up. *An eighteenth-century version of the taker-up.*

Punk. *A common term for a prostitute.*

Queens. *Women working as accomplice prostitutes.*

Rakehell. *A scoundrel.*

Rampsman. *A prostitute's bully.*

Roaring boys and girls. *Young delinquents, constant swearers.*

Rookeries. *Criminal districts in Victorian times.*

Ruffler. *Ablebodied rogue claiming to be ex-soldier.*

Rumper. *A prostitute's client.*

Running bawds. *Mobile vagrant prostitutes.*

Rutter. *A bully in a con game.*

Santar. *Outside accomplice of one who robs shops.*

Setter (or taker-up). *A member of a group of tricksters who strikes up acquaintances with prospective victims.*

Sharper. *Card cheat.*

Shave. *To steal cloaks, swords, and similar articles.*

Shifter. *A member of team of gambling cheats who initiates victims into card and dice games.*

Simpler. *Victim of swindle or blackmail associated with prostitution (crossbiting).*

Slurring. *A dice-cheating technique involving sleight of hand.*

Smoke. *Suspect and accuse.*

Snappings. *The take from a theft.*

Sots and sparks. *Regular frequenters and advertisers of prostitutes.*

Stall. *Decoy.*

Stalling ken. *A place in which stolen goods were received and disposed of.*

Stabbing. *A dice-cheating technique involving sleight of hand.*

Stand. *A budge's lookout man.*

Stew. *Brothel; originally those at Bankside.*

Striked. *Slashed.*

Strumpet and brat. *Blackmail associated with prostitution.*

Swell mobsmen. *Victorian pickpockets.*

Taker or taker-up. *A member of a group of tricksters who strikes up acquaintance with prospective victims.*

Tipping bungs. *Cutting purses.*

'Tis all bob. *The coast is clear for a theft.*

Tomme. *A signal for a burglar to lie still and flat.*

Tongue pad whores. *Prostitutes who mixed commercial sex with confidence cheating.*

Touting the case. *Spotting, marking, and surveying the premises to be robbed.*

Traffic. *Whore.*

Trapaners. *Prostitutes who lured clients into situations in which they could be robbed.*

Trapping. *A dice-cheating technique involving sleight of hand.*
Trugging-house. *Brothel.*
Trull. *Prostitute.*
Verser. *Cony-catcher who begins game.*
Vincent. *Victim of bowling alley trickery.*
Warp. *Curber's lookout man.*
Wheedling. *Swindling.*

NOTES

1. Introduction

1. See Frank Aydelotte, *Elizabethan Rogues and Vagabonds*; J. A. S. McPeck, *The Black Book of Knaves and Unthrifts*; Gamini Salgado, *Cony Catchers and Bawdy Baskets*; Gamini Salgado, *The Elizabethan Underworld*.
2. See in particular A. L. Beier, "Social Problems in Elizabethan London"; A. L. Beier, "Vagrants and the Social Order"; P. A. Slack, "Vagrants and Vagrancy in England 1598–1664," pp. 365, 377; Peter Clark, "The Migrant in Kentish Towns 1580–1640," p. 144.
3. For a discussion of this topic see Aydelotte, *Elizabethan Rogues and Vagabonds*, pp. 114–139; Clifford Dobb, "Life and Conditions in London Prisons, 1553–1643, with Special Reference to Contemporary Literature"; T. C. Curtis and F. M. Hale, "English Thinking about Crime, 1530–1620."
4. G. R. Elton, "Crime and the Historian," pp. 1–14.
5. Ibid., p. 6.
6. For examples of work pursuing this tack see J. A. Sharpe, *Crime in Seventeenth Century England: A County Study*; John Beattie, "The Pattern of Crime in England 1660–1800"; John Beattie, "Judicial Records and the Measurement of Crime in Eighteenth Century England."

2. The Making of an Underworld

1. See Lawrence Stone, "Social Mobility in England 1500–1700."
2. See F. J. Fisher, "London as an 'Engine of Economic Growth,'" pp. 205–215.
3. See Alan Everitt, "Social Mobility in Early Modern England."
4. D. C. Coleman, "Labour in the English Economy of the Seventeenth Century," pp. 299–300.
5. Fisher, "London as an 'Engine of Economic Growth,'" pp. 206–207.

6. Stone, "Social Mobility in England 1500–1700," p. 40.
7. Beier, "Vagrants and the Social Order," pp. 3–29.
8. C. Hill, *The World Turned Upside Down: Radical Ideas during the English Revolution*, p. 40.
9. W. K. Jordan, *The Charities of London 1480–1660*, pp. 15–16.
10. P. Clark and P. Slack, *English Towns in Transition 1500–1700*, p. 64.
11. Fisher, "London as an 'Engine of Economic Growth,'" p. 205.
12. This discussion of trade changes is drawn from F. J. Fisher, "London's Export Trade in the Early Seventeenth Century."
13. F. J. Fisher, "Commercial Trends and Policy in Sixteenth Century England"; J. U. Nef, "The Progress of Technology and the Growth of Large-Scale Industry in Great Britain 1540–1640"; Ralph Davis, *The Rise of the English Shipping Industry in the Seventeenth and Eighteenth Centuries*, especially Chapters 1 and 3.
14. See Clark and Slack, *English Towns*, pp. 62–81 for a discussion of industry in London; see also J. D. Gould, *The Great Debasement*.
15. Aydelotte, *Elizabethan Rogues and Vagabonds*, Chapter 1.
16. C. Hill, *Reformation to Industrial Revolution*, pp. 55–60.
17. Fisher, "London as an 'Engine of Economic Growth,'" pp. 208–209.
18. Slack, "Vagrants and Vagrancy in England," p. 373.
19. V. Pearl, *London and the Outbreak of the Puritan Revolution*, pp. 15–17; Davis, *The Rise of the English Shipping Industry*, Chapter 1.
20. Beier, "Vagrants and the Social Order," pp. 3–29.
21. Slack, "Vagrants and Vagrancy in England," pp. 373–375.
22. John Pound, *Poverty and Vagrancy in Tudor England*, p. 59.
23. Ibid., pp. 58–60.
24. Ibid., pp. 23–30.
25. F. J. Fisher, "The Development of London as a Centre of Conspicuous Consumption in the Sixteenth and Seventeenth Centuries," pp. 204–207.
26. Ibid.
27. E. J. Hobsbawm, "The Crises of the Seventeenth Century," pp. 50–51.
28. Fisher, "London as an 'Engine of Economic Growth,'" p. 211.
29. Ibid.
30. *Winter's Tale*, IV, iii.
31. T. C. Barker and C. T. Savage, *An Economic History of Transport in Britain*, Chapter 1.
32. Everitt, "Social Mobility in Early Modern England," p. 68.
33. Fisher, "The Development of London as a Centre of Conspicuous Consumption," pp. 197–207.
34. R. H. Tawney, "The Rise of the Gentry 1558–1640."
35. N. G. Brett-James, *The Growth of Stuart London*.
36. Fisher, "The Development of London as a Centre of Conspicuous Consumption," p. 199.

37. Stone, "Social Mobility in England 1500–1700," p. 43.
38. W. Prest, *The Inns of Court under Elizabeth I and the Early Stuarts 1590–1640.*
39. Stone, "Social Mobility in England 1500–1700," p. 23; J. Cornwall, "The Early Tudor Gentry," pp. 457–461.
40. Stone, "Social Mobility in England 1500–1700," p. 24.
41. W. T. MacCaffrey, "Place and Patronage in Elizabethan Politics," pp. 106–108.
42. Stone, "Social Mobility in England 1500–1700," p. 25.
43. R. S. Roberts, "The Personnel and Practice of Medicine in Tudor and Stuart England."
44. Stone, "Social Mobility in England 1500–1700," p. 44.
45. Prest, *The Inns of Court,* especially Chapters 1 and 2.
46. Fisher, "The Development of London as a Centre of Conspicuous Consumption," pp. 200–201.
47. MacCaffrey, "Place and Patronage," p. 107.
48. Fisher, "The Development of London as a Centre of Conspicuous Consumption," p. 200.
49. Ibid., p. 206.
50. Ibid., pp. 205–207.
51. Peter Burke, "Popular Culture in Seventeenth Century London."
52. Stone, "Social Mobility in England 1500–1700," p. 16.
53. Hill, *Reformation to Industrial Revolution,* pp. 40–41.
54. A. V. Judges, ed., *The Elizabethan Underworld,* especially the introduction.
55. Mary McIntosh, *The Organization of Crime,* pp. 35–36.
56. Robert Greene, "A Notable Discovery of Cozenage," pp. 123–124.
57. Gilbert Walker, "A Manifest Detection of Dice Play," p. 28.
58. J. S. Cockburn, "The Nature and Incidence of Crime in England 1559–1625: A Preliminary Survey," p. 65.
59. William Harrison, *The Description of England,* 1876 ed., bk. 3, pp. 108–109.
60. D. V. Glass, "Two Papers on Gregory King."
61. Donald Lupton, *London and the Country Carbondated and Quartered into Several Characters,* pp. 1–2.
62. Carl Brindenbaugh, *Vexed and Troubled Englishmen 1590–1642,* pp. 161–200.
63. Lupton, *London and the Country,* pp. 112–115.
64. Ibid., p. 4.
65. J. Samaha, *Law and Order in Historical Perspective: The Case of Elizabethan Essex,* pp. 33–36.
66. Ibid., p. 35.
67. Henry Kamen, *The Iron Century: Social Change in Europe 1500–1660,* pp. 430–432.

68. For an examination of the importance of such territories see John Bellamy, *Crime and Public Order in the Later Middle Ages*.
69. A. J. Kempe, *Historical Notices of the Collegiate Church or Royal Free Chapel and Sanctuary of St. Martin-le-Grand*; McIntosh, *The Organization of Crime*, pp. 21–24.
70. David Johnson, *Southwark and the City*, pp. 61–75.
71. Jordan, *The Charities of London*, p. 81.
72. Brindenbaugh, *Vexed and Troubled Englishmen*, p. 168.
73. Ibid., see also Barry E. Supple, *Commercial Crisis and Change in England 1600–1642*, pp. 38–57, 102–123.
74. Kamen, *The Iron Century*, pp. 427–432.
75. Pound, *Poverty and Vagrancy*, pp. 25–26.
76. Ibid., pp. 60–63.
77. Quoted in Hill, *Reformation to Industrial Revolution*, p. 39. Also see Brindenbaugh, *Vexed and Troubled Englishmen*, pp. 375–385.
78. Pound, *Poverty and Vagrancy*, p. 26.
79. E. J. Burford, *Bawds and Lodgings: A History of the Bankside Brothels 900–1675*.
80. Judges, *The Elizabethan Underworld*, especially the introduction.
81. Burford, *Bawds and Lodgings*.
82. As quoted in Aydelotte, *Elizabethan Rogues and Vagabonds*, p. 81.
83. J. J. Jusserand, *English Wayfaring Life in the Middle Ages*.
84. For example, *The Devil's Cabinet Broke Open*, especially the section "A relation of the laws, customs and subtleties of housebreakers, pickpockets."
85. Leslie Sheppard, *The History of Street Literature*, pp. 82–83; J. Jean Hecht, *The Domestic Servant Class in Eighteenth-Century England*; Beier, "Social Problems in Elizabethan London," pp. 214–217. Domestic servants and apprentices appeared in Bridewell with a frequency far in excess of their numbers.
86. For a theoretical interpretation of the role of receivers in organized crime, see Mary McIntosh, "Thieves and Fences: Markets and Power in Professional Crime."
87. Richard Cloward and Lloyd Ohlin, *Delinquency and Opportunity: A Theory of Delinquent Gangs*.
88. M. B. Clinard and D. J. Abbot, *Crime in Developing Countries: A Comparative Perspective*, p. 188.

3. The Labor Market, the Law, and Crime

1. Clark and Slack, *English Towns*, p. 78.
2. Coleman, "Labour in the English Economy," p. 304.
3. Gareth Stedman Jones, *Outcast London: A Study in the Relationship be-*

tween Classes in Victorian Society, demonstrates the importance of basing the analysis on the London casual labor market. See also Supple, *Commercial Crisis and Change*; Gould, *The Great Debasement*; Fisher, "Commercial Trends and Policy."

4. Fisher, "The Development of London as a Centre of Conspicuous Consumption," p. 202.
5. Pearl, *London and the Outbreak of the Puritan Revolution*, p. 16; Supple, *Commercial Crisis and Change*, pp. 38–57; 118–123.
6. Fisher, "London as an 'Engine of Economic Growth,'" p. 214; Nef, "The Progress of Technology."
7. Joan Parkes, *Travel in England in the Seventeenth Century*, Chapter 11.
8. Pearl, *London and the Outbreak of the Puritan Revolution*, p. 16.
9. Ibid., pp. 15–17. Gould, *The Great Debasement*, p. 125, also lists brewing, leather working, and soap making as growth industries.
10. E. P. Thompson, "Time, Work Discipline and Industrial Capitalism."
11. Hill, *The World Turned Upside Down*, pp. 43–44.
12. W. K. Jordan, *Philanthropy in England 1480–1660: A Study of the Changing Pattern of English Social Aspirations*, pp. 43–44.
13. Brindenbaugh, *Vexed and Troubled Englishmen*, p. 170.
14. Great Britain, Public Record Office, *Calendar of State Papers, Domestic, of the Reign of James I*, 41:537.
15. J. F. Pound, "An Elizabethan Census of the Poor."
16. Coleman, "Labour in the English Economy," p. 304; Hill, *The World Turned Upside Down*, p. 41.
17. George Rudé, *Hanoverian London 1774–1808*; Stedman Jones, *Outcast London*.
18. Fisher, "London as an 'Engine of Economic Growth,'" p. 215.
19. Brindenbaugh, *Vexed and Troubled Englishmen*, pp. 162–175.
20. Ibid.
21. Stone, "Social Mobility in England 1500–1700," pp. 28–29.
22. Quoted in Brindenbaugh, *Vexed and Troubled Englishmen*, p. 188.
23. Hill, *Reformation to Industrial Revolution*, pp. 92–96.
24. Ibid., p. 263.
25. Ibid., p. 262.
26. Ibid., pp. 82–89.
27. Hobsbawm, "The Crises of the Seventeenth Century."
28. Hill, *Reformation to Industrial Revolution*, pp. 82–89.
29. Brindenbaugh, *Vexed and Troubled Englishmen*, pp. 375–385; Kamen, *The Iron Century*, pp. 427–474.
30. Hobsbawm, "The Crises of the Seventeenth Century," pp. 50–58.
31. Brindenbaugh, *Vexed and Troubled Englishmen*, pp. 162–175; Beier, "Social Problems in Elizabethan London," pp. 214–216.
32. For the characteristics of the casual labor market see Stedman Jones, *Outcast London*, pp. 67–99.

33. Pound, *Poverty and Vagrancy*, p. 59.
34. Beier, "Vagrants and the Social Order," pp. 9–10; Clark, "The Migrant in Kentish Towns," pp. 123–125; Slack, "Vagrants and Vagrancy in England," pp. 365–366. This is also confirmed by Beier's work on Bridewell records. He notes that in London and Norwich young males accounted for about 70 percent of vagrants. By 1600 London was experiencing a large-scale problem of juvenile delinquency, including thieving from shops, market stalls, and the purses and pockets of passersby. "Social Problems in Elizabethan London," p. 210.
35. P. Slack, "Poverty and Politics in Salisbury 1597–1666," pp. 166–168.
36. Hill, *Reformation to Industrial Revolution*, p. 263.
37. Conyers Read, ed., *William Lombarde and Local Government*, p. 169.
38. See E. M. Leonard, *The Early History of English Poor Relief*, for an informative survey.
39. Aydelotte, *Elizabethan Rogues and Vagabonds*, pp. 56–75.
40. Pound, *Poverty and Vagrancy*, p. 59.
41. D. Johnson, *Southwark and the City*, pp. 138–139.
42. Brindenbaugh, *Vexed and Troubled Englishmen*, p. 391.
43. Slack, "Vagrants and Vagrancy in England," p. 366.
44. Brindenbaugh, *Vexed and Troubled Englishmen*, p. 169.
45. Ibid., p. 170; Hecht, *The Domestic Servant Class*.
46. Brindenbaugh, *Vexed and Troubled Englishmen*, p. 164.
47. McIntosh, *The Organization of Crime*, Chapter 3.
48. See Samaha, *Law and Order*, pp. 43–66 for an assessment; and Paul Rock, "Law, Order and Power in Late Seventeenth and Early Eighteenth Century England."
49. W. R. D. Jones, *The Tudor Commonwealth 1529–1559*, p. 216.
50. Ibid., p. 227.
51. Hill, *The World Turned Upside Down*, p. 39.
52. Quoted in ibid., p. 128.
53. Quoted in ibid., p. 127.
54. Ibid., pp. 58–64; and also Rock, "Law, Order and Power," p. 244.
55. Quoted in Jones, *The Tudor Commonwealth 1529–1559*, p. 63.
56. Michel Foucault, *Discipline and Punishment: The Birth of the Prison*, pp. 73–103; Rock, "Law, Order and Power."
57. Samaha, *Law and Order*, p. 55.
58. Thomas Dekker, quoted in Judges, ed., *The Elizabethan Underworld*, p. viii.
59. G. W. Oxley, *Poor Relief in England and Wales 1601–1834*, p. 15.
60. Sidney Webb and Beatrice Webb, *English Poor Law History*, pt. 1: *The Old Poor Law*; and Leonard, *The Early History of English Poor Relief*.
61. W. R. D. Jones, *The Tudor Commonwealth 1529–1559*, Chapter 7.
62. Ibid., p. 109.
63. Jordan, *Philanthropy in England*, pp. 54–56.

64. Leonard, *The Early History of English Poor Relief,* pp. 4–6.
65. W. R. D. Jones, *The Tudor Commonwealth 1529–1559,* pp. 120–121.
66. Ibid.
67. Leonard, *The Early History of English Poor Relief,* pp. 25–26.
68. W. R. D. Jones, *The Tudor Commonwealth 1529–1559,* p. 119.
69. Ibid., pp. 128–129.
70. Ibid., p. 106.
71. Beier, "Vagrants and the Social Order," pp. 26–29.
72. Aydelotte, *Elizabethan Rogues and Vagabonds,* p. 58.
73. Ibid., p. 59.
74. Ibid., p. 63.
75. Ibid., pp. 68–69.
76. Pound, *Poverty and Vagrancy,* pp. 47–48.
77. Oxley, *Poor Relief,* p. 2.
78. C. Hill, *Society and Puritanism in Pre-Revolutionary England,* pp. 251–287.
79. M. James, *Social Problems and Policy during the Puritan Revolution 1640–1660,* pp. 241–302.
80. Slack, "Vagrants and Vagrancy in England"; Beier, "Vagrants and the Social Order"; James, *Social Problems;* Michael Weisser, *Crime and Punishment in Early Modern Europe.*
81. James, *Social Problems,* pp. 241–243; and W. R. D. Jones, *The Tudor Commonwealth 1529–1559,* pp. 123–132.
82. See James, *Social Problems,* pp. 241–302, for an informative assessment.
83. Hill, *Society and Puritanism in Pre-Revolutionary England,* pp. 273–277.
84. Sir William Petty's will quoted in ibid., p. 279.
85. Dod and Cleaver, quoted in ibid., p. 275.
86. Thomas Harman, "A Caveat for Common Cursitors," p. 63.
87. C. Hill, "The Many Headed Monster"; Weisser, *Crime and Punishment.*
88. Hill, *Society and Puritanism,* Chapter 7; and Lawrence Stone, "State Control in Sixteenth Century England," p. 115.
89. Quoted in Aydelotte, *Elizabethan Rogues and Vagrants,* p. 110.
90. Brindenbaugh, *Vexed and Troubled Englishmen,* Chapter 5.
91. Ibid., pp. 390–391.
92. See ibid., Chapters 5 and 10, for a survey.
93. Keith Thomas, *Religion and the Decline of Magic: Studies in Popular Beliefs in Sixteenth and Seventeenth Century England,* p. 18.
94. Quoted in Aydelotte, *Elizabethan Rogues and Vagrants,* p. 104.
95. Brindenbaugh, *Vexed and Troubled Englishmen,* p. 197.
96. Aydelotte, *Elizabethan Rogues and Vagrants,* pp. 105–107.
97. Ibid.
98. Ibid.
99. By 1633 there existed some 211 taverns in the city and liberties and 11 in the ward of Bishopsgate. Brindenbaugh, *Vexed and Troubled Englishmen,* pp. 197–198.

100. Aydelotte, *Elizabethan Rogues and Vagrants*, p. 107.
101. Ibid., pp. 107–109.
102. Ibid., p. 108.
103. Ibid., p. 103.
104. Ibid.
105. Hill, "The Many Headed Monster."
106. Leonard, *The Early History of English Poor Relief*, pp. 238–240.
107. Hill, *The World Turned Upside Down*, Chapter 5.
108. Leonard, *The Early History of English Poor Relief*; and James, *Social Problems*.
109. J. S. Cockburn, *A History of English Assizes, 1558–1714*. For comparative European examples see Bruce Lenman and Geoffrey Parker, "The State, the Community and the Criminal Law in Early Modern Europe."
110. Samaha, *Law and Order*, p. 45.
111. Ibid., pp. 45–48; J. H. Baker, "Criminal Courts and Procedure at Common Law 1550–1800"; Lenman and Parker, "The State, the Community and the Criminal Law."
112. Stated by Justice Hext in A. Rowse, ed., *The England of Elizabeth*, p. 348.
113. Cockburn, "The Nature and Incidence of Crime," pp. 49–71; T. C. Curtis, "Quarter Sessions Appearances and Their Background: A Seventeenth Century Regional Study"; J. A. Sharpe, "Enforcing the Law in the Seventeenth Century English Village"; M. J. Ingram, "Communities and Courts: Law and Disorder in Early Seventeenth Century Wiltshire."
114. Samaha, *Law and Order*, Chapter 2, from which the following analysis is drawn. Various informal methods of social discipline also existed. Employers could fire, physically punish, extract promises from, and pardon their employees. This of course would have resulted in many instances of indictable acts being handled by means other than prosecution.
115. Ibid., pp. 117–118.
116. Ibid., p. 53.
117. Ibid., p. 55.
118. Ibid.
119. Ibid., p. 57.
120. Ibid., pp. 58–59.
121. Ibid., p. 63.
122. Ibid., p. 62.
123. C. B. Firth, "Benefit of Clergy in the Time of Edward IV."
124. Samaha, *Law and Order*, p. 60; A. L. Cross, "The English Criminal Law and Benefit of Clergy during the Eighteenth and Early Nineteenth Centuries."
125. Samaha, *Law and Order*, pp. 60–61.

126. Ibid., pp. 61–62.
127. Ibid. It should be noted that very often being freed by benefit of clergy did entail some other form of punishment, less severe, but including transportation. See Cross, "The English Criminal Law." Also, impressment was used by city and court authorities to rid London of vagrants and criminals, especially after 1618. See Beier, "Social Problems in Elizabethan London," pp. 219–220.
128. Hill, *The World Turned Upside Down*, p. 39.
129. Ibid., p. 33.
130. In particular, Beier, "Vagrants and the Social Order."
131. Philip Jones, *Certaine Sermons preached of late at Cicetor*.
132. Richard Younge, *The Poores Advocate*, Chapter 14, p. 9.
133. Harman, "Caveat for Common Cursitors," p. 61.
134. W. Harrison, *The Description of England*, 1968 ed., p. 194.
135. Quoted in Cockburn, "The Incidence and Nature of Crime," p. 60.
136. Clark, "The Migrant in Kentish Towns," pp. 144–145.
137. Cockburn, "The Incidence and Nature of Crime," p. 60.
138. W. K. Jordan, *The Charities of London*, p. 81.
139. Great Britain, Public Record Office, *Calendar of State Papers, Domestic, of the Reign of Charles I*, 48:433.
140. Quoted in Brindenbaugh, *Vexed and Troubled Englishmen*, p. 388.
141. Kamen, *The Iron Century*, pp. 444–446.
142. See Awdeley, "The Fraternity of Vagabonds," pp. 53–60 for a listing of types of beggars.
143. Kamen, *The Iron Century*, pp. 444–446.
144. As is the tendency in Aydelotte, *Elizabethan Rogues and Vagabonds*, Chapters 2 and 4; and Salgado, *The Elizabethan Underworld*, Chapter 1.

4. Criminal Areas

1. See Brindenbaugh, *Vexed and Troubled Englishmen*, Chapter 5; and Rock, "Law, Order and Power," for ideas on the organization of criminal areas.
2. Kamen, *The Iron Century*, pp. 428–431.
3. Brett-James, *The Growth of Stuart London*.
4. I. D. Thornley, "The Destruction of Sanctuary"; Kempe, *Historical Notices*.
5. Kempe's *Historical Notices* reports on a series of conflicts between church and state and provides some clues about the social composition of the area as well as the life style of its inhabitants.
6. Thornley, "The Destruction of Sanctuary," p. 184; Rock, "Law, Order and Power," p. 246.

7. But, as Thornley argues, these districts maintained a semblance of their rights and were often not effectively managed by the state. See Thornley, "The Destruction of Sanctuary."
8. Brett-James, *The Growth of Stuart London*; William Dugdale, *The History of St. Paul's Cathedral*, pp. 16–18.
9. As quoted in L. F. Salzman, *English Life in the Middle Ages*, p. 230.
10. W. H. Overall and H. C. Overall, eds., *Analytical Index to Remembrancia 1579–1664*, p. 426.
11. Pearl, *London and the Outbreak of the Puritan Revolution*, pp. 31–34.
12. Henry Elliot Malden, ed., *The Victoria History of the Counties of England, Surrey*, vol. 1, pp. 137–144.
13. Pearl, *London and the Outbreak of the Puritan Revolution*, pp. 31–37.
14. Henry Chettle, as quoted in C. T. Onions, ed., *Shakespeare's England*, vol. 2, p. 179.
15. Brett-James, *The Growth of Stuart London.*
16. F. Braudel, *Capitalism and Material Life 1400–1800*, p. 430.
17. Ibid.
18. Quoted in Brindenbaugh, *Vexed and Troubled Englishmen*, p. 185. See also M. J. Power, "East London Housing in the Seventeenth Century."
19. Mary St. Clare Byrne, *Elizabethan Life in Town and Country*, p. 52.
20. Brindenbaugh, *Vexed and Troubled Englishmen*, p. 185.
21. John G. Rule, "Wrecking and Coastal Plunder"; Cal Winslow, "Sussex Smugglers"; E. P. Thompson, *Whigs and Hunters: The Origin of the Black Act.*
22. Kamen, *The Iron Century*, pp. 444–446.
23. A word of caution: the major difficulty is that evidence is fragmentary and of uncertain and uneven reliability. Much of my reconstruction and argument is based on descriptions and assessments left by contemporaries and on local histories. We are dealing with intangible, unmeasurable evidence of questionable quality. Nor are changes over time clear. Nevertheless, the sifting of slender evidence and the accumulation of general impressions do advance our knowledge even if the portrayal is somewhat circumscribed and static.
24. Quoted in R. M. Wingent, *Historical Notes on the Borough of Southwark*, pp. 5–6.
25. Fynes Moryson, *Itinerary of Ten Years Travel . . .* , vol. 4, p. 174.
26. John Stow, *The Survey of London*, p. 359; Brett-James, *The Growth of Stuart London*, p. 57.
27. Burford, *Bawds and Lodgings*, Chapter 11.
28. O. Manning and W. Bray, *History and Antiquities of Surrey*, vol. 3, pp. 530–531.
29. W. B. Rye, *England as Seen by Foreigners in the Days of Elizabeth and James I*, pp. 46–49, 87–89, 123–124.

30. Stow, *The Survey of London*, pp. 10–66.
31. Burford, *Bawds and Lodgings*, Chapter 11.
32. William Rendle and Philip Norman, *The Inns of Old Southwark and Their Associations*.
33. Ibid., pp. 256–283.
34. Wingent, *Historical Notes*, p. 58.
35. Rendle and Norman, *The Inns of Old Southwark*, pp. 339–341.
36. Ibid., Chapter 11.
37. D. Johnson, *Southwark and the City*, pp. 61–75, 332–333.
38. Wingent, *Historical Notes*, p. 14; John Timbs, *Curiosities of London*, pp. 508–509.
39. Rendle and Norman, *The Inns of Old Southwark*, pp. 256–283.
40. Malden, ed., *The Victoria History*, vol. 1, p. 382.
41. Sir Roger Manwood, chief baron of the Exchequer, quoted in Cockburn, "The Nature and Incidence of Crime," pp. 64–67.
42. James Clavell, *Recantations of an Ill Led Life . . .*
43. Stow, *The Survey of London*, pp. 353–355.
44. Robert Greene, "The Second Part of Cony Catching," p. 165.
45. Timbs, *Curiosities of London*, pp. 306, 766–777; W. G. Bell, *Fleet Street in Seven Centuries*, pp. 280–281.
46. See Thomas Shadwell, "The Squire of Alsatia," for a dramatist's representation of the area.
47. Bell, *Fleet Street*, pp. 280–284.
48. Ibid., p. 285.
49. Ibid., pp. 284–285.
50. Ibid., pp. 293–296.
51. Ibid.
52. Shadwell, "The Squire of Alsatia."
53. *The Life and Death of Mrs. Mary Frith commonly called Moll Cutpurse.*
54. Stow, *The Survey of London*, p. 376.
55. Lupton, *London and the Country*, pp. 50–55.
56. Greene, "The Second Part of Cony Catching," p. 165.
57. Brett-James, *The Growth of Stuart London*, Chapter 7. See also Power, "East London Housing."
58. Lupton, *London and the Country*, pp. 50–55.
59. George Whetstone, *A Mirror for Magistrates of Cyties which is Added a Touchstone for the Times*, pp. 35–37.
60. Henry Mayhew, *London Labour and the London Poor*, vol. 1, pp. 246–257.
61. A. H. French, Marybel Moore, Jocelyn Oatley, M. J. Power, D. Summers, and S. C. Tongue, "The Population of Stepney in the Early Seventeenth Century."
62. David Cressey, "Occupations, Migration and Literacy in East London 1580–1640." One estimate showing the increase in numbers in the new

suburbs places the population of the East London parishes of Stepney and Whitechapel at 7,000 in the 1570s, 21,800 in the first decade of the seventeenth century, and 59,000 in the 1670s. See M. J. Power, "The Urban Development of East London, 1550 to 1700."

63. Quoted in E. K. W. Ryan, *Cripplegate, Finsbury and Moorfields*, p. 25.
64. Ibid., pp. 26–27.
65. Stow, *The Survey of London*, pp. 382–383.
66. Henry Chettle, "Kind-Hartes Dreame: Containing Five Apparitions with Their Invectives against Abuses Reigning."
67. Ryan, *Cripplegate, Finsbury and Moorfields*, p. 23.
68. Lupton, *London and the Country*, pp. 50–55.
69. Walker, "A Manifest Detection of Dice Play," p. 41.
70. Greene, "A Notable Discovery of Cozenage," pp. 123–124; Thomas Dekker, "O Per Se O," pp. 381–382.
71. Brett-James, *The Growth of Stuart London*, p. 129.
72. Quoted in G. Laurence Gomme, *London*, p. 225.
73. Quoted in J. E. Smith, *Local Government in Westminster*, pp. 164–166.
74. Kempe, *Historical Notices*, especially the appendix.
75. T. Fuller, *The Beggars Brotherhood*, p. 123.
76. A picture of this building survives in the frontispiece of Nicholas Goodman, *Hollands Leaguer*.
77. E. J. Hobsbawm, *Bandits*, p. 20–22.
78. For a useful introduction to the activities of the highwaymen, see J. L. Raynor and G. T. Crook, eds., *The Complete Newgate Calendar*, especially the life histories in vols. 1 and 2; Cockburn, "The Nature and Incidence of Crime," pp. 64–66.
79. J. Binney, "Thieves and Swindlers," vol. 4, pp. 273–392.
80. Thomas Beames, *The Rookeries of London*, p. 41.
81. Brindenbaugh, *Vexed and Troubled Englishmen*, pp. 181–183.
82. D. Cressey, "Occupations, Migration and Literacy," pp. 53–60. For a discussion of urban villages in London see Power, "The Urban Development of East London."
83. D. Cressey, "Occupations, Migration and Literacy," p. 50.
84. Ibid., p. 52.
85. This is argued by Rock in, "Law, Order and Power," and I have developed his ideas.
86. George Renard, *Guilds in the Middle Ages*, Chapter 4; George Unwin, *Industrial Organization in the Sixteenth and Seventeenth Centuries*; Norman Nymer, *English Town Crafts*.
87. Stow, *The Survey of London*, pp. 10–66.
88. Renard, *Guilds in the Middle Ages*, Chapter 4; Unwin, *Industrial Organization in the Sixteenth and Seventeenth Centuries*, Chapters 8 and 9.

89. A. H. Ditchfield, quoted in Nymer, *English Town Crafts*, p. 3.
90. George Unwin, *The Guilds and Companies of London*, p. 98.
91. Nymer, *English Town Crafts*, p. 3.
92. Kamen, *The Iron Century*, pp. 436–446.
93. Greene, "The Second Part of Cony Catching," pp. 162–172; Awdeley, "The Fraternity of Vagabonds," pp. 51–60; Thomas Dekker, "The Bellman of London," pp. 303–311.
94. See in particular Harman, "A Caveat for Common Cursitors," pp. 61–118; *The Devil's Cabinet Broke Open*, especially the section called "A relation of the laws, customs and subtleties of housebreakers, pickpockets."
95. McIntosh, *The Organization of Crime*, Chapter 3.
96. Pierre Goubert, *The Ancien Regime in French Society 1600–1750*, pp. 103–107.
97. Kamen, *The Iron Century*, pp. 444–445.
98. Goubert, *The Ancien Regime*, p. 104.
99. See Clinard and Abbott, *Crime in Developing Countries*, for a general review.
100 *The Devil's Cabinet Broke Open*.
101. Thompson, *Whigs and Hunters*, p. 248.
102. Ibid.
103. Johnson, *Southwark and the City*, pp. 332–333.
104. Ibid.
105. Thompson, *Whigs and Hunters*, p. 248.
106. R. Steele, ed., *A Bibliography of Royal Proclamations of the Tudor and Stuart Sovereigns . . . 1485–1714*, nos. 511, 701, 739, 871, 910, 1124, 1184.
107. D. H. Bowler, *London Sessions Records 1605–1685*, Introduction.
108. Ibid.
109. Patrick Pringle, *Hue and Cry: The Birth of the British Police*.
110. Luke Hutton, "The Black Dog of Newgate," pp. 265–291.
111. McIntosh, "Thieves and Fences," pp. 256–261.
112. Stow, *The Survey of London*, pp. 106–108.
113. City of London, the Corporation of London, *The Corporation of London, Its Origins, Constitutional Powers and Duties*, pp. 40–42.
114. Pringle, *Hue and Cry*, Chapters 1 and 2.
115. Goodman, *Hollands Leaguer*.
116. City of London, *The Corporation of London*, pp. 28–29, 40.
117. Pearl, *London and the Outbreak of the Puritan Revolution*, p. 58.
118. Ibid., p. 61.
119. City of London, *The Corporation of London*, pp. 42–43.
120. Robert Brenner, "The Civil War Politics of London's Merchant Community."

121. F. F. Foster, *The Politics of Stability: A Portrait of the Rulers in Elizabethan London*, pp. 160–162.
122. Pearl, *London and the Outbreak of the Puritan Revolution*, Chapter 1.
123. Brenner, "Civil War Politics."
124. Foster, *The Politics of Stability*, p. 161.

5. Coercive Institutions

1. Hill, *The World Turned Upside Down*, Chapter 5.
2. R. B. Pugh, *Imprisonment in Medieval England*, Chapters 1 and 2; Penry Williams, "The Northern Borderland under the Early Stuarts."
3. Cockburn, *The History of English Assizes*, p. 40.
4. D. J. Dyos and D. H. Aldcroft, *British Transportation*, p. 21.
5. See F. G. Emmison, *Elizabethan Life: Disorder*.
6. Malden, ed., *The Victoria History*, vol. 1, p. 382.
7. Cockburn, *The History of English Assizes*, pp. 61–62.
8. Everitt, "Social Mobility in Early Modern England," p. 59.
9. Parkes, *Travel in England*, pp. 49–51.
10. G. T. Salisbury-Jones, *Street Life in Medieval England*, pp. 126–166.
11. Julian Cornwall, "Evidence of Population Mobility in the Seventeenth Century," p. 152.
12. French et al., "The Population of Stepney in the Early Seventeenth Century"; E. J. Buckatzsch, "Places of Origins of a Group of Immigrants into Sheffield 1624–1799."
13. D. Cressey, "Occupations, Migration and Literacy."
14. E. A. Wrigley, "A Sample Model of London's Importance in Changing English Society and Economy 1650–1750," pp. 48–50.
15. Hill, *The World Turned Upside Down*, Chapter 5.
16. Brindenbaugh, *Vexed and Troubled Englishmen*, pp. 385–392.
17. This is discussed in T. A. Critchley, *A History of Police in England and Wales 900–1966*; David Rumbelow, *I Spy Blue: The Police and Crime in the City of London from Elizabeth I to Victoria*.
18. Critchley, *A History of Police*, pp. 25–28.
19. Ibid., Chapter 5.
20. W. L. Melville Lee, *A History of Police in England*, p. 99.
21. Great Britain, Public Record Office, *Calendar of State Papers, Domestic, of the Reign of Elizabeth and James I*, Addende 1580–1625, p. 547.
22. George Meriton, *A Guide for Constables, Churchwardens, Overseers of the Poor . . .* ; William Lombarde, *Of the Duties of Constables Within the City of London*, pp. 85–89; T. G. Barnes, *Somerset Assize Orders 1629–1640*; T. G. Barnes, *Somerset 1625–1640: A County's Government during the "Personal Rule"*; A. Hassel Smith, *County and Court: Government and Pol-*

itics in Norfolk, 1588–1603. For a more general and somewhat uncomplimentary assessment of policing practices see E. P. Cheyney, *A History of England from the Defeat of the Armada to the Death of Elizabeth,* vol. 2, pp. 403–408.

23. Brindenbaugh, *Vexed and Troubled Englishmen,* pp. 390–392.
24. Rumbelow, *I Spy Blue,* Chapter 3.
25. Stow, *The Survey of London,* p. 108.
26. City of London, *The Corporation of London,* pp. 126–127. Sharpe notes that the ethos of the constable involved minimum interference from agencies outside the parish. "Enforcing the Law," p. 108.
27. Rumbelow, *I Spy Blue,* Chapters 2 and 3.
28. Quoted in Samaha, *Law and Order,* pp. 86–87.
29. City of London, the Corporation of London, Guildhall Records Office, *Journal of Court of Common Council,* 10 October 1663, "An Act of Common Council for the Better Ordering of the Night Watch."
30. City of London, the Corporation of London, Guildhall Records Office, *Watch and Ward Miscellaneous Manuscripts,* Box 245, "The Humble Petition of Robert Wilkins."
31. Quoted in Samaha, *Law and Order,* p. 87.
32. Samuel Rid, "Martin Markall Beadle of Bridewell," pp. 390–391; see also Thomas Dekker, "Lantern and Candlelight."
33. Quoted in Salgado, *The Elizabethan Underworld,* p. 165.
34. See G. B. Harrison, *The Elizabethan Journals 1591–1603,* 1595, pp. 32–33; Lindsay Boynton, "The Tudor Provost-Marshal."
35. Thomas Allen, *The History and Antiquities of London, Westminster, Southwark, and Parts Adjacent,* pp. 280–281.
36. Ibid., p. 281.
37. Great Britain, Public Record Office, *Acts of the Privy Council,* Elizabeth (I), 25:330.
38. Ibid., p. 438, 22.
39. Ibid., p. 324; Great Britain, Public Record Office, *Acts of the Privy Council,* Elizabeth (I), 26:23; 27:56, 92, 96–97; 29:128, 140.
40. Quoted in Judges, ed., *The Elizabethan UnderWorld,* pp. xxxviii–xxxix.
41. J. C. Jeafferson, ed., *Middlesex Sessions Rolls,* vol. 1, p. 190.
42. Great Britain, Public Record Office, *Acts of Privy Council,* Elizabeth (I), 24:30–31, 193; 27:427–428; 29:128, 414–415.
43. William Fleetwood, quoted in R. H. Tawney and E. Power, eds., *Tudor Economic Documents,* vol. 2, p. 335.
44. Great Britain, Public Record Office, *Acts of Privy Council,* Elizabeth (I), 29:128, 140; Boynton, "The Tudor Provost-Marshal."
45. City of London, the Corporation of, Guildhall Records Office, *Repertoires of the Court of Aldermen,* vol. 23, fol. 548.

46. Ibid., vol. 26, fol. 1979.
47. Ibid., vol. 34, fol. 125 and 183.
48. Allen, *The History and Antiquities*, p. 334; Great Britain, Public Record Office, *Calendar of State Papers, Domestic, of the Reign of James I*, 42:244.
49. Samaha, *Law and Order*, Chapter 3.
50. City of London, the Corporation of, Guildhall Records Office, *Lord Mayor's Proclamations*, 30 September 1603.
51. The quality of policing is discussed in Rumbelow, *I Spy Blue*, particularly Chapter 3.
52. Ibid.
53. City of London, the Corporation of, Guildhall Library, *King's Proclamations*, 17 February 1628, 17 September 1630, 12 February 1634, 25 November 1642.
54. City of London, the Corporation of, Guildhall Library, *Miscellaneous Proclamations*, London 1649. "Instructions to be Observed by the Several Justices of the Peace in the Several Counties within the Commonwealth for the Better Prevention of Robberies, Burglaries and Other Outrages."
55. Great Britain, Public Record Office, *King's Proclamations*, 25 May 1627, "A Proclamation for the Better Execution of the Office of His Majesties Exchanger, and Reformation of Sundry Abuses and Frauds Practiced upon His Majesties Coins."
56. Ibid.
57. City of London, the Corporation of, Guildhall Library, *Miscellaneous Proclamations*, 8 November 1649, "Two Orders of Parliament: The one, Appointing the Giving of Ten Pounds to Every One who shall bring in a High-way-man; The Other: Referring to the Council of State to give Reprieves to Persons Guilty of Robberies, if they Shall Discover any of their Accomplices"; see also City of London, the Corporation of, Guildhall Library, *Miscellaneous Proclamations*, 10 January 1650, "Two Orders of Parliament Concerning the Apprehending of Thieves."
58. City of London, the Corporation of, Guildhall Library, *Miscellaneous Proclamations*, 8 November 1649, "Two Orders of Parliament." See also City of London, the Corporation of, Guildhall Library, *Miscellaneous Proclamations*, 10 January 1650, "Two Orders of Parliament."
59. Great Britain, Public Record Office, *King's Proclamations*, 25 May 1627.
60. Steven Spitzer and Andrew Scull, "Privatization and Capitalist Development: The Case of the Private Police."
61. Steven Spitzer and Andrew Scull, "Social Control in Historical Perspective: From Private to Public Responses to Crime."
62. K. Swart, *The Sale of Offices in the Seventeenth Century*; J. Hurstfield, "Political Corruption in Modern England: The Historian's Problem"; T. E.

Hartley, "Under-Sheriffs and Bailiffs in Some English Shrievalties 1580 to 1625"; C. H. Karraker, *The Seventeenth Century Sheriff*.

63. MacCaffrey, "Place and Patronage."
64. The following discussion is taken from Rumbelow, *I Spy Blue*, pp. 50–51.
65. City of London, the Corporation of, Guildhall Library, *Miscellaneous Proclamations*, by the Protector, 9 August 1655, "A Proclamation Commanding a Speedy and Due Execution of the Laws."
66. City of London, The Corporation of, Guildhall Library, *Lord Mayor's Proclamations*, 20 January 1656, "A Proclamation Against Neglect of Executing Laws Against Rogues."
67. L. Boynton, *The Elizabethan Militia*.
68. Hill, *Reformation to Industrial Revolution*, pp. 25–43.
69. John Hale, "War and Public Opinion in the Fifteenth and Sixteenth Centuries"; Michael Roberts, *The Military Revolution 1560–1660*.
70. Lawrence Stone, *The Crisis of the Aristocracy 1553–1641*, pp. 199–270.
71. Ibid., p. 215.
72. Ibid., pp. 224–226.
73. Cockburn, "The Nature and Incidence of Crime," pp. 58–59.
74. W. Harrison, *The Description of England*, 1968 ed., pp. 237–238.
75. V. G. Kiernan, "Foreign Mercenaries and Absolute Monarchy," pp. 77–78.
76. Hill, *Reformation to Industrial Revolution*, p. 30.
77. Kiernan, "Foreign Mercenaries," p. 73.
78. G. R. Aylmer, "Office Holding," pp. 81–86.
79. Stone, *The Crisis of the Aristocracy*, p. 259.
80. Boynton, *The Elizabethan Militia*, pp. 244–297.
81. Ibid., pp. 290–293; Barnes, *Somerset 1625–1640*, pp. 144–147, 339–342, 401–402.
82. Brian Manning, *The English People and the English Revolution 1640–1649*.
83. Stone, *The Crisis of the Aristocracy*, J. S. Morrill, "Mutiny and Discontent in English Provincial Armies, 1645–1647."
84. Boynton, *The Elizabethan Militia*, p. 249.
85. Morrill, "Mutiny and Discontent," presents a full analysis of how militias could become problems for social control.
86. J. Western, *The English Militia in the Eighteenth Century*, pp. 70–73.

6. The Canting Crew

1. Aydelotte, *Elizabethan Rogues and Vagabonds*; McPeck, *The Black Book of Knaves and Unthrifts*; Salgado, *The Elizabethan Underworld*; P. Linebaugh, "The Ordinary of Newgate and His Account."
2. Sheppard, *The History of Street Literature*.

3. For an example of this tendency see Beier, "Vagrants and the Social Order."
4. The best reconstruction of unofficial worlds is in Peter Burke, *Popular Culture in Early Modern Europe.*
5. Kamen, *The Iron Century*, pp. 436–446.
6. C. J. Ribton-Turner, *A History of Vagrants and Vagrancy*; J. P. Clebert, *The Gypsies.*
7. Harman, "A Caveat for Common Cursitors," pp. 113–114.
8. Ibid.
9. Greene, "A Notable Discovery of Cozenage," p. 133.
10. See Shadwell, "The Squire of Alsatia," for an example.
11. Maurice Merleau-Ponty, *Signs*, Chapter 2.
12. Linebaugh, "The Ordinary of Newgate," pp. 246–269.
13. Greene, "A Notable Discovery of Cozenage," p. 136; Greene, "The Second Part of Cony Catching," pp. 149–50; Rid, "Martin Markall Beadle," p. 395.
14. David Maurer, "The Argot of the Dice Gambler"; David Maurer, *Whiz Mob: A Correlation of the Technical Argot of Pickpockets with Their Behaviour Patterns.*
15. Mary McIntosh, "Changes in the Organization of Thieving," pp. 98–133.
16. J. S. Cockburn, "Early Modern Assize Records as Historical Evidence," pp. 223–224.
17. Linebaugh, "The Ordinary of Newgate," pp. 265–266.
18. Aydelotte, *Elizabethan Rogues and Vagabonds*, Chapter 6; Dobb, *Life and Conditions in London Prisons*, Appendix.
19. R. Kwant, *Phenomenology of Language*, pp. 143–145.
20. F. W. Chandler, *The Literature of Roguery*, vol. 1.
21. See in particular the works of Dekker, Nashe, and Greene.
22. Hans-Georg Gadamer, "The Historicity of Understanding."
23. P. Rock, "Some Problems of Interpretative Historiography."
24. Gadamer, "The Historicity of Understanding," p. 128.
25. Rock, "Some Problems of Interpretative Historiography."
26. McIntosh, *The Organization of Crime*, pp. 18–27, 35–41; John L. McMullan, "Criminal Organization in Sixteenth and Seventeenth Century London."
27. Greene, "A Notable Discovery of Cozenage," pp. 135–136; Greene, "The Second Part of Cony Catching," pp. 149–150.
28. Greene, "The Second Part of Cony Catching," pp. 162–165.
29. Ibid.
30. B. E., *The Canting Crew*; Captain Alexander Smith, "The Thieves' New Canting Dictionary," pp. 201–210.
31. Robert Greene, "A Disputation between a He Cony Catcher and a She Cony Catcher," pp. 211–212.

32. Greene, "The Second Part of Cony Catching," p. 162.
33. Greene, "A Disputation," pp. 211–212; *The Wandering Whore,* no. 3.
34. Greene, "A Notable Discovery of Cozenage," pp. 206–207. Crossbiting appears as a precursor to the "buttock and twang" of the eighteenth century. Gerald Howson, *Thief-Taker General; The Rise and Fall of Jonathan Wild,* pp. 44–48.
35. Greene, "A Notable Discovery of Cozenage," pp. 139–149; Greene, "A Disputation," pp. 218–219; *The Wandering Whore,* no. 2.
36. Captain Alexander Smith, "The Thieves' Grammar," pp. 594–596. A. Smith, "The Thieves' New Canting Dictionary," p. 201.
37. Greene, "The Second Part of Cony Catching," pp. 175–178.
38. For present-day similarities see Neal Shrover, "The Social Organization of Burglary"; and Peter Letkenmann, *Crime as Work.*
39. Whetstone, *A Mirror for Magistrates,* pp. 594–595; B. E., *The Canting Crew;* A. Smith, "The Thieves' Grammar," pp. 594–595; *The Devil's Cabinet Broke Open.*
40. A. Smith, "The Thieves' Grammar," p. 595.
41. Greene, "The Second Part of Cony Catching," pp. 170–172.
42. Walker, "A Manifest Detection of Dice Play," pp. 47–50; Greene, "A Notable Discovery of Cozenage," pp. 119–134; *The Holborn Hector;* J. Aberndoerfer, *An Anatomye of the true Physition and Counterfeit Mountebanke.*
43. "Thieving Detected," reprinted in G. Armitage, *The History of the Bow Street Runners,* Appendix 2.
44. Walker, "A Manifest Detection of Dice Play," pp. 40–42; Whetstone, *A Mirror for Magistrates.*
45. *The Country Gentleman's Vade Mecum.*
46. *Memoirs of the Life and Death of the Famous Madam Charlton.*
47. Walker, "A Manifest Detection of Dice Play," pp. 41–42.
48. Charles Cotton, "The Compleat Gamester or Instructions on How to Play Billiards, Trucks, Bowls, and Chess."
49. Ibid.
50. Ibid.
51. Awdeley, "The Fraternity of Vagabonds," pp. 53, 55; Harman, "A Caveat for Common Cursitors," pp. 81, 84, 93.
52. Dekker, "O Per Se O," p. 374.
53. Ibid., p. 375.
54. Henry T. Rhodes, *The Craft of Forgery,* pp. 6–19.
55. *The Cheating Sollicitor Cheated.*
56. *The Arraignment, Tryal and Condemnation of Frost, the Broker;* Great Britain, Public Record Office, King's Proclamation, *A Proclamation for Restraint of the Exportation, Waste, and Consumption of Coine and Bullion,* 11 June 1622; *A Proclamation for Restraint of Consumption of Coyne and Bullion and Deceitful Making of Gold Thread,* 18 January 1635. For a discus-

sion of the organization of counterfeiting see Alan Macfarlane, *The Justice and the Mare's Ale: Law and Disorder in Seventeenth Century England*. For a later example see John Styles, "Our Traiterous Money-Makers: The Yorkshire Coiners and the Law 1760–83."

57. Greene, "The Second Part of Cony Catching," p. 165.
58. Whetstone, "A Mirror for Magistrates," pp. 35–37.
59. Quoted in Tawney and Power, eds., *Tudor Economic Documents*, pp. 335–356.
60. Quoted in Aydelotte, *Elizabethan Rogues and Vagabonds*, pp. 164–165.
61. Greene, "A Disputation," p. 226.
62. Quoted in Aydelotte, *Elizabethan Rogues and Vagabonds*, pp. 167–173.
63. Greene, "The Second Part of Cony Catching," pp. 171–172.
64. Quoted in Aydelotte, *Elizabethan Rogues and Vagabonds*, p. 164.
65. Greene, "The Second Part of Cony Catching," p. 171.
66. Ibid., pp. 171–172.
67. Dekker, "O Per Se O," p. 367.
68. *Some Account of a Remarkable old House formerly existing in Chick Lane, Clerkenwell, with a description of the various rooms*.
69. Greene, "The Second Part of Cony Catching," p. 171.
70. Aydelotte, *Elizabethan Rogues and Vagabonds*, p. 81.
71. Harman, "A Caveat for Common Cursitors," p. 71.
72. Robert Greene, "The Third Part of Cony Catching," p. 186.
73. Greene, "The Second Part of Cony Catching," pp. 166–167; Greene, "The Third Part of Cony Catching," pp. 195–196.
74. Ivy Pinchbeck and Margaret Hewitt, *Children in English Society*, vol. 2, pp. 91–104.
75. Walker, "A Manifest Detection of Dice Play," pp. 36–43.
76. Reginald Scot, *A Discovery of Witchcraft*.
77. Quoted in Tawney and Power, eds., *Tudor Economic Documents*, pp. 335–336.
78. Ibid., p. 335.
79. See Raynor and Crook, eds., *The Complete Newgate Calendar*, vol. 2, for a description of his life history.
80. Pinchbeck and Hewitt, *Children in English Society*, vol. 2, pp. 91–104.
81. Robert C. Johnson, "The Transportation of Vagrant Children from London to Virginia 1618–1622."
82. *The Life and Death of Mary Frith*.
83. See Raynor and Crook, eds., *The Complete Newgate Calendar*, vol. 2, for various histories.
84. *The Cheating Sollicitor Cheated*.
85. John Taylor, *Comparison Between a Thiefe and a Booke*, p. 115.
86. John Taylor, *Brood of Commorants*.
87. Greene, "A Notable Discovery of Cozenage," pp. 133–134.

88. Robert Greene, "The Defence of Cony Catching," p. 377.
89. Letter sent by Court of Aldermen to archbishop of Canterbury, 25 February 1592 in Overall and Overall, eds., *Analytical Index*, p. 353. For a general discussion of these low-life haunts see Robert Ashton, "Popular Entertainment and Social Control in Later Elizabethan and Early Stuart London."
90. Burford, *Bawds and Lodgings*.
91. *The Wandering Whore*, no. 2; *Select City Quaries: Discovering Several Cheats, Abuses and Subtleties of City Bawds, Whores and Trapanners*.
92. Fennor, "The Counter's Commonwealth," pp. 423–487. Beier suggests that Bridewell and Work hospitals also "corrupted rather than corrected." Recidivism rates were apparently high and grew worse in the early seventeenth century. "Social Problems in Elizabethan London," pp. 217–218.
93. Ibid.
94. John Taylor, *The Praise and Virtue of Jayles and Jaylers*. See also Thomas Nashe, *Strange Newes of the Intercepting Certain Letters and a Convoy of Verses*.
95. Henry Chettle, *Discoverie of the Knights of the Post*; John Taylor, *The True Cause of Waterman's Suit*.
96. Donald R. Cressey, *Criminal Organization*, p. 51.
97. Ibid.
98. Greene, "The Second Part of Cony Catching," p. 165.
99. For some important ideas that guided my thinking see McIntosh, "Thieves and Fences," pp. 257–266; Duncan Chappell and Marilyn Walsh, " 'No Questions Asked': A Consideration of the Crime of Criminal Receiving"; Karl B. Klockars, *The Professional Fence*.
100. McIntosh, "Thieves and Fences," pp. 261–263. See also Sharpe, *Crime in Seventeenth Century England*.
101. McIntosh, "Thieves and Fences," pp. 261–262.
102. Hutton, "The Black Dog of Newgate."
103. Rock, "Law, Order and Power," pp. 257–265.
104. *The Life and Death of Mary Frith*.
105. Hutton, "The Black Dog of Newgate."
106. Maurer, *Whiz Mob*, Edwin Sutherland, *The Professional Thief*; Werner J. Einstadter, "The Social Organization of Armed Robbery."
107. S. K. Weinberg, "Juvenile Delinquents and Non-Delinquents," p. 480.
108. S. S. Scivostata, *Juvenile Vagrancy: A Socio-Ecological Study of Juvenile Vagrants in the Cities of Kampur and Lucknow*, pp. 121–212; see Pinchbeck and Hewitt, *Children in English Society*, vol. 2, pp. 91–104, for a comparison.
109. Paul F. Cressey, "The Criminal Tribes of India."
110. C. M. Rasonquist and E. I. Megaree, *Delinquency in Three Cultures*.

111. Frank Robertson, *Triangle of Death: The Inside Story of the Triads—the Chinese Mafia*, pp. 142–169.
112. C. B. Mamoria, *Social Problems and Social Disorganization in India*, p. 229.
113. J. C. Mitchell, "The Concept and Use of Social Networks," pp. 28–29; A. W. Southall, "Kinship, Friendship and the Network of Relations in Kisenyi," p. 227; Clark, "The Migrant in Kentish Towns," pp. 139–142.
114. Anton Blok, *The Mafia of a Sicilian Village, 1860–1960: A Study of Violent Peasant Entrepreneurs.*
115. A recent example of this tendency is Salgado, *The Elizabethan Underworld*, Chapter 1.
116. For a debate on this question see J. F. Pound, "Vagrants and the Social Order in Elizabethan England"; A. L. Beier, "A Rejoinder." See also Beier, "Social Problems in Elizabethan London."
117. A more general point needs to be made in this context. Unfortunately, social historians' recent work on crime in early modern England comes dangerously close to categorizing much, if not all, illegality as composed of essentially random, unplanned, individualistic, and opportunistic acts. Some historians are cautious and claim this interpretation holds only for local village communities or rural counties; others say it applies to London and smaller towns as well. The major flaw in this argument is that it is often guided entirely by official legal categories of crime and is not concerned with the assumptions about associations, exchanges, and structural relationships that are essential to organizational analysis. Legal records, also, have their own inherent biases. For one thing they are not particularly informative about crimes of the powerful. For another they tend to represent and report acts of crime as discrete events, dislocated from any socioeconomic context. This has the effect of minimizing the importance of the "able criminal," who may or may not get caught, but who is rational, competent, and in varying degrees organized about crime, even if his criminal activities overlap with the activities of tramps, casual laborers, and officeholders. It is hardly a cause for surprise that criminal organization does not surface in legal records. For some useful ideas on this question see John Mack, *The Crime Industry*; Albert Cohen, "The Concept of Criminal Organization"; and Joel Best and David F. Luckenbill, *Organizing Deviance.*

7. Infamous Commerce

1. Thomas Nashe, as quoted in Brindenbaugh, *Vexed and Troubled Englishmen*, p. 373.
2. Clare Williams, ed., *Thomas Platter's Travels in England*, especially pp. 153–180.

3. Phillip Stubbes, *Anatomy of Abuses in Shakespeare's Youth*, pt. 1, Chapters 5 and 9.
4. Brindenbaugh, *Vexed and Troubled Englishmen*, p. 373.
5. *Wonderful Strange Newes from Woodstreet Counter; The Wandering Whore*, no. 2.
6. *Anti Moixea: or the Honest and Joynt Design . . . for the General Suppression of Bawdy Houses.*
7. Quoted in Brindenbaugh, *Vexed and Troubled Englishmen*, p. 373.
8. Charles MacKay, ed., *A Collection of Songs and Ballads Relative to the London Prentices and Trades; and to the Affairs of London Generally during the Fifteenth, Sixteenth and Seventeenth Centuries*, p. 49.
9. Thomas Nashe, quoted in Brindenbaugh, *Vexed and Troubled Englishmen*, p. 374.
10. Harman, "A Caveat for Common Cursitors," pp. 98–107.
11. Greene, "A Disputation," pp. 206–207.
12. *The Black Book of Newgate*, pp. 248, 254, 259.
13. Ibid., pp. 239, 248; *The Trial and Conviction of Mary Butler alias Stickland for Counterfeiting of a Bond of £40,000 of Sir Robert Clayton, Kt. Alderman of London.* See also the accounts of Mary Carleton and Moll Jones in Raynor and Crook, eds., *The Complete Newgate Calendar*, vol. 11.
14. *The Wandering Whore*, no. 3.
15. Brindenbaugh, *Vexed and Troubled Englishmen*, p. 373.
16. Ibid.
17. Ibid.
18. *Strange Newes from Bartholomew Fair, or the Wandering Whore Discovered, her Cabinet Unlock't, her Secrets Laid Open.*
19. Burford, *Bawds and Lodgings*.
20. F. Henriques, *Prostitutes and Society*, vol. 2, Chapters 1 and 2.
21. Ibid.
22. Ibid. For comparative examples from France, see Jacques Rossiaud, "Prostitution, Youth and Society, in the Towns of Southeastern France in the Fifteenth Century."
23. *The Country Gentleman's Vade Mecum.*
24. Newes from the New Exchange or the Commonwealth of Ladies Drawn to the Life in their Several Characters and Concernments.
25. Ibid.
26. William Taylor, *Annals of St. Marie Overy: An Historical and Descriptive Account of St. Saviours Church and Parish*, pp. 140–143.
27. John Dunton, *The Night Walker or Evening Rambles in Search after Lewd Women, etc.*, vol. 1, no. 4.
28. Ibid., vol. 2, no. 2.
29. *Newes from the New Exchange.*
30. Burford, *Bawds and Lodgings*.

31. Dunton, *The Night Walker*, vol. 1, no. 1.
32. Ibid.
33. *A Morning Ramble or Islington Wells Burlesqt'.*
34. For a description, see Dunton, "The Night Walker, vol. 1, no. 2.
35. E. J. Burford, *Queen of the Bawds.*
36. Dunton, *The Night Walker*, vol. 1, no. 2.
37. Ibid., vol. 2, no. 1.
38. Ibid.
39. *The Art of Wheedling; The Country Gentleman's Vade Mecum*, letter 11.
40. *The Country Gentleman's Vade Mecum*, especially letters 7, 11, 15.
41. *Newes from the New Exchange.*
42. Ibid; Burford, *Queen of the Bawds.*
43. *Strange Newes from Bartholomew Fair.*
44. Dunton, *The Night Walker*, vol. 1, no. 4.
45. Burford, *Bawds and Lodgings.*
46. *Select City Quaries*, pts. 1 and 2.
47. *The Seven Women Confessors, or a Discovery of the Seven White Devils which lived at Queen Street in Covent Garden.*
48. Quoted in Burford, *Queen of the Bawds*, pp. 86–87.
49. *The Wandering Whore*, no. 3.
50. *Strange and True Newes from Jack-a-Newberries. Six Windmills: or the Crafty Impudent Common Whore (Turned Bawd), Anatomised.*
51. *A Conference Between Damrose Page and Pris Fotheringham—by Megg Spenser, Overseer of the Whores and Hectors on Bankside.*
52. Greene, "A Notable Discovery of Cozenage," pp. 137–143.
53. Dunton, *The Night Walker*, vol. 1, no. 3.
54. Burford, *Bawds and Lodgings*, pp. 141–142.
55. *Wonderful Strange Newes from Woodstreet Counter.*
56. *Strange and True Newes from Jack-a-Newberries.*
57. Whetstone, *A Mirror for Magistrates.*
58. *Strange and True Newes from Jack-a-Newberries.*
59. This is suggested by a number of pamphlets. See *A Conference Between Damrose Page and Pris Fotheringham; Strange and True Newes from Jack-a-Newberries.*
60. Ibid; *The Wandering Whore*, nos. 2, 3.
61. Kelow Chesney, *The Victorian Underworld*, Chapter 10.
62. Ibid.
63. John I. Tobias, *Crime and Industrial Society in the Nineteenth Century*, p. 105.
64. Beames, *The Rookeries of London*; Mayhew, *London Labour and the London Poor*, vol. 4.
65. Mayhew, *London Labour and the London Poor*, vol. 4, pp. 237–238.
66. Quoted in Tobias, *Crime and Industrial Society*, p. 105.

67. L. O. Pike, *A History of Crime in England*, vol. 2, p. 527.
68. For present-day examples demonstrating these continuities in the practice of prostitution, see James H. Bryan, "Apprenticeships in Prostitution"; Barbara Heyl, "The Madam as Entrepreneur"; Susan Hall, *Ladies of the Night*.
69. Burford, *Bawds and Lodgings*, Chapter 11.
70. Goodman, *Hollands Leaguer*.
71. J. W. Ebsworth, ed., *The Bagford Ballads*, vol. 1, p. 491.
72. The following discussion is based on a description of brothel life found in Goodman, *Holland Leaguer*; see also Burford, *Queen of the Bawds*.
73. Greene, "The Second Part of Cony Catching," pp. 162–171.
74. Goodman, *Hollands Leaguer*.
75. F. Kirkman, *The Wits or Sport upon Sport in Selected Pieces of Drollery*, pt. 1.
76. McKay, ed., *A Collection of Songs and Ballads*, p. 37.
77. *The Wandering Whore*, no. 2.
78. F. J. Furnivall, ed., *Queen Elizabeth's Academy and Epigrames*.
79. Dunton, *The Night Walker*, vol. 1, no. 4.
80. Ibid., vol. 1, no. 2.
81. *Wandering Whore*, nos. 1, 2.
82. *Newes from the Newe Exchange*.
83. Dunton, *The Night Walker*, vol. 2, no. 3.
84. Ibid.
85. See the pamphlets by Dunton; and also Whetstone, *A Mirror for Magistrates*.
86. Francis Thynne, *Emblemes and Epigrames*, p. 62.
87. Lupton, *London and the Country*, p. 50–55.
88. *Tom Tell Truths Come*.
89. See Rid, "Martin Markall Beadle of Bridewell," pp. 417–418.
90. McKay, ed., *A Collection of Songs and Ballads*, p. 47.
91. *The Seven Women Confessors*.
92. *Tom Tel Troths Come*.
93. Dunton, *The Night Walker*, vol. 2, no. 1.
94. Ibid., vol. 1, no. 4.
95. Ibid.; Stubbes, *Anatomy of Abuses*.
96. *The Wandering Whore*, no. 3.
97. *Select City Quaries*.
98. Whetstone, *A Mirror for Magistrates*.
99. J. W. Ebsworth, ed., *The Roxburghe Ballads*.
100. Greene, "A Notable Dicovery of Cozenage," p. 137.
101. Mayhew, *London Labour and the London Poor*, vol. 4, pp. 237–239.
102. Chesney, *The Victorian Underworld*, p. 394. See also Judith R. Walkowitz, *Prostitution and Victorian Society; Women, Class, and the State*, Chapter 1.

103. Tobias, *Crime and Industrial Society*, pp. 104–107, 144–162; Frances Finnegan, *Poverty and Prostitution; A Study of Victorian Prostitutes in York*, Chapter 2.
104. Chesney, *The Victorian Underworld*, p. 405.
105. Ibid., p. 397; Finnegan, *Poverty and Prostitution*, Chapter 3.
106. Mayhew, *London Labour and the London Poor*, vol. 4, pp. 237–239.
107. Ibid., p. 253.
108. *The Wandering Whore*, nos. 2, 3.
109. See Chapter Six for a further discussion.
110. See the pamphlets by Dunton.
111. Greene, "The Second Part of Cony Catching."
112. *Select City Quaries; Newes from the New Exchange*.
113. For present-day research, see Diana Gray, "Turning Out: A Study of Teenage Prostitution"; Bryan, "Apprenticeships in Prostitution."
114. This discussion is drawn from Burford, *Queen of the Bawds*.
115. *The Wandering Whore*, nos. 1, 2.
116. Burford, *Queen of the Bawds*.
117. For a study of present-day brothel life see Barbara Heyl, "The Madam as Teacher: The Training of House Prostitutes."
118. Thomas Macaulay, *History of England*, vol. 1, p. 143. For a general survey of brothels and their significance see Ashton, "Popular Entertainment and Social Control."
119. Henriques, *Prostitutes and Society*, vol. 2, pp. 107–108.
120. *The Country Gentlemen's Vade Mecum*, letters 7, 8.
121. Ibid.; Henriques, *Prostitutes and Society*, vol. 2, p. 104.
122. Henriques, *Prostitutes and Society*, vol. 2, p. 106.
123. Shadwell, "The Squire of Alsatia." A general survey of theaters and a discussion of their significance can be found in Ashton, "Popular Entertainment and Social Control."
124. Thomas Middleton, and Thomas Dekker, "The Roaring Girle."
125. Bridenbaugh, *Vexed and Troubled Englishmen*, p. 199.
126. *The Country Gentleman's Vade Mecum*, letter 15.
127. Whetstone, *Mirror for Magistrates*, pp. 23–37. See Ashton, "Popular Entertainment and Social Control" for a general survey of these institutions and their significance.
128. Stephen Gosson, *The School of Abuse*.
129. Burford, *Bawds and Lodgings*, pp. 151–153.
130. Ibid., p. 150.
131. J. P. Collier, ed., *Philip Henslowe's Diary*.
132. Burford, *Bawds and Lodgings*, p. 156.
133. For the history of the Hollands' involvements see Burford, *Queen of the Bawds*, Chapter 8.
134. Ibid., pp. 101–103.

135. Ibid. This seems a possible conclusion although Burford is convinced that there existed a "brothel racket" which suggests considerably more social organization than I am implying.
136. J. P. Collier, ed., *Edward Alleyn's Papers.*
137. Burford, *Bawds and Lodgings,* Chapter 10.
138. Burford, *Queen of the Bawds,* Chapter 8.
139. Burford, *Bawds and Lodgings,* Chapter 12; Shakerley Marmion, "Holland's Leaguer."
140. Burford, *Bawds and Lodgings,* Chapters 11 and 12.
141. *The Wandering Whores,* nos. 1, 2, 3.
142. Dunton, *The Night Walker,* vol. 1, no. 1; *the Insinuating Bawd: or the Repenting Harlot.*
143. Burford, *Bawds and Lodgings,* p. 172.
144. "London's Ordinary: or Everyman in his Humor," in MacKay, ed., *A Collection of Songs and Ballads,* p. 64.
145. Burford, *Queen of the Bawds,* pp. 95–96, 120–121.
146. M. W. Beresford, "The Common Informer, the Penal Statutes and Economic Regulation."
147. This is discussed at length in Chapter 8.
148. *The Country Gentleman's Vade Mecum,* letter 16.

8. The Mediation of Crime

1. Howson, *Thief-Taker General,* pp. 34–35. See also Chapter 5.
2. MacCaffrey, "Place and Patronage," p. 97; Karraker, *The Seventeenth-Century Sheriff.*
3. MacCaffrey, "Place and Patronage," p. 98.
4. Joel Hurstfield, *Freedom, Corruption and Government in Elizabethan England.*
5. Menna Prestwich, *Cranfield: Politics and Profits under the Early Stuarts;* E. Moir, *The Justice of the Peace.*
6. Lawrence Stone, "The Fruits of Office: The Case of Robert Cecil."
7. Hurstfield, *Freedom, Corruption and Government,* pp. 304–305.
8. MacCaffrey, "Place and Patronage," p. 123; Joel Hurstfield, *Liberty and Authority under Elizabeth I.*
9. Barnes, *Somerset 1625–1640.* See also Keith Wrightson, "Two Concepts of Order: Justices, Constables and Jurymen in Seventeenth Century England."
10. J. Plumb, *The Growth of Political Stability in England,* p. 51.
11. MacCaffrey, "Place and Patronage," p. 125.
12. See Dobb, *Life and Conditions in London Prisons,* for a discussion of patronage inside the prison administration. See also Moir, *The Justice of*

the Peace; J. H. Gleason, *The Justices of the Peace in England, 1558 to 1640,* Chapters 3 and 4.

13. Salgado, *The Elizabethan Underworld,* p. 71.
14. Rock, "Law, Order and Power," pp. 255–257; Spitzer and Scull, "Social Control in Historical Perspective."
15. K. R. Andrews, *Elizabethan Privateering: English Privateering during the Spanish War 1585–1603.*
16. Blok, *The Mafia in a Sicilian Village.*
17. Hobsbawm, *Bandits.*
18. Armitage, *The History of the Bow Street Runners;* Rock, "Law, Order and Power," p. 256.
19. Hill, *Reformation to Industrial Revolution,* p. 97.
20. G. R. Elton, *Policy and Police: The Enforcement of the Reformation in the Age of Cromwell,* Chapter 8.
21. Beresford, "The Common Informer," p. 221.
22. E. P. Thompson, "The Moral Economy of the English Crowd in the Eighteenth Century."
23. G. R. Elton, "Informing for Profit."
24. Ibid.
25. M. G. Davies, *The Enforcement of English Apprenticeship 1563–1642,* p. 47.
26. Beresford, "The Common Informer," p. 222; Davies, *The Enforcement of English Apprenticeship,* pp. 61–62.
27. Elton, "Informing for Profit"; Davies, *The Enforcement of English Apprenticeship,* p. 49.
28. Davies, *The Enforcement of English Apprenticeship,* Chapter 2.
29. Ibid., pp. 55–58; Elton "Informing for Profit."
30. Pringle, *The Thief-Takers,* pp. 15–17.
31. Beresford, "The Common Informer," p. 231.
32. Davies, *The Enforcement of English Apprenticeship,* p. 58.
33. Ibid., pp. 58–76.
34. Hutton, "The Black Dog of Newgate," pp. 265–295.
35. *The Character of a Sham-Plotter or Man Catcher;* John Dunton, *The Informer's Doom.*
36. Dobb, *Life and Conditions in London Prisons,* pp. 141–143, 160.
37. Hutton, "The Black Dog of Newgate," p. 271.
38. The officers of the fleet, marshalcy, and Newgate as well as the messenger of the Privy Council and bishop's pursuants had the power to make arrests upon warrant.
39. See Rock, "Law, Order and Power," for the late seventeenth century and Spitzer and Scull, "Social Control in Historical Perspective" for an overview.
40. Davies, in her study of professional informers, notes that "net yearly

income may have compared favourably with average incomes of the lower middle classes." *The Enforcement of English Apprenticeship*, p. 57.

41. Greene, "The Second Part of Cony Catching," pp. 165–166; Pringle, *The Thief-Takers*, Chapters 1 and 2. For a discussion of a later use of the general warrant for avowedly political purposes see John Brewer, "The Wilkites and the Law 1763–74: A Study of Radical Notions of Governance."
42. Greene, "The Second Part of Cony Catching," p. 165.
43. Rock, "Law, Order and Power."
44. Dobb, *Life and Conditions in London Prisons*, p. 161.
45. *A Brief Collection of Some Part of Executions, Extortions and Excesses.*
46. This discussion is summarized from Hutton, "The Black Dog of Newgate," pp. 265–291; see Howson, *Thief-Taker General*, for a later confirmation of this system.
47. Greene, "The Second Part of Cony Catching," p. 165.
48. This role is mentioned as early as 1552. Walker, "A Manifest Detection of Dice Play, pp. 49–50; Clifford Dobb, "London Prisons."
49. See Fennor, "The Counter's Commonwealth," for a full discussion of related practices.
50. Hutton, "The Black Dog of Newgate," pp. 289–290.
51. Pringle, *The Thief Takers*; Howson, *Thief-Taker General*.
52. Armitage, *History of the Bow Street Runners*.
53. In particular, *The Life and Death of Mrs. Mary Frith*; Raynor and Crook, eds., *The Complete Newgate Calendar*, vol. 1, pp. 169–179.
54. McIntosh, "Thieves and Fences," pp. 257–261; McMullan, "Criminal Organization in London," pp. 317–320.
55. Spitzer and Scull, "Privatization and Capitalist Development," pp. 18–29.
56. Raynor and Crook, eds., *The Complete Newgate Calendar*, vol. 2, p. 145.
57. McIntosh, "Thieves and Fences", pp. 259–260.
58. Howson, *Thief-Taker General*, p. 145.
59. Klockars, *The Professional Fence*, Chapters 4, 5, 7.

9. Continuity and Change

1. Alan Macfarlane, *The Origins of English Individualism: The Family, Property and Social Transition.*
2. John Brewer and John Styles, eds., *An Ungovernable People: The English and Their Law in the Seventeenth and Eighteenth Centuries*, p. 18.
3. Barbara Hanawalt, *Crime and Conflict in English Communities 1300–1348*, pp. 32–52.
4. Keith Wrightson and Davis Levine, *Poverty and Piety in an English Village: Terling, 1525–1700.*

5. Douglas Hay, ed., *Albion's Fatal Tree: Crime and Society in Eighteenth Century England*; Thompson, *Whigs and Hunters*.
6. See Hanawalt, *Crime and Conflict*; James S. Cockburn, ed., *Crime in England 1550–1800*; David Philips, *Crime and Authority in Victorian England: The Black Country 1835–1860*; Sharpe, *Crime in Seventeenth Century England*.
7. Raphael Samuel, *East End Underworld: Chapters in the Life of Arthur Harding*.
8. Bellamy, *Crime and Public Order*; Hanawalt, *Crime and Conflict*, Chapter 6; Howson, *Thief-Taker General*; Rock, "Law, Order and Power"; Tobias, *Crime and Industrial Society*; Donald A. Low, *Thieves' Kitchen: The Regency Underworld*.
9. Hanawalt, *Crime and Conflict*, Chapters 3 and 6.
10. Chesney, *The Victorian Underworld*; Tobias, *Crime and Industrial Society*; Tobias, *Crime and Police in England 1700–1900*.
11. Howson, *Thief-Taker General*; John J. Tobias, *Prince of Fences*; Michael Weisser, *Crime and Punishment in Early Modern Europe*.
12. Hanawalt, *Crime and Conflict*; Maurice Keen, *The Outlaws of Medieval Legend*; Bellamy, *Crime and Public Order*.
13. Hanawalt, *Crime and Conflict*, p. 193.
14. Howson, *Thief-Taker General*, p. 36.
15. Ibid.; Tobias, *Prince of Fences*; McIntosh, "Thieves and Fences," pp. 256–261.

WORKS CITED

Aberndoerfer, J. *An Anatomye of the True Physition and Counterfeit Mountebanke.* London, 1602.

Allen, Thomas. *The History and Antiquities of London, Westminster, Southwark and Parts Adjacent.* London: Rouse and Strange, 1827.

Andrews, Kenneth R. *Elizabethan Privateering: English Privateering during the Spanish War 1585–1603.* Cambridge: Cambridge University Press, 1964.

Anti Moixea: or the Honest and Joynt Design . . . for the General Suppression of Bawdy Houses. London, 1691.

Armitage, George. *The History of the Bow Street Runners.* London: Wisehart and Co., 1932.

The Arraignment, Tryal and Condemnation of Frost, the Broker. London, 1675.

The Art of Wheedling. London, 1656.

Ashton, Robert. "Popular Entertainment and Social Control in Later Elizabethan and Early Stuart London." *London Journal,* 9:1 (1983): 3-20.

Awdeley, John. "The Fraternity of Vagabonds." In *The Elizabethan Underworld,* edited by A. V. Judges. London: Routledge and Sons, 1930.

Aydelotte, Frank. *Elizabeth Rogues and Vagabonds.* Oxford: Clarendon Press, 1913.

Aylmer, G. R. "Office Holding." *Social Change and Revolution in England 1540–1640,* edited by Lawrence Stone. London: Longmans, 1965.

Baker, J. H. "Criminal Courts and Procedure at Common Law 1550–1800. In *Crime in England 1550–1800,* edited by J. S. Cockburn. London: Methuen and Co., 1977.

Barker, T. C., and C. T. Savage. *An Economic History of Transport in Britain.* London: Hutchison, 1969.

Barnes, T. G. *Somerset Assize Orders 1629–1640.* Somerset: Somerset Record Society, 1959.

Works Cited

————. *Somerset 1625–1640: A County's Government during the "Personal Rule."* London: Oxford University Press, 1961.

B. E. *The Canting Crew.* London, 1698.

Beames, Thomas. *The Rookeries of London.* London: Thomas Bosworth, 1850.

Beattie, John. "Judicial Records and the Measurement of Crime in Eighteenth Century England." In *Crime and Criminal Justice in Europe and Canada,* edited by Louis A. Knafla. Waterloo: Wilfrid Laurier Press, 1981.

————. "The Pattern of Crime in England 1660–1800." *Past and Present,* no. 72 (1974):47–95.

Beier, Alan L. "A Rejoinder." *Past and Present,* no. 71 (1975):130–134.

————. "Social Problems in Elizabethan London." *Journal of Interdisciplinary History,* 9:2 (1978):203–221.

————. Vagrants and the Social Order." *Past and Present,* no. 64 (1974):3–29.

Bell, W. G. *Fleet Street in Seven Centuries.* London: Pitman and Sons, 1912.

Bellamy, John. *Crime and Public Order in the Later Middle Ages.* London: Routledge and Kegan Paul, 1973.

Beresford, M. W. "The Common Informer, the Penal Statutes and Economic Regulation." *Economic History Review,* 10, 2d ser. (1957–1958):221–237.

Binney, J. "Thieves and Swindlers." In Henry Mayhew, *London Labour and the London Poor.* Vol. 4. London: Griffin Bohm Co., 1861–1862.

The Black Book of Newgate. London, 1676.

Blok, Anton. *The Mafia of a Sicilian Village, 1860–1960: A Study of Violent Peasant Entrepreneurs.* Oxford: Basil Blackwell, 1974.

Bowler, D. H. *London Sessions Records 1605–1685.* London: Catholic Record Society, 1934.

Boynton, L. *The Elizabethan Militia.* London: Routledge and Kegan Paul, 1967.

————. "The Tudor Provost-Marshal." *English Historical Review,* 77 (1962):442–446.

Braudel, Fernand. *Capitalism and Material Life 1400–1800.* London: Fontana Collins, 1973.

Brenner, Robert. "The Civil War Politics of London's Merchant Community." *Past and Present,* no. 58 (1973):53–107.

Brett-James, Norman G. *The Growth of Stuart London.* London: Allen and Unwin, 1935.

Brewer, John. "The Wilkites and the Law 1763–74: A Study of Radical Notions of Governance." In *An Ungovernable People: The English and Their Law in the Seventeenth and Eighteenth Centuries,* edited by John Brewer and John Styles. London: Hutchison, 1980.

Brewer, John, and John Styles, eds. *An Ungovernable People: The English and Their Law in the Seventeenth and Eighteenth Centuries.* London: Hutchison, 1980.

A Brief Collection of Some Part of Executions, Extortions and Excesses. London, 1620.

Brindenbaugh, Carl. *Vexed and Troubled Englishmen 1590–1642.* Oxford: University Press, 1968.

Bryan, James H. "Apprenticeships in Prostitution." *Social Problems,* 12 (Winter 1965):287–297.

Buckatzsch, E. J. "Places of Origins of a Group of Immigrants into Sheffield 1624–1799." *Economic History Review,* 11, 2d ser. (1950):145–150.

Burford, E. J. *Bawds and Lodgings: A History of the Bankside Brothels 900–1675.* London: Peter Owen, 1976.

———. *Queen of the Bawds.* London: Spearman, 1973.

Burke, Peter. *Popular Culture in Early Modern Europe.* London: Temple Smith, 1978.

———. "Popular Culture in Seventeenth Century London." *London Journal,* 3, (1977):143–162.

Byrne, Mary St. Clare. *Elizabethan Life in Town and Country.* London: Methuen, 1947.

Chandler, F. W. *The Literature of Roguery.* 2 vols. London: Constable, 1907.

Chappell, Duncan, and Marilyn Walsh. "'No Questions Asked': A Consideration of the Crime of Criminal Receiving." *Crime and Delinquency,* 20, no. 2 (1974):157–168.

The Character of a Sham-Plotter or Man Catcher. London, 1656.

The Cheating Sollicitor Cheated. London, n.d.

Chesney, Kelow. *The Victorian Underworld.* Middlesex: Penguin Books, 1970.

Chettle, Henry. *Discoverie of the Knights of the Post.* London, 1597.

———. "Kind-Hartes Dreame: Containing Five Apparitions with their Invectives against Abuses Reigning." Percy Society Series. London: Percy Society, 1841.

Cheyney, E. P. *A History of England from the Defeat of the Armada to the Death of Elizabeth.* Vol. 2. London: Longmans, 1926.

City of London, the Corporation of. *The Corporation of London, Its Origins, Constitutional Powers and Duties.* London: Oxford University Press, 1967.

———. Guildhall Library. *King's Proclamations,* 17 February 1628, 17 September 1630, 12 February 1634, 25 November 1642.

———. *Lord Mayor's Proclamations,* 20 January 1656, "A Proclamation Against Neglect of Executing Laws Against Rogues. . . ."

———. *Miscellaneous Proclamations,* 8 November 1649, "Two Orders of Parliament: The one, Appointing the Giving of Ten Pounds to Every One who shall bring in a High-way-man; The Other: Referring to the Council of State to give Reprieves to Persons Guilty of Robberies, if they Shall Discover any of their Accomplices."

———. *Miscellaneous Proclamations,* 10 January 1650, "Two Orders of Parliament Concerning the Apprehending of Thieves."

————. *Miscellaneous Proclamations*, by the Protector, 9 August 1655, "A Proclamation Commanding a Speedy and Due Execution of the Laws . . ."

————. *Miscellaneous Proclamations*, London 1649, "Instructions to be Observed by the Several Justices of the Peace in the Several Counties within the Commonwealth for the Better Prevention of Robberies, Burglaries and Other Outrages."

————. Guildhall Records Office. *Journal of Court of Common Council*, 10 October 1663, "An Act of Common Council for the Better Ordering of the Night Watch within ye City of London and the Liberties Thereof."

————. *Lord Mayor's Proclamations*, 30 September 1603. P.D. 10.48, 10.49, 10.73, 16.71.

————. *Repertories of the Court of Aldermen*. Vol. 23, fol. 548; vol. 26, fol. 1979; vol. 34, fols. 125 and 183.

————. *Watch and Ward Miscellaneous Manuscripts*. Box 245, "The Humble Petition of Robert Wilkins about Miscarriages of Watching."

Clark, Peter. "The Migrant in Kentish Towns 1580–1640." In *Crisis and Order in English Towns 1500–1700*, edited by Peter Clark and Paul Slack. London: Routledge and Kegan Paul, 1972.

Clark, Peter, and Paul Slack. *English Towns in Transition 1500–1700*. London: Oxford University Press, 1976.

Clavell, James. *Recantations of an Ill Led Life* . . . London, 1628.

Clebert, J. P. *The Gypsies*. London: Vista Books, 1963.

Clinard, M. B., and D. J. Abbot. *Crime in Developing Countries: A Comparative Perspective*. New York: John Wiley and Sons, 1973.

Cloward, Richard, and Lloyd Ohlin. *Delinquency and Opportunity: A Theory of Delinquent Gangs*. Glencoe, Ill.: Free Press, 1960.

Cockburn, James S. "Early Modern Assize Records as Historical Evidence." *Journal of Society of Archivists*, 5 (1975):215–231.

————. *A History of English Assizes, 1558–1714*. Cambridge: Cambridge University Press, 1972.

————. "The Nature and Incidence of Crime in England 1559–1625: A Preliminary Survey." In *Crime in England 1550–1800*, edited by J. S. Cockburn. London: Methuen and Co., 1977.

————, ed. *Crime in England 1550–1800*. London: Methuen and Co., 1977.

Coleman, D. C. "Labour in the English Economy of the Seventeenth Century." In *Essays in Economic History*, edited by E. M. Carus-Wilson, vol. 2. London: Edward Arnold, 1962.

Collier, J. P., ed. *Edward Alleyn's Papers*. Shakespeare Society Publications, no. 18. London, 1843.

————, ed. *Philip Henslowe's Diary*. Shakespeare Society Publications, no. 28. London, 1845.

A Conference Between Damrose Page and Pris Fotheringham—by Megg Spenser, Overseer of the Whores and Hectors on Bankside. London, 1660.

Cornwall, Julian. "The Early Tudor Gentry." *Economic History Review*, 17, 2d ser. (1964–1965):456–475.

———. "Evidence of Population Mobility in the Seventeenth Century." *Bulletin of the Institute of Historical Research*, 40, no. 102 (1967):143–152.

Cotton, Charles. "The Compleat Gamester or Instructions on How to Play Billiards, Trucks, Bowls, and Chess." Reprinted in *Games and Gamesters of the Restoration*, edited by C. H. Hartman. London: Routledge and Sons, 1930.

The Country Gentleman's Vade Mecum. London: John Harris, 1699.

Cressey, David. "Occupations, Migration and Literacy in East London 1580–1640." *Local Population Studies*, no. 5 (1970):53–60.

Cressey, Donald R. *Criminal Organization.* London: Heinemann Educational Books, 1972.

Cressey, Paul F. "The Criminal Tribes of India." *Sociology and Social Research*, 20 July-August 1936):503–511.

Critchley, T. A. *A History of Police in England and Wales 900–1966.* London: Constable and Co., 1967.

Cross, A. L. "The English Criminal Law and Benefit of Clergy during the Eighteenth and Early Nineteenth Centuries." *American Historical Review*, 22 (1916–1917):544–565.

Curtis, T. C. "Quarter Sessions Appearances and Their Background: A Seventeenth Century Regional Study." In *Crime in England 1550–1800*, edited by J. S. Cockburn. London: Methuen and Co., 1977.

Curtis, T. C., and F. M. Hale. "English Thinking about Crime, 1530–1620." In *Crime and Criminal Justice in Europe and Canada*, edited by Louis A. Knafla. Waterloo: Wilfrid Laurier Press, 1981.

Davies, M. G. *The Enforcement of English Apprenticeship 1563–1642.* Cambridge, Mass.: Harvard University Press, 1956.

Davis, Ralph. *The Rise of the English Shipping Industry in the Seventeenth and Eighteenth Centuries.* Newton Abbot: David and Charles, 1962.

Dekker, Thomas. "The Bellman of London." Reprinted in *The Elizabethan Underworld*, edited by A. V. Judges. London: Routledge and Sons, 1930.

———. "Lantern and Candlelight." Reprinted in *the Elizabethan Underworld*, edited by A. V. Judges. London: Routledge and Sons, 1930.

———. "O Per Se O." Reprinted in *The Elizabethan Underworld*, edited by A. V. Judges. London: Routledge and Sons, 1930.

The Devil's Cabinet Broke Open. London: Henry Marsh, 1658.

Dobb, Clifford. "Life and Conditions in London Prisons, 1553–1643 with Special Reference to Contemporary Literature." B. Litt. dissertation, Oxford University, 1953.

———. "London Prisons." In *Shakespeare in His Own Age*, Shakespeare Survey 17, edited by A. Nicoll. Cambridge: Cambridge University Press, 1964.

Works Cited

Dugdale, William. *The History of St. Paul's Cathedral.* London, 1658.

Dunton, John *The Informer's Doom.* London, n.d.

――――. *The Night Walker or Evening Rambles in Search after Lewd Women, etc.* Vol. 1, nos. 1–4, vol. 2, nos. 1, 3. London, 1696.

Dyos, D. J., and D. H. Aldercroft. *British Transportation.* Surrey: Leicester University Press, 1969.

Ebsworth, J. W., ed. *The Bagford Ballads.* Reprinted by the Ballad Society, vol. 1. London: S. Austin, 1878.

――――. *The Roxburghe Ballads.* 9 vols. Reprinted by the Ballad Society. London: S. Austin, 1871–1899.

Einstadter, Werner J. "The Social Organization of Armed Robbery." *Social Problems,* 17 (Summer 1969):64–83.

Elton, G. R. "Crime and the Historian." In *Crime in England 1550–1800,* edited by J. S. Cockburn. London: Methuen and Co., 1977.

――――. "Informing for Profit." In *Star Chamber Stories,* edited by G. R. Elton. London: Methuen, 1958.

――――. *Policy and Police: The Enforcement of the Reformation in the Age of Cromwell.* Cambridge: Cambridge University Press, 1972.

Emmision, F. G. *Elizabethan Life: Disorder.* Chelmsford: Chelmsford Essex County Council, 1970.

Everitt, Alan. "Social Mobility in Early Modern England." *Past and Present,* no. 33 (1966):56–73.

Fennor, William. "The Counter's Commonwealth." Reprinted in *The Elizabethan Underworld,* edited by A. V. Judges. London: Routledge and Sons, 1930.

Finnegan, Frances. *Poverty and Prostitution: A Study of Victorian Prostitutes in York.* Cambridge: Cambridge University Press, 1979.

Firth, C. B. "Benefit of Clergy in the Time of Edward IV." *English Historical Review,* 32 (1917):175–191.

Fisher, Frederick J. "Commercial Trends and Policy in Sixteenth Century England." *Economic History Review,* 10 (1940):95–117.

――――. "The Development of London as a Centre of Conspicuous Consumption in the Sixteenth and Seventeenth Centuries." In *Essays in Economic History,* vol. 2, edited by E. M. Carus-Wilson. London: Edward Arnold, 1962.

――――. "London as an Engine of Economic Growth." In *the Early Modern Town,* edited by P. Clark. London: Longmans, 1976.

――――. "London's Export Trade in the Early Seventeenth Century." *Economic History Review,* 3, 2d ser. (1950–1951):151–161.

Foster, F. F. *The Politics of Stability: A Portrait of the Rulers in Elizabethan London.* London: Royal Historical Society, 1977.

Foucault, Michel. *Discipline and Punishment: The Birth of the Prison.* New York: Vintage Books, 1979.

French, A. H., Marybel Moore, Jocelyn Oatley, M. J. Power, D. Summers, and S. C. Tongue. "The Population of Stepney in the Early Seventeenth Century." *Local Population Studies*, no. 3 (1969):39–52.

Fuller, Thomas. *The Beggars Brotherhood*. London: Allen and Unwin, 1936.

Furnivall, F. J., ed. *Queen Elizabeth's Academy and Epigrames*. Early English Text Society no. 8. London: E. E. T. S., 1898.

Gadamer, Hans-Georg. "The Historicity of Understanding." In *Critical Sociology*, edited by Paul Connerton. Middlesex: Penguin Books, 1976.

Glass, David V. "Two Papers on Gregory King." In *Population in History*, edited by D. V. Glass and D. E. C. Eversley. Chicago: Aldine and Co., 1969.

Gleason, J. H. *The Justices of the Peace in England, 1558 to 1640*. Oxford: Clarendon Press, 1969.

Gomme, G. Laurence. *London*. London: Williams and Norgate, 1914.

Goodman, Nicholas. *Hollands Leaguer*. London, 1632.

Gosson, Stephen. *The School of Abuse*. Edited by J. P. Collier, Shakespeare Society Publications, no. 2. London, 1841.

Goubert, Pierre. *The Ancien Regime in French Society 1600–1750*. New York: Harper and Row, 1969.

Gould, J. D. *The Great Debasement*. Oxford: Clarendon Press, 1970.

Gray, Diana. "Turning Out: A Study of Teenage Prostitution." *Urban Life and Culture*, 1 (January 1973):401–425.

Great Britain. Public Record Office. *Acts of the Privy Council*, Elizabeth (I). Vol. 24 (1594–1595); vol. 25 (1595); vol. 26 (1596–1597); vol. 27 (1597–1598); vol. 29 (1598–1599).

———. *Calendar of State Papers, Domestic, of the Reign of Charles I*. Vol. 48 (1631–1633).

———. *Calendar of State Papers, Domestic, of the Reign of Elizabeth and James I*. Addende 1580–1625.

———. *Calendar of State Papers, Domestic, of the Reign of James I*. Vol. 41 (1611–1618); vol. 42 (1619–1623).

———. King's Proclamation. *A Proclamation for Restraint of Consumption of Coyne and Bullion and Deceitful Making of Gold Thread*, 18 January 1635.

———. *A Proclamation for Restraint of the Exportation, Waste, and Consumption of Coine and Bullion*, 11 June 1622.

———. *King's Proclamations*, 25 May 1627, "A Proclamation for the Better Execution of the Office of His Majesties Exchanger, and Reformation of Sundry Abuses and Frauds Practiced upon His Majesties Coins."

Greene, Robert. "The Defence of Cony Catching." Reprinted in *Cony Catchers and Bawdy Baskets*, edited by Gamini Salgado. Middlesex: Penguin Books, 1972.

———. "A Disputation between a He Cony Catcher and a She Cony Catcher." Reprinted in *The Elizabethan Underworld*, edited by A. V. Judges. London: Routledge and Sons, 1930.

———. "A Notable Discovery of Cozenage." Reprinted in *The Elizabethan Underworld*, edited by A. V. Judges. London: Routledge and Sons, 1930.

———. "The Second Part of Cony Catching." Reprinted in *The Elizabethan Underworld*, edited by A. V. Judges. London: Routledge and Sons, 1930.

———. "The Third Part of Cony Catching." Reprinted in *The Elizabethan Underworld*, edited by A. V. Judges. London: Routledge and Sons, 1930.

Hale, John. "War and Public Opinion in the Fifteenth and Sixteenth Centuries." *Past and Present*, no. 22 (1962):19–33.

Hall, Susan. *Ladies of the Night*. New York: Trident Press, 1973.

Hanawalt, Barbara. *Crime and Conflict in English Communities 1300–1348*. Cambridge, Mass.: Harvard University Press, 1979.

Harman, Thomas. "A Caveat for Common Cursitors." Reprinted in *The Elizabethan Underworld*, edited by A. V. Judges. London: Routledge and Sons, 1930.

Harrison, G. B. *The Elizabethan Journals 1591–1602*. London: Routledge, 1955.

Harrison, William. *The Description of England*. London: North Shropshire Society, 1876. Edited by George Edelon, Ithaca: Cornell University Press, 1968.

Hartley, T. E. "Under-Sheriffs and Bailiffs in Some English Shrievalties 1580 to 1625." *Bulletin of the Institute of Historical Research*, 47 (1974):164–185.

Hay, Douglas, ed. *Albion's Fatal Tree: Crime and Society in Eighteenth Century England*. Middlesex: Penguin Books, 1977.

Hecht, J. Jean. *The Domestic Servant Class in Eighteenth-Century England*. London: Routledge and Kegan Paul, 1956.

Henriques, F. *Prostitutes and Society*. Vol. 2. London: MacGibbon and Kee, 1963.

Heyl, Barbara. "The Madam as Entrepreneur." *Sociological Symposium*, 11 (Spring 1974):61–82.

———. "The Madam as Teacher: The Training of House Prostitutes." *Social Problems*, 24 (June 1977):545–555

Hill, Christopher. "The Many Headed Monster." In *Change and Continuity in Seventeenth Century England*. London: Weidenfeld and Nicolson, 1974.

———. *Reformation to Industrial Revolution*. Middlesex: Pelican Books, 1969.

———. *Society and Puritanism in Pre-Revolutionary England*. London: Panther, 1964.

———. *The World Turned Upside Down: Radical Ideas during the English Revolution*. Middlesex: Pelican Books, 1972.

Hobsbawn, Eric J. *Bandits*. Middlesex: Penguin, 1972.

———. "The Crisis of the Seventeenth Century." In *Crises in Europe*

1560–1660, edited by Trevor Ashton. New York: Doubleday & Co., 1967.

The Holborn Hector. London, 1675.

Howson, Gerald. *Thief-Taker General: The Rise and Fall of Jonathan Wild*. London: Hutchison, 1970.

Hurstfield, Joel. *Freedom, Corruption and Government in Elizabethan England*. London: Jonathan Cape, 1973.

———. *Liberty and Authority under Elizabeth I*. London: University College, 1960.

———. "Political Corruption in Modern England: The Historian's Problem." *History*, no. 52 (1967):16–34.

Hutton, Luke. "The Black Dog of Newgate." Reprinted in *The Elizabethan Underworld*, edited by A. V. Judges. London: Routledge and Sons, 1930.

Ingram, M. J. "Communities and Courts: Law and Disorder in Early Seventeenth Century Wiltshire." In *Crime in England 1550–1800*, edited by J. S. Cockburn. London: Methuen and Co., 1977.

The Insinuating Bawd: or the Repenting Harlot. London, n.d.

Jackson, Bruce. *A Thief's Primer*. New York: Macmillan, 1969.

James, Margaret. *Social Problems and Policy during the Puritan Revolution 1640–1660*. London: Routledge and Sons, 1930.

Jeafferson, J. C., ed. *Middlesex Sessions Rolls*. Vol. 1. London, 1886.

Johnson, David. *Southwark and the City*. London: Oxford University Press, 1969.

Johnson, Robert C. "The Transportation of Vagrant Children from London to Virginia 1618–1622." In *Early Stuart Studies in Honor of D. G. Willson*, edited by Howard Reinmuth. Minneapolis: University of Minnesota Press, 1970.

Jones, Gareth Stedman. *Outcast London: A Study in the Relationship between Classes in Victorian Society*. Middlesex: Penguin Books, 1976.

Jones, Philip. *Certaine Sermons preached of late at Cicetor*. London, 1588.

Jones, W. R. D. *The Tudor Commonwealth 1529–1559*. London: Athlone Press, 1970.

Jordan, Wilbur K. *The Charities of London 1480–1660*. London: Allen and Unwin, 1960.

———. *Philanthropy in England 1480–1660: A Study of the Changing Pattern of English Social Aspirations*. London: Allen and Unwin, 1959.

Judges, Arthur V., ed. *The Elizabethan Underworld*. London: Routledge and Sons, 1930.

Jusserand, Jean Jules. *English Wayfaring Life in the Middle Ages*. London: Methuen, 1961.

Kamen, Henry. *The Iron Century: Social Change in Europe 1550–1660*. London: Cardinal, 1976.

Karraker, C. H. *The Seventeenth Century Sheriff.* Chapel Hill: University of North Carolina Press, 1930.

Keen, Maurice. *The Outlaws of Medieval Legend.* Toronto: University of Toronto, 1961.

Kempe, Alfred J. *Historical Notices of the Collegiate Church or Royal Free Chapel and Sanctuary of St. Martin-le-Grand.* London: Longmans, 1825.

Kiernan, V. G. "Foreign Mercenaries and Absolute Monarchy." *Past and Present*, no. 11 (April 1957):66–86.

Kirkman, Francis. *The Wits or Sport upon Sport in Selected Pieces of Drollery.* London, 1671.

Klockars, Karl B. *The Professional Fence.* London: Tavistock Publications, 1975.

Kwant, R. *Phenomenology of Language.* Pittsburgh: Duquesne University Press, 1965.

Lee, W. L. Melville. *A History of Police in England.* London: Methuen, 1901.

Letkenmann, Peter. *Crime as Work.* Englewood Cliffs, N.J.: Prentice-Hall, 1973.

Lenman, Bruce, and Geoffrey Parker. "The State, the Community and the Criminal Law in Early Modern Europe." In *Crime and the Law: The Social History of Crime in Western Europe since 1500*, edited by V. A. C. Gatrell, Bruce Lenman, and Geoffrey Parker. London: Europa Publications, 1980.

Leonard, E. M. *The Early History of English Poor Relief.* Cambridge: University Press, 1900.

The Life and Death of Mrs. Mary Frith, commonly called Moll Cutpurse. London, 1612.

Linebaugh, Peter. "The Ordinary of Newgate and His Account." In *Crime in England 1550–1800*, edited by J. S. Cockburn. London: Methuen and Co., 1977.

Lombarde, William. *Of the Duties of Constables Within the City of London.* London, 1668.

Lupton, Donald. *London and the Country Carbondated and Quartered into Several Characters.* London: N. Okes, 1632.

Macaulay, Thomas. *History of England.* Vol. 1. London: Everyman Edition, 1906.

MacCaffrey, William T. "Place and Patronage in Elizabethan Politics." In *Elizabethan Government and Society; Essays Presented to Sir John Neal*, edited by Stanley T. Bindoff, Joel Hurstfield, and Charles Williams. London: Athlone Press, 1969.

Macfarlane, Alan. *The Justice and the Mare's Ale: Law and Disorder in Seventeenth Century England.* Oxford: Blackwell's, 1981.

———. *The Origins of English Individualism: The Family, Property, and Social Transition.* Oxford: Oxford University Press, 1978.

McIntosh, Mary. "Changes in the Organization of Thieving." In *Images in Deviance*, edited by S. Cohen. Middlesex: Penguin Books, 1971.

———. *The Organization of Crime*. London: Macmillan, 1975.

———. "Thieves and Fences: Markets and Power in Professional Crime." *British Journal of Criminology*, 16, (July 1976):257–266.

Mack, John. *The Crime Industry*. London: Saxon House, 1974.

MacKay, Charles, ed. *A Collection of Songs and Ballads Relative to the London Prentices and Trades; and to the Affairs of London Generally during the Fifteenth, Sixteenth and Seventeenth Centuries*. Percy Society, no. 7. London, 1841.

McMullan, John L. "Criminal Organization in Sixteenth and Seventeenth Century London." *Social Problems*, 29 (February 1982):311–323.

McPeck, J. A. S. *The Black Book of Knaves and Unthrifts*. London: Storrs, 1969.

Malden, Henry Elliot, ed. *The Victoria History of the Counties of England, Surrey*. Vol. 1. London: Constable and Co., 1902.

Mamoria, C. B. *Social Problems and Social Disorganization in India*. Allahabad: Kitab Mahal, 1960.

Manning, Brian. *The English People and the English Revolution 1640–1649*. London: Heinemann, 1976.

Manning, O., and W. Bray. *History and Antiquities of Surrey*. Vol. 3. London: Nichols, Son and Bentley, 1814.

Marmion, Shakerley. "Holland's Leaguer." In *The Dramatic Works of Shakerley Marmion*, edited by J.Maidmont and W. H. Logan. London: H. Sotheran, 1875.

Maurer,David. "The Argot of the Dice Gambler." *Annals of the American Academy of Political and Social Science*, no. 269 (May 1950):114–133.

———. *Whiz Mob: A Correlation of the Technical Argot of Pickpockets with Their Behaviour Patterns*. New Haven: College and University Press, 1955.

Mayhew, Henry. *London Labour and the London Poor*. Vols. 1, 4. London: Griffin Bohm Co., 1861–1862.

Memoirs of the Life and Death of the Famous Madam Charlton. London, 1673.

Meriton, George. *A Guide for Constables, Churchwardens, Overseers of the Poor* . . . London, 1668.

Merleau-Ponty, Maurice. *Signs*. Evanston, Ill.: Northwestern University Press, 1964.

Middleton, Thomas, and Thomas Dekker. "The Roaring Girle." In *The Works of Thomas Middleton*, edited by Alexander Dyee. Vol. 2, pp. 427–562. London: Lumley, 1840.

Mitchell, J. C. "The Concept and Use of Social Networks." In *Social Networks in Urban Situations*, edited by J. C. Mitchell. Manchester: University of Manchester Pres, 1969.

Moir, E. *The Justice of the Peace*. Middlesex: Penguin Books, 1969.

A Morning Ramble or Islington Wells Burlesq't': London, 1624.

Works Cited

Morrill, J. S. "Mutiny and Discontent in English Provincial Armies 1645–1647." *Past and Present,* no. 56 (1972):49–74.

Moryson, Fynes. *Itinerary of Ten Years Travel . . .* Vol. 4. Glasgow: Mac-Lehase, 1907–1908.

Nashe, Thomas. *Strange Newes of the Intercepting Certain Letters and a Convoy of Verses.* London: John Dunton, 1592.

Nef, J. U. "The Progress of Technology and the Growth of Larage-Scale Industry in Great Britain 1540–1640." In *Essays in Economic History,* edited by E. M. Carus-Wilson. London: Edward Arnold, 1954.

Newes from the New Exchange or the Commonwealth of Ladies Drawn to the Life in their Several Characters and Concernments. London, 1650.

Nymer, Norman. *English Town Crafts.* London: B. T. Batsford, 1949.

Onions, C. T., ed. *Shakespeare's England.* Oxford: Clarendon Press, 1916.

Overall, William H., and Henry C. Overall, eds. *Analytical Index to Remembrancia 1579–1664.* London: Corporation of London, 1878.

Oxley, G. W. *Poor Relief in England and Wales 1601–1834.* London: Davis and Charles, 1974.

Parkes, Joan. *Travel in England in the Seventeenth Century.* London: Oxford University Press, 1925.

Pearl, Valerie L. *London and the Outbreak of the Puritan Revolution.* London: Oxford University Press, 1961.

Philips, David. *Crime and Authority in Victorian England: The Black Country 1835–1860.* London: Croom Helm, 1977.

Pike, L. O. *A History of Crime in England.* Vol. 2. London: Smith Elder and Co., 1876.

Pinchbeck, Ivy, and Margaret Hewitt. *Children in English Society.* Vol. 2. London: Routledge and Kegan Paul, 1969.

Plumb, J. *The Growth of Political Stability in England.* London: Macmillan, 1967.

Pound, John F. "An Elizabethan Census of the Poor." *University of Birmingham Historical Journal,* 8 (1962):135–151.

———. *Poverty and Vagrancy in Tudor England.* London: Longmans, 1971.

———. "Vagrants and the Social Order in Elizabethan England." *Past and Present,* no. 71 (1975):126–129.

Power, M. J. "East London Housing in the Seventeenth Century." In *Crisis and Order in English Towns 1500–1700,* edited by Peter Clark and Paul Slack. London: Routledge and Kegan Paul, 1972.

———. "The Urban Development of East London, 1550 to 1700." Ph.D. thesis, University of London, 1971.

Prest, William. *The Inns of Court under Elizabeth I and the Early Stuarts 1590–1640.* London: Longmans, 1972.

Prestwich, Menna. *Cranfield: Politics and Profits under the early Stuarts, the Career of Lionel Cranfield, Earl of Middlesex.* Oxford: Clarendon Press, 1966.

Pringle, Patrick. *Hue and Cry: The Birth of the British Police*: London: Museum Press, 1955.

——. *The Thief-Takers*. London: Museum Press, 1958.

Pugh, R. B. *Imprisonment in Medieval England*. Cambridge: Cambridge University Press, 1968.

Rasonquist, C. M., and E. I. Megaree. *Delinquency in Three Cultures*. Austin: University of Texas Press, 1969.

Raynor, J. L., and G. T. Crook, eds. *The Complete Newgate Calendar*. 5 vols. London: Navarre Society, 1926.

Read, Conyers, ed. *William Lombarde and Local Government*. New York: Ithaca Press, 1962.

Renard, George. *Guilds in the Middle Ages*. London: A. Bell and sons, 1918.

Rendle, William, and Philip Norman. *The Inns of Old Southwark and Their Associations*. London: Longmans Green and Co., 1888.

Rhodes, Henry T. *The Craft of Forgery*. London: John Murray, 1934.

Ribton-Turner, C. J. *A History of Vagrants and Vagrancy*. London: Chapman and Hall, 1887.

Rid, Samuel. "Martin Markall Beadle of Bridewell." Reprinted in *The Elizabethan Underworld*, edited by A. V. Judges. London: Routledge and Sons, 1930.

Roberts, Michael. *The Military Revolutions 1560–1660*. Belfast: University of Belfast Press, 1956.

Roberts, R. S. "The Personnel and Practice of Medicine in Tudor and Stuart England." *Medical History*, 8 (1964):217–234.

Robertson Frank. *Triangle of Death: The Inside Story of the Triads—the Chinese Mafia*. London: Routledge and Kegan Paul, 1977.

Rock, Paul. "Law, Order and Power in Late Seventeenth and Early Eighteenth Century England." *Annals of Criminology*, 16, nos. 1, 2 (1977):233–265.

——. "Some Problems of Interpretative Historiography." *British Journal of Sociology*, 27 (1976):353–369.

Rossiaud, Jacques. "Prostitution, Youth and Society, in the Towns of Southeastern France in the Fifteenth Century." In *Deviants and the Abandoned in French Society*, edited by R. Forster and O. Ranum. Baltimore: John Hopkins University Press, 1978.

Rowse, Alan, ed. *The England of Elizabeth*. New York: Macmillan, 1967.

Rudé, George. *Hanoverian London 1774–1808*. London: Martin Secker and Warburg, 1971.

Rule, John C. "Wrecking and Coastal Plunder." In *Albion's Fatal Tree: Crime and Society in Eighteenth Century England*, edited by Douglas Hay. Middlesex: Penguin Books, 1977.

Rumbelow, David. *I Spy Blue: The Police and Crime in the City of London from Elizabeth I to Victoria*. London: Macmillan Press, 1971.

Works Cited

Ryan, E. K. W. *Cripplegate, Finsbury and Moorfields*. London: Adams Brothers and Shardlow, 1917.

Rye, W. B. *England as Seen by Foreigners in the Days of Elizabeth and James I*. London: John Russell Smith, 1865.

Salgado, Gamini, ed. *Cony Catchers and Bawdy Baskets*. Middlesex: Penguin Books, 1972.

————. *The Elizabethan Underworld*. London: Methuen, 1977.

Salisbury-Jones, G. T. *Street Life in Medieval England*. Oxford: Pen-In-Hand Publishing Company, 1938.

Salzman, Louis F. *English Life in the Middle Ages*. London: Oxford University Press, 1924.

Samaha, Joel. *Law and Order in Historical Perspective: The Case of Elizabethan Essex*. London: Academic Press, 1974.

Samuel, Raphael. *East End Underworld: Chapters in the Life of Arthur Harding*. London: Routledge and Kegan Paul, 1981.

Scivostata, S. S. *Juvenile Vagrancy: A Socio-Ecological Study of Juvenile Vagrants in the Cities of Kampur and Lucknow*. New York: Asia Publishing House, 1963.

Scot, Reginald. *A Discovery of Witchcraft*. London, 1632.

Select City Quaries: Discovering Several Cheats, Abuses and Subtleties of City Bawds, Whores and Trapanners. Pts. 1 and 2. London, 1660.

The Seven Women Confessors, or a Discovery of the Seven White Devils which lived at Queen Street in Covent Garden. London, 1641.

Shadwell, Thomas. "The Squire of Alsatia." In *The Complete Works of Thomas Shadwell*, edited by M. Summers, vol. 4. London: Fortune Press, 1927.

Shakespeare, William. *The Winter's Tale*. Middlesex: Penguin Books, 1973.

Sharpe, J. A. *Crime in Seventeenth Century England: A County Study*. Cambridge: University of Cambridge Press, 1983.

————. "Enforcing the Law in the Seventeenth Century English Village." In *Crime and the Law: The Social History of Crime in Western Europe since 1500*, edited by V. A. C. Gatrell, Bruce Lenman, and Geoffrey Parker. London: Europa Publications, 1980.

Sheppard, Leslie. *The History of Street Literature*. Newton Abbot: David and Charles, 1973.

Shrover, Neal. "The Social Organization of Burglary." *Social Problems*, 20 (Spring 1973):499–514.

Slack, Paul. "Poverty and Politics in Salisbury 1597–1666." In *Crisis and Order in English Towns 1500–1700*, edited by Peter Clark and Paul Slack. London: Routledge and Kegan Paul, 1972.

————. "Vagrants and Vagrancy in England 1598–1664." *Economic History Review*, 27, 2d ser. (1974):360–379.

Smith, A. Hassel. *County and Court: Government and Politics in Norfolk, 1588–1603*. Oxford: Clarendon Press, 1974.

Smith, Alexander. "The Thieves' Grammar." Reprinted in *A Complete History of the Lives and Robberies of the Most Notorious Highwaymen, Footpads, Shoplifts and Cheats of Both Sexes*, edited by Arthur L. Hayward. London: Routledge and Sons, 1926.

——. "The Thieves' New Canting Dictionary." Reprinted in *A Complete History of the Lives and Robberies of the Most Notorious Highwaymen, Footpads, Shoplifts and Cheats of Both Sexes*, edited by Arthur L. Hayward. London: Routledge and Sons, 1926.

Smith, J. E. *Local Government in Westminster*. London: Wightman, 1889.

Some Account of a Remarkable Old House formerly existing in Chick Lane, Clerkenwell, with a description of the various rooms. London, n.d.

Southall, A. W. "Kinship, Friendship and the Network of Relations in Kisenyi." In *Social Change in Modern Africa*, edited by A. W. Southall. Oxford: University Press, 1961.

Spitzer, Stephen, and Andrew Scull. "Privatization and Capitalist Development: The Case of the Private Police." *Social Problems*, 25 (1977): 18–29.

——. "Social Control in Historical Perspective: From Private to Public Responses to Crime." In *Corrections and Punishment*, edited by David Greenberg. Beverly Hills: Sage, 1980.

Steele, R., ed. *A Bibliography of Royal Proclamations of the Tudor and Stuart Sovereigns . . . 1485–1714*. Oxford: Oxford University Press, 1910.

Stone, Lawrence. *The Crisis of the Aristocracy 1553–1641*. Oxford: Clarendon Press, 1965.

——. "The Fruits of Office: The Case of Robert Cecil, First Earl of Salisbury, 1596–1612." In *Essays in the Economic and Social History of Tudor and Stuart England*, edited by Frederick J. Fisher. Cambridge: Cambridge University Press, 1961.

——. "Social Mobility in England 1500–1700." *Past and Present*, no. 33 (1966):16–55.

——. "State Control in Sixteenth Century England." *Economic History Review*, 17 (1947):103–120.

Stow, John. *The Survey of London*. London: J.M. Dent, 1958.

Strange and True Newes from Jack-a-Newberries Six Windmills: or the Crafty Impudent, Common Whore (Turned Bawd), Anatomised. London, 1660.

Strange Newes from Bartholomew Fair, or the Wandering Whore Discovered, her Cabinet Unlock't, her Secrets Laid Open. London, 1661.

Stubbes, Philip. *Anatomy of Abuses in Shakespeare's Youth*. Reprinted by the Shakespeare Society. Edited by F. J. Furnivall. London: Trubner and Co., 1877–1879.

Styles, John. "Our Traiterous Money-Makers: The Yorkshire Coiners and the Law 1760–83." In *An Ungovernable People: The English and Their Law in the Seventeenth and Eighteenth Centuries*, edited by John Brewer and John Styles. London: Hutchison, 1980.

Supple, Barry E. *Commercial Crisis and Change in England 1600–1642.* Cambridge: Cambridge University Press, 1959.

Sutherland, Edwin. *The Professional Thief.* Chicago: University of Chicago Press, 1956.

Swart, Kenneth. *The Sale of Offices in the Seventeenth Century.* The Hague: Martinus Nijhoff, 1949.

Tawney, R. H. "The Rise of the Gentry 1558–1640." *Economic History Review,* 11 (1941):1–38.

Tawney, R. H., and Eileen Power, eds. *Tudor Economic Documents.* Vol. 2. London: Longmans, 1924.

Taylor, John. *Brood of Commorants.* London, 1632.

———. *Comparison Between a Thiefe and a Booke.* London, 1622.

———. *The Praise and Virtue of Jayles and Jaylers.* London, 1623.

———. *The True Cause of Waterman's Suit.* London, 1632.

Taylor, William. *Annals of St. Marie Overy: An Historical and Descriptive Account of St. Saviours Church and Parish.* London: Nichols and Son, 1833.

Thomas, Keith. *Religion and the Decline of Magic: Studies in Popular Beliefs in Sixteenth and Seventeenth Century England.* Middlesex: Penguin Books, 1973.

Thompson, Edward P. "The Moral Economy of the English Crowd in the Eighteenth Century." *Past and Present,* no 50 (1971):76–136.

———. "Time, Work Discipline and Industrial Capitalism." *Past and Present,* no 38 (December 1967):56–97.

———. *Whigs and Hunters: The Origins of the Black Act.* Middlesex: Penguin Books, 1977.

Thornley, Isobel D. "The Destruction of Sanctuary." In *Tudor Studies Presented to A. F. Pollard,* edited by R. W. Seton-Watson. London: Longmans, 1924.

Thynne, Francis. *Emblemes and Epigrames.* Edited by F. J. Furnivall. Early English Text Society, no. 35. London: E.E.T.S., 1876.

Timbs, John. *Curiosities of London.* London: David Bogue, 1855.

Tobias, John J. *Crime and Industrial Society in the Nineteenth Century:* Middlesex: Penguin Books, 1972.

———. *Crime and Police in England 1700–1900.* Dublin: Gill and Macmillan, 1979.

———. *Prince of Fences.* Middlesex: Penguin Books, 1974.

———. *Tom Tell Truths Come.* London, 1643.

The Trial and Conviction of Mary Butler alias Stickland for Counterfeiting of a Bond of £40,000 of Sir Robert Clayton, Kt. Alderman of London. London, 1699.

Unwin, George. *The Guilds and Companies of London.* London: Frank Cass, 1908.

———. *Industrial Organization in the Sixteenth and Seventeenth Centuries.* Oxford: Clarendon Press, 1904.

Walker, Gilbert. "A Manifest Detection of Dice Play." Reprinted in *The Elizabethan Underworld*, edited by A. V. Judges. London: Routledge and Sons, 1930.

Walkowitz, Judith R. *Prostitution and Victorian Society: Women, Class, and the State*. Cambridge: Cambridge University Press, 1980.

The Wandering Whore. Nos. 1–3. London, 1660.

Webb, Sidney, and Beatrice Webb. *English Poor Law History*. London: Longmans, Green and Company, 1927.

Weinberg, S. K. "Juvenile Delinquency in Ghana: A Comparative Analysis of Delinquents and Non-Delinquents." *Journal of Criminal Law, Criminology and Police Science*, 55 (December 1964):471–481.

Weisser, Michael. *Crime and Punishment in Early Modern Europe*. Sussex: Harvester Press, 1979.

Western, J. *The English Militia in the Eighteenth Century*. London: Routledge and Kegan Paul, 1965.

Whetstone, George. *A Mirror for Magistrates of Cyties which is Added a Touchstone for the Times*. London, 1584.

Williams, Clare, ed. *Thomas Platter's Travels in England*. London: Jonathan Cape, 1937.

Williams, Penry. "The Northern Borderland under the Early Stuarts." In *Historical Essays 1600–1750. Presented to David Ogg*, edited by H. E. Bell and R. L. Ollard. London: Adam and Charles Black, 1963.

Wingent, R. M. *Historical Notes on the Borough of Southwark*. London: Ash and Co., 1913.

Winslow, Cal. "Sussex Smugglers." In *Albion's Fatal Tree: Crime and Society in Eighteenth Century England*, edited by Douglas Hay. Middlesex: Penguin Books, 1977.

Wonderful Strange Newes from Woodstreet Counter. London, 1642.

Wrightson, Keith. "Two Concepts of Order: Justices, Constables and Jurymen in Seventeenth Century England. In *An Ungovernable People: The English and Their Law in the Seventeenth and Eighteenth Centuries*, edited by John Brewer and John Styles. London: Hutchison, 1980.

Wrightson, Keith, and David Levine. *Poverty and Piety in an English Village: Terling, 1525–1700*. New York: Academic Press, 1979.

Wrigley, E. A. "A Sample Model of London's Importance in Changing English Society and Economy 1650–1750." *Past and Present*, no. 37 (1967):44–70.

Younge, Richard. *The Poores Advocate*. London, 1654.

INDEX